Marx and Other Four-Letter Words

Also available, edited by Georgina Blakeley and Valerie Bryson

Contemporary Political Concepts: A Critical Introduction

Marx and Other Four-Letter Words

Edited by
Georgina Blakeley and Valerie Bryson

Pluto  Press
LONDON • ANN ARBOR, MI

First published 2005 by Pluto Press
345 Archway Road, London N6 5AA
and 839 Greene Street, Ann Arbor, MI 48106

www.plutobooks.com

British Library Cataloguing in Publication Data
A catalogue record for this book is available from the British Library

ISBN   0 7453 2253 0 hardback
ISBN   0 7453 2252 2 paperback

Library of Congress Cataloging in Publication Data applied for

10   9   8   7   6   5   4   3   2   1

Designed and produced for Pluto Press by
Chase Publishing Services, Fortescue, Sidmouth, EX10 9QG, England
Typeset from disk by Stanford DTP Services, Northampton, England
Printed and bound in the European Union by
Antony Rowe Ltd, Chippenham and Eastbourne, England

Contents

Acknowledgements

The editors would like to thank all those who took part in the Huddersfield University 'Class and Other Four-Letter Words' conference, which gave rise to this book, for making this such a stimulating and enjoyable occasion. Thanks also to Politics students and colleagues for their continuing enthusiasm for critical and scholarly debate.

Introduction

Georgina Blakeley and Valerie Bryson

Until the late 1980s, socialist and Marxist theories were an important strand in academic and public policy debates in the west. A rich, complex and fiercely contested body of thought, they provided a language and an analytical basis for radical critiques of both western and so-called communist societies, and claimed to provide the key to understanding both how societies function and how they might be changed for the better. As such, they were the starting point for a wide range of radical political movements. Concepts such as capitalism, imperialism, oppression and class were underpinned by a distinctive methodology that was grounded in conditions of material life and that rejected the individualistic assumptions of liberal thought. This gave rise to an analysis of the class-based nature of state power, linked to radical interpretations of equality and democracy, which many believed could only be achieved through international class struggle and revolution.

In recent years, however, such approaches have been widely abandoned, shorn of their radical associations or replaced by such newly fashionable concepts as social capital, empowerment and the 'Third Way'. These 'new' concepts do not align themselves clearly with discrete ideological perspectives, but are used and endorsed by those from both the left and the right of the political spectrum. In contrast, the classic concepts of the left often seem to be the 'four-letter words' of political discourse, no longer to be articulated in polite company. Their theoretical building blocks have also fallen into a degree of disuse and disrepute, while the previously radical vocabulary of democracy and equality has been watered down to such an extent that even conservatives can claim these concepts as their own.

It would, however, be premature to consign radical approaches to the dustbin of history. Some theorists and activists have always insisted on their relevance. More generally, and contrary to the 'End of History' heralded by Fukuyama, we are living in an era in which the assumptions of liberal democracy and free market capitalism are facing national and international challenges, and the growing worldwide anti-capitalist movements show that belief in the possibility of emancipatory politics is certainly not dead. In this context, there has been something of a revival of interest in alternatives to liberalism, and it seems timely to re-examine the rich and complex perspectives provided by socialist and Marxist theory.

This volume, which brings together the work of academics from a range of disciplines, reflects both a desire to think beyond the narrow confines of liberalism and the belief that, although the classic concepts of the left have sometimes been misused and misunderstood, they can make important contributions to radical political analysis today. Its starting point is an agreement with Marx's claim that theory should not be an abstract end in itself, but a means to understanding society in order to improve it. It therefore aims at providing a critical exposition of key concepts and ideas which is not only accessible but also grounded in practical concerns, so that concepts are applied to specific historical situations rather than treated as universal abstractions, and particular contemporary issues and debates can be understood in a wider context. As such, it is relevant for all those interested in exploring radical alternatives to existing society, be they academics, students, political activists or simply concerned citizens.

However, the authors are aware that the traditional left has not always provided a welcoming home for radicals. Rather, it has often seemed inhospitably jargon-ridden and dogmatic, with a rigid and impenetrable theoretical framework which allows no space for new forms of political engagement or creativity and may be hostile to non-class-based movements such as feminism. This book, therefore, aims to disentangle the potential insights of Marxist thought from the rigid interpretations of some of Marx's more dogmatic followers; in this context it is worth remembering that, according to Engels, Marx said 'I am not a Marxist' (1970:679).

The contributors are united by the belief that western liberal democracy is not 'as good as it gets', and many explicitly criticise the shortcomings of dominant conceptions of democracy and equality. They are also agreed that traditional Marxist approaches provide a starting point from which to understand and critique the world in which we live. In particular, there is general agreement on the need to ground theory in materialist analysis.

A number of other themes also run through the book. Perhaps the most important of these is the above-mentioned belief that theory should be judged by its usefulness, and that it should therefore be applicable to specific historical situations. Rather than indulging in what E.P. Thompson (1978:384) eloquently referred to as 'Capital navel scrutinising', the authors believe that concepts are only useful if they can be applied to the 'reality' around us rather than treated as universal abstractions. Marx, after all, was as much a practitioner as he was a theorist. Moreover, a useful theory is one that recognises complexity and ambiguity rather than attempting to provide neat categories that gloss over these, and the contributors believe that if Marxism is to be useful, it should not be seen as a rigid and formulaic doctrine. They therefore take the ambiguities in Marx's work seriously and none offers an entirely uncritical defence of his thought. Much of the contemporary repudiation of Marxist theory comes from the mistaken, almost messianic, belief, shared by critics as much as by followers, that it constitutes a universal 'meta-theory'. On the contrary, we should not expect it to provide answers to all of the questions thrown up by the world around us.

General agreement at this level means that none of the contributors interprets Marxism as a doctrine of economic determinism. This in turn means that such issues as the relationship between objective interests and class consciousness, or the extent to which the state, politics and ideology may be autonomous from class interests, are not predetermined but are likely to be highly variable – and such variation is something to be explored. It also means that local, national and global concerns cannot be understood separately: for local and national issues occur in a global context, while global issues are experienced in specific national and local situations.

Another running theme, more explicit in some chapters than others, is the belief that capitalism is an increasingly inefficient, conflict-ridden and self-destructive mode of production. This is linked to a sense of moral concern and indignation about the hypocrisies and suffering of capitalist class societies, and the belief that, as well as providing indispensable tools of analysis, Marxism can help provide an alternative set of ethical values and goals.

The contributors to the volume are not, however, in full agreement on all issues. On the contrary, they disagree over the likelihood or desirability of proletarian revolution, the nature and significance of non-class-based oppressions, and the possibility of achieving meaningful social change short of revolution. They also place differing degrees of emphasis on ideology and the role of ethical theory. The importance of these differences should not be understated. Nevertheless, all are agreed that Marxist thought still provides a relevant starting point for both interpretations of the world and attempts to change it.

Deciding in which order to present the chapters has not been straightforward. Historical materialism provided the methodological foundations for Marx's thought, while capitalism was the primary focus of his analysis. As such, they were the obvious choices for the first two chapters. The concepts and issues discussed in later chapters are, however, inherently interconnected, with debates in one area having consequences for and being influenced by those in others. The chapter ordering that follows might be logically defended as a progression from key concepts, to issues of political practice, to the analysis of goals. However, this would be to impose the kind of schematic reductionism that we are anxious to avoid. Like the 'reality' it seeks to analyse, the world of theory is inherently messy: the chapters do not fit into neat categories, and they could have been ordered quite differently.

THE CHAPTERS

The theme of historical specificity is clearly established in Philip Wood's opening chapter on *historical materialism*. Rather than treating this as an abstract theory of economic determinism, he advocates a more open-ended approach which, through a 'turn to the concrete', can acknowledge and analyse the role of politics and ideas as well as economics in producing particular outcomes. He applies this to the racialisation and expansion of the American prison system, and argues convincingly that, while there are clear problems with using a more rigid and orthodox version of historical materialism to interpret this, a revisionist approach provides a sound basis for analysis.

Keith Faulks similarly refuses to reduce *capitalism* to either an abstract set of principles or to its economic arrangements. Drawing on humanistic elements in Marxist thought as well as Marx's economic analysis, Faulks analyses capitalism's changing historical manifestations and the distinctive political/value system that these have entailed. In terms of the world today, this enables him to combine a trenchant critique of the dehumanising consequences of capitalist values with an analysis of capitalism's increasingly negative economic consequences, particularly its generation of large-scale inequalities and its inability to confront such global problems as environmental damage. He finds that Marx's diagnosis of the 'deeply pathological nature' of capitalism remains powerfully relevant today, and argues that it should be central to building an alternative. Faulks is in broad agreement with the authors of later chapters in maintaining that the state both consistently serves capitalist interests and does so in a range of ways, and that capitalism is in stark opposition to key principles of democracy. However, in contrast to Paul Blackledge's later chapter, he does not see proletarian revolution as a likely or desirable way forward. Indeed, he argues that a resort to violence will be counter-productive, and that radicals should instead work to connect more closely with mainstream politics.

As with the first two chapters, Peter McLaverty's discussion of *class* interprets Marxism as a flexible theory and rejects the view that politics can simply be 'read off' from economics. He argues both that defining the working class can never be straightforward, and that there is no necessary link between economic class position, political interest and political action. While he agrees that class remains critically important to the analysis of contemporary society and that class should not be written off as a mobilising force, he insists that there is nothing inevitable about the development of class-based politics. This provides the basis for an open-ended approach to contemporary society which recognises that interests cannot always be reduced to class position and stresses the importance of subjectivity in the development of political consciousness. This in turn means that we must recognise the continuing relevance of ethics and ideas of social justice to the development of progressive politics, and that the relationship between traditional forms of class politics and new movements against global capitalism remains an open question.

Andrew Taylor's chapter on *the state* is even more pessimistic about the potential for radical working-class consciousness and anti-capitalist change. Drawing on the analyses of Marx, Engels, Lenin and Gramsci, he both rejects the view that the nature and activities of the state are economically determined and argues that the modern representative state does nevertheless have a universal function in serving the interest of the economically dominant capitalist class by maintaining a class compromise. This compromise means that capitalists no longer rule directly, and may indeed have to accept particular state policies that are against their immediate interests. However, it secures the long-term interests of capitalism, by securing ideological domination and the integration of the working class into the state. In particular, Taylor uses rational choice theory to argue that the democratic electoral cycle protects capitalism, because, although workers would benefit in the long term from a move to socialism, in the short term such a move would produce acute economic costs; a government that introduced socialist measures would therefore not be re-elected. The short-term costs of revolution would be even greater; most workers therefore support state repression of revolutionaries, who are seen as a threat to their economic security. This explains why class compromise has been able to survive so much longer than Marx expected, and Taylor agrees with Lenin that democracy provides 'the best political shell' for capitalism. However, the modern representative state remains inherently both coercive and unstable: because the conditions in which compromise emerged were historically specific, class compromise can never be final and the interests of capitalists and workers remain opposed.

A useful concept alerts us to things we might not otherwise see, and may help us challenge dominant versions of 'reality'. Graham Harrison's chapter suggests that *imperialism* can perform this function by exposing the violently negative impact of capitalism as it has expanded beyond the west. Harrison provides a powerful exposition of the hypocrisy that lies at the heart of global capital accumulation by contrasting the dominant rhetoric of development and progress with the reality of mass dispossession, insecurity, war and environmental degradation. Although Marx himself did not use the term imperialism, Harrison traces this critique of bourgeois hypocrisy back to original Marxism and finds it to be a common theme as the concept of imperialism has developed. However, its history has also been highly erratic and uneven, leading Harrison to describe imperialism as a 'radically elastic' concept, giving rise to a range of competing approaches and strong disagreement over the nature, causes and significance of the economic processes involved. The concept also has a shifting relationship (sometimes complementary, sometimes conflicting) with dependency theory. Despite these difficulties, and although the full potential of imperialism as a concept has yet to be explored, Harrison argues that it remains the most appropriate theoretical starting point for developing a critique of the double standards of global capitalism. Not only does the concept highlight the misery and destruction that theories of globalisation ignore or marginalise, but it enables us to see these as the historically structured outcomes of a capitalist 'heartland' and to analyse the ways in which inequalities of power between states are intertwined with the combined and uneven development of capitalism. Such analysis places the 'war against terrorism' in a wider politico-economic context and suggests that we have to understand it in relation to strategic economic thinking in the United States. It also leads us to expect that, as well as producing inequality, the processes of global capitalist expansion will produce resistance, although Harrison does not attempt to discuss whether or not we can expect this to succeed.

Marx's critique of the manufacturing *division of labour*, explored in Renzo Llorente's chapter, was central to his condemnation of capitalism as both destructive of human potential and ultimately inefficient. Llorente shows that although classical economists and sociologists such as Smith and Durkheim claimed that an extensive division of labour was economically and socially beneficial, they acknowledged that it also had harmful effects, such as the loss of mental, social and physical capacity on the part of the worker. Llorente draws on recent research to support Marx's analysis of the detrimental effects of the extensive division of labour on human well-being. He agrees with Marx both that such human impoverishment and disempowerment are not a price worth paying, and that after a point the division of labour hinders the greater productivity, autonomy and social cohesion it is supposed to provide. Although the division of labour has received only limited attention on the left in recent years, Llorente argues that its critique remains highly relevant, particularly in formulating and justifying demands for people to be enabled to realise their potential through 'a right to meaningful work'. As such, it will, he says 'rightly continue to provide inspiration and orientation for emancipatory social theory'.

Marxist analysis has usually focused on class as the primary social division, and in her chapter on *oppresssion* Mary Davis agrees that this is right. However, she also argues that class has usually been seen through a white and male lens, and that the specific oppression of women and black people is not reducible to their class position. Understanding this, she says, enables us to see the ways in which class exploitation is maintained by sex and race oppressions. Not only are these oppressions materially linked to capitalist class interests (as they enable the super-exploitation of women and black people at the point of production), but they also serve a critical ideological function by preventing the unity of the working class. This means both that if we are to analyse class society we must examine oppression, and that oppression cannot be understood outside of its class context. At a practical level, it means that working-class politics must be based on the recognition that most workers are not white men, while those opposing racist and sexist divisions can only hope to do so as part of a wider movement aimed at ending class society.

The claim that male perspectives see only half the picture is reiterated by Valerie Bryson in her chapter on *production and reproduction*. She returns to the classic concept of historical materialism, and argues that the insights therein have been limited by a narrow view of productive work which excludes the socially necessary labour that is disproportionately performed by women. She argues that biological reproduction, domestic work, caring activities and human sexuality are neither naturally given nor by-products of productive activity as conventionally understood. On the contrary, they are a part of human history and at times have their own dynamic. This means that they must be included in any materialist analysis, and she introduces the term '(re)production' to refer to this hitherto invisible aspect of productive life. From this reformulated materialist perspective, challenging oppressive conditions of (re)production is a central economic issue which should be treated as a political priority by men as well as women.

The first eight chapters agree that capitalism's inhumanity and/ or exploitation should be condemned and that it is in the long-term interests of the majority to challenge it. However, while there is a general sense that the growing anti-capitalist movements give some grounds for optimism, none appears to think radical change is imminent, and several are decidedly pessimistic. In contrast, Paul Blackledge's chapter on *revolution* argues that the revolutionary transformation of society is not only possible but necessary and desirable, although not inevitable. He argues that, although involvement in reform movements should not be rejected, reform alone cannot bring about a radically better society: it cannot solve the economic crises inherent in the capitalist system, it cannot achieve any fundamental change to its social relations, and it is only by participating in the democratic revolutionary process that working people will become fit to rule themselves. Blackledge does not see working-class revolution or victory as any kind of automatic outcome of capitalist development. Rather, he argues that it will be fiercely opposed and, like Andrew Taylor, he expects the ruling class to use all the coercive and ideological weapons at its disposal. Nevertheless, unlike Taylor, he finds grounds for optimism about the prospects for the growth of a mass revolutionary socialist movement. If such a movement is to achieve its goals, he says, it must be led by ordinary workers, grounded in workers' own experience of capitalism and expressing a collective growth of class consciousness. In reaching this understanding, Blackledge draws on contemporary theory, but argues that it is necessary to return to the key concepts of original Marxism to understand the ways in which the socialist political project must be informed by a scientific analysis of capitalism, but cannot be reduced to it.

For Blackledge, the revolutionary proletarian movement is clearly international, and there is general agreement amongst the contributors that, because capitalism is a global economic system, effective movements for change will have to transcend national boundaries. This point is addressed directly by Mark O'Brien in his chapter on *working-class internationalism*. He accepts Marx's original claim that capitalism's increasingly international character means both that working-class struggle has an international dimension and that in their own interests workers in imperialist nations should support movements elsewhere against colonial oppression. He also agrees with Marx that this will not be an automatic development, and he cautions that in terms of practical strategy the relevance of internationalism will be highly variable. In surveying the uneven history of internationalism, O'Brien stresses its ideological as well as economic significance. Like McLaverty in Chapter 3, he sees the importance of ethical ideals of social justice in the development of consciousness and unity. He argues that working-class internationalism has the potential to provide such a transformative vision, and he finds particular grounds for optimism in the involvement of organised labour in a range of new international movements against capitalism and for social justice.

As the final two chapters show, the concepts of *equality* and *democracy* have long provided the inspiration for such a transformatory vision. Both have, however, frequently been used in much more limited ways, and the chapters argue that the radical potential of these concepts should be reclaimed. Brendan Evans identifies a continuum from Marxist to social-democratic to social-liberal conceptions of equality within the socialist tradition, and argues that only the first enables us either to think beyond the confines of the status quo or to understand its nature. He argues that the contemporary focus on equality of opportunity represents a degradation of the concept, which seeks to redistribute inequalities rather than challenge them and obscures the underlying reality that 'the dynamic of capitalism is unequal rewards' and that the needs of capital and labour are inevitably in conflict. In contrast, Marx's vision of a society in which people contribute what they can and receive according to their needs may be utopian at present, but it is the basis both for more robustly egalitarian policies and for alternative ethical values.

As Georgina Blakeley shows, the concept of democracy today is equated with liberal democracy, and its original Athenian meaning, which linked it to the working class, has been forgotten. Marxist analysis, however, enables us to see that liberal democracy is simply one historically specific and very limited form of democracy, which has been made possible by capitalism's separation of economic and political power. At the same time, Marxism enables us both to envision a radically different model of working-class democracy, and to understand that this cannot be realised without fundamental economic change. Blakeley argues that, by abandoning material analysis, post-Marxists have lost these insights, and are left with a severely impoverished theory of democracy. Echoing Wood's arguments in the opening chapter, she also insists that, if it is to help us develop effective political strategies, democratic theory must undertake the difficult task of 'returning to the concrete', rather than remaining at the level of abstraction. Moreover, as Blakeley argues, the challenge lies in applying Marxist theory to those parts of the world where capitalism appears in its most blatant form. In this respect, though liberal democracy may well have triumphed over communism in the short term, the celebrations which accompanied this victory may well have been premature. The problems which inspired the communist challenge in the first place are still very much apparent, and it is indeed questionable whether or not liberal democracy, as opposed to Marxism, can provide either the 'means or ideals' to confront them.

CONCLUSION

The chapters in this book show that radical debate today is alive and well. Taken together, they provide a powerful argument for the continuing relevance and importance of classical Marxism, not only as a means of understanding the contemporary world and developing more realistic political strategies, but also as a rich source of inspiration that enables us to think beyond the ethical limitations of existing society. This does not mean that Marxism provides all the answers or any ready-made formulae. The problems the chapters are grappling with are much too complex for that, and Marxism itself is full of ambiguities. It is however an indispensable starting point.

REFERENCES

Marx, K. and Engels, F. (1970) *Selected Works* (London: Lawrence and Wishart).
Thompson, E.P. (1978) *The Poverty of Theory* (London: Merlin Press).

1
Historical Materialism

Philip Wood

The purpose of this chapter is to examine the role of historical materialism in social explanation. The first part discusses two ways of interpreting Marx's methodological writings. Orthodox historical materialism largely ignores the ambiguities in Marx's writings in order to build an abstract theory of history useful in the defence of 'actually existing socialism'. Recent changes, however, have magnified the importance of race, gender, nationalism, the environment and other factors alien to the orthodoxy, and a second, revisionist, interpretation has emerged, suggesting a non-deterministic empirical Marxism. The second half of the chapter assesses the merits of these two approaches in terms of their ability to explain one of the most significant tendencies in contemporary American politics: the expansion and racialisation of prisons.

HISTORICAL MATERIALISM: TRADITIONAL AND MODERN

Despite its importance, Karl Marx nowhere provided a systematic treatment of his general methodological position. The term 'historical materialism' comes to us from Engels, who systematised Marx's ideas in the decades around his friend's death. The problem that Engels faced was that Marx's methodological writings are both ambitious and ambiguous. For one thing, they are scattered through writings whose purposes are historically specific, spanning a long period of large-scale political and intellectual change. For another, the task Marx set himself – to understand social and economic development; to explain historical events and long-term structural change; to combine English and Scottish political economy, French materialism and German idealism; and to unify science with political practice – is so grand that analytical rigour seems an unlikely outcome.

Attempts to encapsulate historical materialism in a clear and concise set of methodological statements inevitably founder on these shoals. The most famous of these attempts belongs to Engels, who wrote in 1892 that historical materialism:

designate[s] that view of the course of history which seeks the ultimate cause and the great moving power of all important historic events in the economic development of society, in the changes in the modes of production and exchange, in the consequent division of society into distinct classes, and in the struggles of these classes against one another. (Marx and Engels 1968:382–3)

The ambiguities that result are easy to find. How do economic development, changes in modes of production and exchange, class divisions and class struggles combine to explain historical social change? What weight is to be attached to each? Does the word 'consequent' imply that class divisions and struggles simply reflect the level of economic development and changes in the modes of production and exchange? What is meant by the terms 'ultimate cause' and 'great moving power', and do they imply economic determinism? Does the materialist cast of the summary imply no part in the explanation of historical social change for individuals, ideas, politics and the state? Is the statement to be taken as one of logic and philosophy or as a more open-ended suggestion about the direction of concrete historical research?

Engels' statement, in other words, contains in summary form the same kinds of ambiguity that are found in Marx's work as a whole. For instance, in a preface to the first volume of *Capital*, Marx states that he has inverted Hegel's argument that social reality reflects the realm of ideas, implying in the process, however, that he accepts his predecessor's philosophical approach to history (1976:103). Elsewhere, however, he stresses the need for concrete historical analysis and suggests that trans-historical or philosophical abstractions are of limited value. With respect to the role of ideas, the Marx of *The German Ideology* argues that consciousness is a reflection of material life, while in the *Theses on Feuerbach* the argument is amended to allow 'sensuous' and 'practical-critical' activity to play a role in building material reality (Marx and Engels 1976:36–7, 5). Similarly, Marx's theory of socio-historical change in the *Preface* is a scientifically-knowable theory of the interplay of forces (technology, scientific knowledge, skills and so on) and relations of production (master–slave, lord–serf, capitalist–wage worker), in which human agency plays no part. In contrast, in *The Communist Manifesto*, Marx gives class struggles and subjectivity priority, so that history can be modified by conscious human action, and outcomes are uncertain

(Marx and Engels 1968:180–4, 35–63). How should we deal with these ambiguities?

Orthodox historical materialism

The traditional response, referred to by Larrain as 'orthodox historical materialism', has been to stress the universal, the structural and the philosophical at the expense of the conjunctural, the social and the practical (1986: Chapter 2). The origins of this are disputed. Colletti (1972) argues that they can be traced back to Engels' letters on historical materialism after the death of Marx. In these letters, Colletti argues, Engels' defence of historical materialism stressed the reciprocal role of ideas and politics, the interplay of individual wills and the state's relative autonomy. But he also insisted that the economic was the determining factor 'in the last instance', suggesting an abstract distinction between economic and non-economic relations. In addition, the first post-Marx generation of Marxists, such as Kautsky and Plekhanov, had their own axes to grind. They 'were concerned in different ways to systematise historical materialism as a comprehensive theory of history, capable of replacing rival bourgeois disciplines and providing the workers' movement with a broad and coherent vision of the future that could be easily grasped by its militants' (Anderson 1976:6). For Colletti, Engels' letters were thus an invitation to stress the economic while largely ignoring all the other, non-economic, factors, and inaugurated a view of historical materialism as a grand materialist philosophy, divorced from its critical historical origins and universally applicable. For Larrain, historical materialism was thus transformed into a 'theory which is derived from supposedly universal laws of dialectics inherent in nature, which conceives of consciousness as a mere reflection of material life, which propounds a kind of technological determinism, and which results in a general, teleological and unilinear theory of history which sketches the necessary path of development of all nations' (1986:59). This became the orthodoxy of the Second International, was transformed into the philosophy of dialectical materialism during the Stalinist period, and was given new life in the second half of the last century by the structuralism of Althusser and Balibar (1970) and the analytic Marxian philosophy of Cohen (1978).

Predictably, this approach was of limited value in understanding capitalism or the societies in which it had emerged. Sayer agrees that the source is to be found in Engels' letters, but argues that they have been misread. The crucial point, often ignored, is that the letters 'repeatedly, and emphatically, underline the limitations of any general theory or model when it comes to analysing particular historical events, processes or societies' (Sayer 1987:10). In his letter to Bloch, Engels accepts that he and Marx are at fault for emphasising the material in their debates with idealism, 'but when it came to presenting an era of history, i.e. to making a particular application, it was a different matter and there no error could be permitted'. Again, in a letter to Schmidt: 'our conception of history is above all a guide to study, rather than a lever for construction after the manner of the Hegelian' (Marx and Engels 1968:683, 679).

For Sayer, the letters are less an invitation to economic determinism than 'a general warning against a certain pre-emptive use of theory, and a plea for empirical, and in particular for historical study' (1987:11). It is no accident, he argues, that Engels refers his readers to Marx's *The Eighteenth Brumaire* as a classic example of historical materialism in action. This is not inconsistent with Marx himself, who presents the 1859 preface, taken by many as the definitive text, as 'a few brief indications concerning the course of my politico-economic studies' and 'a guiding thread for my studies', not a fully elaborated theory of history (Marx and Engels 1968:180–1). Years earlier, in *The German Ideology*, Marx argued that '[e]mpirical observation must in each separate instance bring out empirically, and without any mystification and speculation, the connection of the social and political structure with production' (Marx and Engels 1976:35). And years later, his work on Russia led him to consider the possibility of different evolutionary paths. In a letter to Mikhailovsky, Marx rejected abstract historicism: 'one will never arrive [at a proper historical understanding] by using as one's master-key a general historico-philosophical theory, the supreme virtue of which consists in being super-historical' (McLellan 1977:571–2).

Revisionist historical materialism

The key turning point in the history of Marxism, according to Anderson, occurred in the 1960s and 1970s. Relative economic decline, racial upheavals, the women's, peace and environmental movements, and the 1968 events in France and Prague left orthodox Marxism ill-equipped and unable to respond, 'clearing the way for another sort of Marxism to emerge'. In this context, there developed a 'sudden zest, a new appetite, for the concrete' which revived political economy, especially in Britain and America (1983:18, 21).

This attempt to concretise historical materialism is best exemplified in the work of Larrain (1986) and Sayer (1987). Both use Cohen's interpretation of the 1859 preface as a technological theory of history as a model of orthodox historical materialism. Cohen's argument rests on a radical distinction between productive forces, which he says are material things used in the productive process, and productive relations, which involve the exercise of power and control. These, in turn, are distinguished from the superstructure, which is an ensemble of legal and institutional relations. The productive forces, defined as technologies, have causal primacy, functionally determining the rise and fall of production relations. The production relations that emerge in a given epoch do so because they enhance the development of the productive forces. In turn, the legal and institutional superstructure arises to reinforce the system of forces and relations. Both the social relations of production and the superstructure, in this image, are ultimately dependent on the way in which technological development unfolds.

Whatever the merits of Cohen's work in terms of clarity and analytical rigour, Larrain and Sayer argue that it is inadequate as a method of political economy. Precisely delimited definitions and finite, one-way causal sequences abstract from a complex and evolving reality which contextualises concepts in relational and historical settings. An assembly line is a productive force, but it also materialises the ideas of F.W. Taylor (the father of scientific management in America), and the class struggles and intellectual milieu in which he worked. Forms of cooperation and scientific knowledge of various kinds can, in other words, be productive forces (Marx 1973:706; Larrain 1986:78–80; Sayer 1987:26). The list of non-material productive forces discussed by Marx is a long one, as Sayer indicates (1987:29).

A similar logic holds for productive relations. Cohen's power-based definition neglects the broader issue of the phenomena – laws, the state, ideas, culture, morality and so on – that shape them. For Marx, the economic structure was a much broader totality of social relations than the orthodoxy suggests, and his writings are full of references to non-economic relations that constitute the *social* relations of production (see, for instance Marx 1973:471–514).

Sayer concludes that there is 'no good reason for excluding any kind of social relation from being a possible relation of production, or for arbitrarily assigning some social relations to the "base" and others to the "superstructure" of society a priori' (1987:75). This opens up new lines of thinking, and facilitates the integration of research from intellectual traditions usually thought external to Marxism. Sayer discusses human reproduction here, but the point could equally be extended to race, ethnicity, and other factors.

There are also implications for the analysis of superstructures. Cohen's view restricts the category to non-economic institutions. Marx used the term broadly however, to encompass ideas and forms of consciousness as well as their institutionalisation in the state, religion, culture and the law. Marx's arguments about the superstructure are similar to his view of ideas generally: he denies both the validity of the distinction between the ideal and the material, and the cause–effect image of their relationship. Material reality and superstructural relations are not distinct entities connected in a causal sequence, but rather two sides of the same coin. The components of the superstructure are ideological forms of appearance of social relations. These 'phantoms' have 'the semblance of independence', but this is illusory. Consciousness 'can never be anything else than conscious existence' (Marx and Engels 1976:47). Likewise 'all struggles within the State, the struggle between democracy, aristocracy and monarchy, the struggle for the franchise, etc., are merely the illusory forms in which the real struggles of the different classes are fought out among one another'. Nevertheless, they are 'empirically verifiable and bound to material premises' (Marx and Engels 1976:54, 47). These material premises, in turn, must be grasped 'in definite historical form … If material production itself is not conceived in its specific historical form, it is impossible to understand what is specific in the spiritual production corresponding to it and the reciprocal influence of one on the other. Otherwise one cannot get beyond inanities' (Marx 1963:285).

The formation of superstructures connects ideas and institutions with the production and reproduction of material and social life through human thought and practice. Cultural and institutional relations are products of 'a process of continuous reanimation of ideas in the context of new practices' (Larrain 1986:71). Ideas and institutional activity may be anticipatory or reflective, or they may be survivals from the past that have adapted to new conditions. They have their own life histories, produced in relationship with human practice. The cultural and institutional legacies of the past are powerful building blocks of the present, creating a stock of ideas and practices that can be drawn upon for use in political and other battles.

The result of this turn to the concrete is an image of historical materialism that is different from the orthodoxy. In place of a universal causal chain of technological forces, economic relations and superstructures, we now confront a more complicated and historically variable set of relational possibilities. Any significant relation between classes may be a production relation, with a part to play in the development of the productive forces. In place of abstract causal links that operate outside the historical process, we confront 'a rich totality of many determinations and relations' (Marx 1973:100) with structured agency and indeterminacy at its core. Production is a social process, in the broadest sense of the word.

This in turn alters the way we explain historical phenomena. The 'turn to the concrete' privileges conditional human agency rather than abstract economic forces. Since material forces are not ultimately determining, history does not guarantee that crises will be resolved through the movement to a higher level of technological development, either within capitalism, or by means of its supersession. Capitalist crises are typically crises of both the economic and the political order, and give rise to competing efforts at resolution (Hall 1978). Empirically, a shift to a higher level of technological development is only one possible outcome and if it is blocked, 'morbid symptoms' (Gramsci 1971:226) can appear, usually in the form of the resurrection of old ideas and practices long thought extinct.

HISTORICAL MATERIALISM AND THE PRISON GHETTO

The goal of the 'turn to the concrete' was to reconstruct historical materialism as an empirical 'guiding thread'. This section uses one of the morbid symptoms of the post-1970s crisis, the expansion and racialisation of the American prison system, as a way to assess the relative merits of the orthodox and revisionist approaches.

The American prison boom is a complex phenomenon. We focus here on two themes: the size of the prison population and its racial make-up. For most of the last century, the state and federal prison population varied between 100,000 and 200,000 inmates. After 1972 it increased six and a half times, reaching 1.3 million in 2000, while the incarceration rate (prisoners per 100,000 population) increased from 93 to 478 (*Sourcebook of Criminal Justice Statistics Online [SCJSO]*, Table 6.26; Beck and Glaze 2001). If we add inmates of local and municipal jails, those incarcerated surpassed 2 million in 2000 (*Manchester Guardian Weekly* 2000:1). The growth rate of the prison population has been falling since its peak (8.7 per cent) in 1994, but the numbers are so large that a 1.3 per cent growth rate in 2000 (the lowest since 1972) added about 27,000 inmates (Beck and Harrison 2001). The number under all forms of correctional control (in prison, jail, on parole or probation) grew by 117,000 in 2000 and stands at 6.5 million people, or 3.1 per cent of the adult population (US Department of Justice 2001).

The second dimension is the prison population's racial make-up. The racist use of the law and prisons for purposes of social control, proletarianisation and exploitation has a long pedigree, stretching back as far as the post-Reconstruction era (Lichtenstein 1996). The current racial make-up is more recent, however. Since 1950, when whites outnumbered non-whites roughly 2:1, the ratio has reversed (Cahalan 1987; Harrison and Beck 2002). Racial profiling, a drug war that targets black neighbourhoods and 'three strikes' legislation have created a prison population at odds with the profile of modern America.

In the 1990s, African-Americans made up about 12 per cent of the US population. On 31 December 2000, 46.2 per cent of state and federal prisoners were black, up from 44.5 per cent in 1990. Another 18 per cent were Hispanic. The percentage of young black males in prison varies between 7 and 10 per cent, depending on their age category, compared with a range of 0.8 to 1.2 per cent for white males in the same age categories (Beck and Harrison 2001). In 1997 in the South, 63 per cent of state prison inmates whose race was known were black (US Bureau of Justice Statistics 2000: Table 5.6).

How do we account for these patterns? We can quickly pass over conventional social science approaches, which see prison expansion as a result of increasing crime, or of rising violent and/or black crime, for the simple reason that none can stand up to empirical testing (Ladipo 2001). In the 27 years since the incarceration rate began to rise in the early 1970s, the overall crime rate fell 14 times (SCJSO, Table 3.120), and in 1999 was at 71.7 per cent of its peak. Similar patterns can be found in violent crime data. Minority crime rates are higher than those for whites, but they do not explain all of the disproportionality among the incarcerated. Moreover, racial differences in crime rates are stable over time, and cannot explain the recent racial transformation (Sabol 1989; Tonry 1995). Rather, the latter is a product of three decades of political change and legislation designed to redefine crime to encompass behaviour not previously criminalised (Parenti 1999; Ladipo 2001).

Approaches drawn from orthodox historical materialism

Materialist explanations examine punishment in the context of the business cycle and the effect of technology on the size of the surplus population. Rusche and Kirchheimer argue that crime is only part of the explanation of penal regimes. Rather, '[e]very system of production tends to discover punishments which correspond to its productive relationships. It is thus necessary to investigate the origin and fate of penal systems, the use or avoidance of specific punishments, and the intensity of penal practices as they are determined by social forces, above all by economic and then fiscal forces' ([1939] 1968:5). The crucial factor is the labour market, especially the size of the population that is surplus to economic requirements, and the technological factors that affect it. While there is no close fit between material factors and ideas about punishment, labour market conditions determine which ideas are activated at which times.

For the contemporary period, Quinney (1977:2) follows Rusche and Kirchheimer in stressing the size of the surplus population, but adds the inadequacy of the welfare state and the effect of the business cycle on unemployment into the mix. Similarly, Gordon and others find the roots of the incarceration boom in the shift from a 'Golden Age' of American capitalism (1945 to the late 1960s) to a succeeding period of crisis and decline (Marglin and Schor 1990; Gordon 1996). In the first period, social order was maintained by means of a virtuous circle of rising employment, productivity, profits, wages, standards of living, and consumption. Since work and work incentives are forms of social control, incarceration rates were low and falling. In contrast, the second period has been characterised by high unemployment, longer hours, falling real wages, work insecurity and poverty, dangerous levels of consumer debt, and comparative stagnation. In these later conditions, as the size of the surplus population has grown, control by incentives has given way to the 'stick' (Gordon 1996).

In contrast with conventional social science arguments, the advantages of these accounts are clear: they take seriously the epoch-making character of the prison boom and its concern with the marginalised and with race and class, and try to explain these as part of the restructuring that defines the age.

That said, the argument is wanting in several respects. First, the relationship between unemployment and incarceration rates is ambiguous. Since the 1970s, increasing incarceration rates have coincided with both rising and falling unemployment. It is the racial dimension, usually explained as a function of above average rates of marginality among minority populations, which is crucial however. David Gordon, for instance, argues that it is their structural economic position among the poor and blue-collar workers that leads blacks to crime as a way to survive, while also making them vulnerable to the attentions of zero-tolerance, drug-war policing (1996:141–2). Tonry (1995) has demonstrated the weaknesses of this type of argument. But it is also spurious, since if the function of prisons is to control the surplus population, the key test is not the poverty rate of blacks, but the size of the black component of those who are poor and/or marginal. Whether we focus on the official definition of poverty (US Bureau of the Census 2001:7), or a low family budget-based definition (Boushey et al. 2001:14), or the working-poor (Schwarz and Volgy 1992:74–5) or low-wage workers (Mishel et al. 2001, Table 5.19), the results are similar: the black share varies between 16 per cent and 24 per cent, no more than about half the black share of the incarcerated. The white proportion varies between three fifths and two thirds. If the prison population reflected the racial make-up of the surplus population, its profile would look more like it did in 1950 than it does now. Economic explanations may be a good starting point, but there is a large unexplained racial residual.

Revisionist historical materialism and the prison ghetto

A first step towards improvement is to follow Sayer and Larrain, recognising that restructuring is a broadly social process that can be driven by various non-material factors, and that the stock of ideas and practices is not simply a reflection of material reality. Brenner (1998) argues that the dominant response to the crisis that emerged in the 1970s was to reduce labour costs, increase the intensity of work and raise the rate of exploitation. The historical origins of this strategy can be found in a distinct Southern accumulation strategy that was eclipsed at the national level during the New Deal, but was reanimated beginning in the 1980s. This strategy was based on low-wage, labour-intensive, high-exploitation production, and hostility to unions. Social and political control and capital accumulation rested on the manipulation of racial antagonisms and the use of the law, the courts and forced prison labour to create low-wage labour forces for agriculture and industry (Wood 1986; Lichtenstein 1996). The South's 'de facto industrial policy' was to provide a haven for 'footloose' capital using relocation incentives and a business climate that protected employers from Fordist regulation, high wages, unions and tax rates (Lyson 1989).

One consequence of this was that the South had a significant interest in imprisoning black people. In 1971, at the end of a period of liberal criminal justice policy at the national level, the Southern incarceration rate was over three times as high as that in the Northeast. Though state incarceration rates have since converged, Southern states still top the list (Beck and Harrison 2001).

From the New Deal on, Southern accumulation was threatened by attempts to nationalise Fordism. Later, the civil rights legislation of the mid 1960s promised to undermine its political foundations, and tight metropolitan labour markets threatened the low-wage economy. Southern sociologists began to speculate about the 'Americanization of Dixie' (Egerton 1974). But in the crisis of the 1970s, the South became the fastest growing region in the country as firms searched for 'good business climates'. In the process, the region's political weight grew and by 1981 its development strategy had become the template for national policy.

Reaganomics responded to crisis by reconfiguring the balance of power between capital and labour, reducing wages, raising the rate of exploitation and moving towards export-oriented growth. Tax reform was skewed to benefit the wealthiest and the income and wealth distributions quickly polarised. High interest rates produced an industrial shakeout, raised unemployment and underemployment, and increased poverty. This increased insecurity also made it possible to attack the wages and benefits of those still employed. In addition, the labour and civil rights movements came under attack and environmental, workplace and consumer protections were weakened. Public services were cut back or privatised. Confined to the bottom of the job ladder and reliant on state services, minority workers were the main victims. Unemployment among blacks increased from 12 per cent in 1979 to 20 per cent by 1983 (US Council of Economic Advisers 2001). According to Cummings (1998:x), 'the economic ... policies that we have implemented in the United States over the past three decades have taken on the characteristics of an up-to-date, modified version of those that have been in effect in the American South for decades'. As a result, observers now stress the 'dixification of America' (Applebome 1996).

The key to both Southern accumulation and its nationalisation was racial politics. Racism had come under pressure in the 1960s and 1970s, but has since been revitalised. The source of this is to be found less in the economic crisis itself and more in the way it was 'lived': as a dual crisis not just of economic relations but also of the hierarchical building blocks of the social order: gender, the family, the domination of the military and especially race. The nationalisation of the Southern political formula since 1980 is not only economically motivated, it is also an attempt to restore order by combating the social movements that emerged in the 1960s.

The key to this effort was the law-and-order politics that emerged within the Republican Party in the late 1960s, usually referred to as the 'Southern strategy'. Its goal was to criminalise where possible, and demonise where not, social movements – civil rights, peace, women – that challenged the limits of American capitalist democracy and especially those that challenged the large-scale disfranchisement that was its foundation. It also involved a concerted attack on the courts, whose decisions in the 1960s had expanded rights for defendants, African-Americans and women. The strategy's symbolic goal was to present popular mobilisations as evidence of social breakdown, crime and moral decay. Its narrower, but crucial, purpose was to detach Southern white conservatives from the Democratic Party, thus facilitating the rollback of the liberal reforms of the 1960s.

Barry Goldwater's 1964 presidential campaign married an authoritarian law-and-order campaign with states' rights and opposition to civil rights legislation. In 1968 and 1972 George Wallace took up the standard, demonising civil rights activists in the same breath as the liberal elite, pornographers, muggers and the courts, and forced Richard Nixon to play the same game in order to protect his right flank (Carter 1996). This set the political agenda of the Republican Party for a generation. Though the initial audience was Southern, Nixon discovered that coded racism played well elsewhere. And the Republican Party discovered a way to reshape itself, and the electoral system, around the anxieties of the white Southern male. By the 1990s, according to Lind (1995:173), the supply-side wing of the Republican Party had been defeated by 'culture war conservatism', whose main concerns were with '[r]ace, sex, breeding, class ... the classic themes of the Tidewater reaction'. Racial backlash was now 'the common currency of American political rhetoric' (Carter 1996:19).

In the process, several policy issues – taxes, welfare, crime and policing, rights, affirmative action, drug enforcement, public housing – came to be seen in racial terms (Edsall and Edsall 1991). Angry taxpayers, hard pressed by a low-wage economic strategy, were persuaded (even though the facts are wrong) that their hard work was supporting young, addicted, welfare-dependent black women who were in the process of giving birth to an unsocialisable, violent predatory 'underclass'. The rhetorical coupling of race and welfare with drugs and crime came easily, as Diana Gordon's history of campaigns against the 'dangerous classes' demonstrates (1994:24–6 and Chapter 11). In the 1980s and 1990s, race, drugs and crime became the master-metaphors of the age, justifying 'war' on drug use, and prompting David Gordon to suggest that 'the U. S. criminal justice system, and perhaps large portions of the citizenry as well, believes that many African-Americans simply belong behind bars' (1996:141).

As if on cue, scholarly justification appeared. Though racial hereditarian ideas have lost scientific credibility, they can be reanimated when the circumstances are right. The most recent manifestation is *The Bell Curve*, a self-conscious response to the mobilisations of the 1960s (Herrnstein and Murray 1994:7–9). It appeared in 1994, the year that the Republican Party's 'Contract with America' announced the abolition of affirmative action and the welfare state. The authors argue (1994:523) that black poverty results from the race-structured inheritability of intelligence rather than social structure, public policy, or racism. If so, they say, the welfare state is both futile and immoral, and should be abandoned.

These views also reinforce the case for a racialised prison system. What is needed, according to Herrnstein and Murray, is a 'custodial state', to warehouse the underclass, provide for its welfare, take over childcare, and act as a 'high tech and more lavish version of the Indian reservation for some substantial minority of the nation's population, while the rest of America tries to go about its business' (1994:526). The authors are optimistic about their chilling utopia, which is already under construction.

CONCLUSION

Though the prison boom and neo-liberal economic restructuring are linked, economic explanations of the penal state are inadequate. This is not to say that controlling the surplus population is unimportant. Nor is it to deny the importance of everyday economic interests. Prison building provides many opportunities for profit. Politicians receive campaign contributions and benefit from the 'endless dramaturgical possibilities' (Downes 2001:213) that result from being 'tough on crime'. Conservative Southern politicians thrive on

black electorates artificially reduced by felony disfranchisement laws
(Shapiro 1997). Small towns seek prison projects to offset decades
of economic decline (Huling 2000). For the national economy, the
prison industrial complex acts like its military counterpart as an
automatic Keynesian stabiliser (Downes 2001:220).

Yet in the end, none of this would be possible without fear of the
black underclass and the ideas and practices that it has reanimated.
A racialised penal system, the result of an ideology of race and
class hierarchy and of a low-wage, high-exploitation accumulation
strategy, has been part of the Southern landscape since the end of
Reconstruction, when 'Southern prisons turned black overnight'
(Waquant 2002:53). Both have now been nationalised in response
to democratic mobilisations, economic crisis and globalisation, and a
racialised penal punitiveness has been nationalised in the process.

Historical materialism can explain these patterns, but not in its
orthodox form. To do so, it must make concessions that are alien to
the orthodox model: that ideas are not simply reflections of material
circumstances, but rather have their own life-process, and can be
reanimated in new circumstances; that development is complex
and uneven, both because of the coexistence of distinct regional
growth models and the way that aspects of a modern economy are
combined with the ideas and practices of the last century; and that the
historical process is simultaneously both open-ended, allowing such
combinations to be made in practice, but also structured and path-
dependent, since not all combinations are equally likely. Above all, it
must reject thinking in abstract categories and sequences, and admit
the possibility that relations formerly considered superstructural might
shape the development of the productive forces, as they manifestly
do in the empirical world. None of this requires the abandonment
of Marx's emphasis on social production and reproduction, but it
does require that we stop thinking about the world in abstract and
mechanical ways.

GUIDE TO FURTHER READING

Larrain (1986) provides the best general introduction to the issues
around historical materialism discussed here. Anderson (1976) fills
in some of the historical background. The literature on the American
prison system and on the more recent rise of a 'prison-industrial
complex' is vast. The best single guide is Parenti (1999), while Tonry
(1995) is a good introduction to the race issue. Waquant (2002) provides

important insights into the changing institutional forms taken by strategies of racial control from slavery to the judicial ghetto.

REFERENCES

Althusser, L. and Balibar, E. (1970) *Reading Capital* (London: New Left Books).

Anderson, P. (1976) *Considerations on Western Marxism* (London: New Left Books).

—— (1983) *In the Tracks of Historical Materialism* (London: Verso).

Applebome, P. (1996) *Dixie Rising* (New York: Harcourt, Brace).

Beck, A. and Glaze, L. (2001) *Correctional Populations in the United States, 1980–2000* (US Department of Justice, Bureau of Justice Statistics).

Beck, A. and Harrison, P. (2001) 'Prisoners in 2000', *Bureau of Justice Statistics Bulletin*, August (Washington: US Department of Justice).

Boushey, H. et al. (2001) *Hardships in America* (Washington: Economic Policy Institute).

Brenner, R. (1998) 'Uneven Development and the Long Downturn', *New Left Review*, No. 229.

Cahalan, M. (1987) *Historical Corrections Statistics in the United States 1850–1984* (Rockville, MD: Westat Inc.).

Carter, D. (1996) 'Legacy of Rage: George Wallace and the Transformation of American Politics', *Journal of Southern History*, Vol. LXII, No. 1.

Cohen, G. (1978) *Karl Marx's Theory of History* (Oxford: Clarendon Press).

Colletti, L. (1972) *From Rousseau to Lenin* (New York: Monthly Review Press).

Cummings, S. (1998) *The Dixification of America* (Westport, CT: Praeger).

Downes, D. (2001) 'The Macho Penal Economy: Mass Incarceration in the United States', in Anthony Giddens (ed.), *The Global Third Way Debate* (Cambridge: Polity Press).

Edsall, T.B. with Edsall, M. (1991) *Chain Reaction* (New York: Norton)

Egerton, J. (1974) *The Americanization of Dixie* (New York: Harper's Magazine Press).

Gordon, David (1996) *Fat and Mean* (New York: The Free Press).

Gordon, Diana (1994) *The Return of the Dangerous Classes* (New York: Norton).

Gramsci, A. (1971) *Selections from the Prison Notebooks*, edited by Quintin Hoare and Geoffrey Nowell Smith (New York: International Publishers).

Hall, S. (1978) *The Hard Road to Renewal* (London: Verso).

Harrison, P. and Beck, A. (2002) *Prisoners in 2001* (Washington: US Bureau of Justice Statistics, July 2002), <http://www.ojp.usdoj.gov/bjs/pub/pdf/p01.pdf>.

Herrnstein, R. and Murray, C. (1994) *The Bell Curve* (New York: The Free Press).

Huling, T. (2000) 'Prisoners of the Census', *Mother Jones*, May 10, <http://www.motherjones.com/realitycheck/census.html>.

Ladipo, D. (2001) 'The Rise of America's Prison-Industrial Complex', *New Left Review*, No. 7.

Larrain, J. (1986) *A Reconstruction of Historical Materialism* (London: Allen and Unwin).

Lichtenstein, A. (1996) *Twice the Work of Free Labour* (London: Verso).

Lind, M. (1995) 'Brave New Right', in Steven Fraser (ed.) *The Bell Curve Wars* (New York: Basic Books).

Lyson, T. (1989) *Two Sides to the Sunbelt* (New York: Praeger).

Manchester Guardian Weekly (2000) 'US Jails Two Millionth Inmate', 17 February.

Marglin, S. and Schor, J. (1990) *The Golden Age of Capitalism* (New York: Oxford University Press).

Marx, K. (1963) *Theories of Surplus Value*, Part I (Moscow: Progress Publishers).

—— (1973) *Grundrisse* (Harmondsworth: Penguin).

—— (1976) *Capital*, Vol. 1. (Harmondsworth: Penguin).

Marx, K. and Engels, F. (1968) *Selected Works* (Moscow: Progress Publishers).

—— (1976) *Collected Works*, Vol. 5 (New York: International Publishers).

McLellan, D. (ed.) (1977) *Karl Marx: Selected Writings* (Oxford: Oxford University Press).

Mishel, L. et al. (2001) *The State of Working America 2000–2001* (Ithaca, NY: ILR Press).

Parenti, C. (1999) *Lockdown America* (London: Verso).

Quinney, R. (1977) *Class, State and Crime* (New York: David McKay).

Rusche, G. and Kirchheimer, O. ([1939] 1968) *Punishment and Social Structure* (New York: Russell and Russell).

Sabol, W. (1989) 'Racially Disproportionate Prison Populations in the United States: an overview of historical patterns and review of contemporary issues', *Contemporary Crises*, Vol. 13.

Sayer, D. (1987) *The Violence of Abstraction* (Oxford: Blackwell).

Schwarz, J. and Volgy, T. (1992) *The Forgotten Americans* (New York: Norton).

Shapiro, A. (1997) 'The Disenfranchised', *The American Prospect*, No. 35.

Sourcebook of Criminal Justice Statistics Online, US Bureau of Justice Statistics, <http://www.albany.edu/sourcebook/index.html>.

Tonry, M. (1995) *Malign Neglect* (New York: Oxford University Press).

US Bureau of Justice Statistics (2000) *Correctional Populations of the United States 1997* (Washington: USGPO).

US Bureau of the Census (2001) *Poverty in the United States 2000*, Current Population Report (Washington: USGPO).

US Council of Economic Advisers (2001) *Economic Report to the President, 2001* (Washington: USGPO), <http://w3.access.gpo.gov/usbudget/fy2002/pdf/2001_erp.pdf>.

US Department of Justice (2001) 'National Correctional Population Reaches New High', Press Release, 26 August.

Waquant, L. (2002) 'From Slavery to Mass Incarceration: Rethinking the "race question" in the US', *New Left Review*, No. 13.

Wood, P. (1986) *Southern Capitalism* (Durham, NC: Duke University Press).

2
Capitalism

Keith Faulks

Capitalism is the primary target of the political left. This is because capitalism, despite its undoubted productive capacities, creates vast inequalities of wealth and power that have damaging consequences for the political, cultural and ecological foundations of society. The need for a coherent critique of capitalism has never been greater because capitalism has, in recent decades, become truly global in its impact, if not in the benefits it brings to the people of the world. Marx's forensic diagnosis of the ills of capitalism retains much of its power and provides a firm basis upon which such a critique can be built. Marx's characterisation of capitalism as inherently alienating and dehumanising seems of particular relevance in a world where the very existence of the planet is threatened by the pursuit of profit over all other human and ecological considerations. Capitalism alienates us from other people and from the natural world that sustains our lives, and blinds us to the plight of those suffering, through no fault of their own, the inequities of the system. What is routinely described today as economic *globalisation* is in reality *polarisation*, as inequality both within and between nations grows wider. This excessive inequality is linked to both the growth in global risks, such as the destruction of the natural environment, and to the weakening of democratic governance. Before exploring these criticisms in more detail it is necessary to define capitalism and to outline its various stages of development.

WHAT IS CAPITALISM?

Capitalism emerged as a concept in the mid nineteenth century, with the *Oxford English Dictionary* citing 1854 as the date when the term was first used. Significant elements of what came to be called capitalism, such as wage labour and private property, have of course existed in a variety of human societies and historical epochs well before the nineteenth century. It was however through the work of the French social theorist Saint Simon and, in particular, the German revolutionary Karl Marx that capitalism developed its contemporary meaning as a distinctly modern form of economic and social organisation. As an economic system, 'pure' capitalism is characterised by the following four main features:

1. The means by which the goods necessary to fulfil our material and cultural needs are produced are owned and controlled by relatively few people, known as capitalists.
2. The primary objective of capitalists is to maximise profit by producing and selling goods and services for as little cost as possible, and selling them on to consumers for as much profit as possible.
3. Profits are achieved largely through the exploitation of wage labour. Those who do not own the means of production sell their labour to capitalists for wages, which are paid at a rate invariably lower than the actual value of their work to the production process. In Marxist theory this excess is known as surplus value and is appropriated by the capitalist to reinvest or spend as they please.
4. The exchange system through which profit is obtained is the 'free' market, where commodities are brought and sold according to the laws of supply and demand, and for a value determined not by their intrinsic worth but by their market value. Crucially, labour is a commodity like any other, to be sold to the highest bidder.

In developing a critique of capitalism, it is important to understand that capitalism not only entails a set of economic arrangements. It is also a distinctive political/value system. In fact, capitalism today is a highly pervasive 'way of life' which many people now accept as how things are, how they should be, and how they will always be. With the collapse of the Soviet bloc in the late twentieth century, this new common sense has been turned into an influential theory that asserts that the triumph of capitalism over its main ideological rival marks the 'end of history' (Fukuyama 1992).

Politically, capitalism demands as much freedom from government interference as possible. Pure capitalism is therefore almost synonymous with classical liberalism, the principles of which Marx saw as the ideological shell of capitalism. Many influential liberals are sceptical about politics, with Thomas Paine asserting that government is but a 'necessary evil' and Hayek arguing that 'democracy may set up the most complete despotism imaginable'

(Faulks 1998). Nevertheless, because capitalism requires a framework of laws to protect the sanctity of contracts and private property, the great majority of capitalists accept the need for what the US theorist Nozick (1974) calls a 'nightwatchman state'. Such a state seeks only to secure order and thereby maintain the necessary conditions for the free market. To extend the role of government beyond this function, to redistribute wealth for example, is to violate the freedoms that capitalism both demands and helps to sustain. By refusing to accept that the market should be rooted in and subject to regulation by the community within which it operates, Nozick seeks in effect to depoliticise capitalism and exempt it from democratic scrutiny.

The values championed by capitalism are focused primarily upon the autonomy of the self-interested individual, who acts rationally to maximise his or her wealth and therefore happiness. Thus capitalism entails a modern, materialist conception of human nature. From this perspective, against a background of laws enforced by the state, I seek to compete with others to accumulate as much wealth and as many commodities as possible and my status in society will largely depend on my personal success in the market. Adam Smith (1976), in his famous tract on the merits of the free market, first published in 1776, asserted that such self-interest not only benefits the individual; it would, via the 'invisible hand' of the forces of supply and demand, meet the wider needs of the community by providing consumers, through competition between producers, with a wide choice of product.

Defenders of capitalism, then, see it as the best economic and social system ever devised; one which delivers both prosperity, through competition and the rigours of the market, and personal freedom, through limited government (Saunders 1995).

STAGES IN THE DEVELOPMENT OF CAPITALISM

So far I have outlined an idealised vision of capitalism, what the sociologist Max Weber calls an 'ideal type'. In practice, 'pure' capitalism has never, and probably will never, exist. Of particular significance in determining the particular form capitalism takes has been the role played by the state in regulating the market. Since even defenders of capitalists like Nozick grudgingly concede the need for *some* kind of state, the purity of capitalism at any given time and place is a question of degree. The extent to which citizenship (rights and obligations exercised within the political community) has supported or, at some junctures, challenged the logic of the capitalist system is therefore crucial to explaining the different historical forms taken by capitalism.

Classical capitalism

The form of capitalism found in Britain from around 1750 until the 1870s is the closest approximation to pure capitalism that the world has seen. Sometimes referred to as anarchic capitalism, this phase was marked by a multitude of relatively small-scale producers, an unorganised and mobile labour force, and largely unrestrained free markets (Faulks 1998:101–3). Even at this early stage of industrial capitalism, it is important not to overlook the repressive role played by the state in creating and protecting the conditions necessary for capitalist exploitation. As Gray observes, 'the mid-Victorian free market was an artefact of state coercion' (1998:8).

The forced enclosure of common land was essential in furthering capitalist interests and could only be carried out by a highly repressive state intent upon promoting those market rights necessary to capitalist accumulation. Although liberals such as Marshall ([1950] 1992) have painted a positive picture of the implications of early capitalism for citizens' rights, his claim that an extensive package of civil rights had developed in Britain by the end of the eighteenth century is false. Market rights, such as the protection of contract and private property, necessary to facilitate the smooth operation of the market, were granted to (male) citizens, whereas civil rights such as protest or free association were suppressed. Between 1816 and 1820, for example, the Conservative government of Lord Liverpool embarked upon a series of reactionary legislation in response to several instances of relatively minor civil unrest, notably the Luddite Riots[1] and Peterloo Massacre.[2] Habeas Corpus was suspended and the so-called 'Six Acts' gave granted magistrates draconian powers including rights to search houses without warrants and to restrict the scope of demonstrations.

The dominance of the market over citizenship during this period is well illustrated by the Poor Law Act of 1834, which formed the centrepiece of the British welfare system until the First World War. This legislation detached welfare relief from the notion of social citizenship by setting benefits at levels lower than the lowest wage available in the market. Recipients of benefits were also denied basic civil rights through their enforced confinement to the poor house, which insisted upon families living apart. The abstract nature of human relationships in a free market system is well illustrated by such legislation. The apparent 'freedom' of the wage labourer to sell their productive capacity to the highest bidder masked the structured nature of inequality[3] and reinforced the impression that poverty and unemployment could be explained by individual idleness. Even radical liberals like J.S. Mill defended the harshness of the poor house as a necessary inducement to work (Faulks 1998:34).

The form taken by the state during the classical period of capitalist development closely approximates that described by Marx and Engels in *The Communist Manifesto* of 1848. The state did primarily act as a 'committee for managing the affairs of the whole bourgeoisie'. Models of citizenship, based as they were on the promotion of market rights, did nothing to challenge capitalism and were in fact a necessary precondition of it. Only with the extension of political rights to the working class in the nineteenth century[4] did a more developed sense of citizenship begin to modify the excesses of classical capitalism.

Politically regulated capitalism

The role played by the state in the regulation of capitalism increased dramatically from the 1870s onwards and this regulated approach dominated capitalist societies until the mid 1970s. This stage involved much greater state intervention in the economy, including the direct provision by the state of certain key utilities and state-funded training, education and welfare. It also entailed the emergence of huge corporations, which sought to concentrate production to maximise profitability, and the associated development of organised labour. As Marx and Engels comment, 'with the development of industry the proletariat not only increases in number; it becomes concentrated in greater mass, its strength grows, and it feels that strength more' (1985:89). Workers were able to utilise their newly won political rights (to vote and to organise politically) to gradually make genuine inroads into the capitalist system by extending citizenship to the social sphere.

The shift to a more politically managed capitalism was, then, the result of both expediency on behalf of the ruling elites *and* struggle by a unionised and politically active working class. The need for an educated labour force and the recognition by employers of the advantages of dealing with organised trade unions, which could generally be peacefully incorporated into the system, encouraged a kind of social contract between owner and worker. The economic advantages of mass, Fordist techniques of production facilitated this compromise, the greatest achievement of which was the establishment of the welfare state. As Marshall ([1950] 1992) comments, this led to the modification of pure capitalism and greater security for workers.

In this context, the primary role of the state shifted from *repression* to *legitimisation*. In Britain the growing strength of the Labour Party gave ordinary workers an influential voice in the political process and to a large extent ensured economic and social grievances were dealt with peacefully and through the mechanisms of parliamentary democracy and industrial arbitration. In other European countries, the taming of pure capitalism was even more pronounced than in Britain. As Albert (1993) has argued, in northern European countries, Germany, Switzerland and the Benelux states, 'Rhine capitalism', which restricts the profit motive by tightly regulating market forces and provides extensive public welfare, successfully challenged the logic of profitability at all costs. Under Rhine capitalism, argues Albert, 'the interests of the community are paramount' (1993:125).

The trade-off between capital and labour, expressed through the extension of citizenship has however been but a temporary phenomenon in many countries. This historic compromise was dependent upon an unprecedented level of economic growth which economists have referred to as the Golden Age of capitalism (Dicken 1998). From the end of the Second World War until the 1970s advanced industrial countries experienced unprecedented levels of economic growth and world trade rose at well over 7 per cent between 1958 and 1968 (Dicken 1998:24). In 1973 however, the Arab oil-producing states, realising their importance to the capitalist system, formed OPEC and subsequently quadrupled oil prices. This action helped trigger a world recession, which saw profitability in the main industrial countries fall drastically. Of particular significance was the decline in the performance of the US economy, which in 1971 saw its trade account fall into deficit for the first time since the nineteenth century. The postwar economic system was built upon the dollar, and the growing interdependence of capitalist economies meant that the decline of the most economically powerful state would create severe problems across the globe. The 'solution' to these problems, however, was not to be tighter political regulation over the economy. Instead, the last few decades have been dominated by a neo-liberal approach to governance, which has sought to greatly restrict democratic controls over the imperatives of capital.

Depoliticised capitalism

Since the late 1970s we have seen a sustained attack on the politically regulated form of capitalism, which ironically had presided over the most sustained period of economic growth in the modern age. The election of Margaret Thatcher in 1979 and Ronald Reagan in 1980 ensured that Britain and the USA, by tradition the two countries most committed to a pure form of capitalism, had two highly committed neo-liberals at the helm of government. These two ideologues set the pattern of governance of capitalism which has remained dominant into the twenty-first century.

The neo-liberals' mission was, in the words of Thatcher, to 'roll back the frontiers of the state'. In effect, to make capitalism safe for capitalists again. Governments across the globe aimed to privatise industries previously owned by the state, reduce personal and business taxation, deregulate financial institutions, remove restrictions on foreign direct investment and reduce public spending, particularly on welfare benefits. The pattern of these changes has been uneven, however, with countries that have followed the so-called Rhine model of capitalism moving slower than the USA and Britain in accepting deregulation and foreign capital. Albert notes, however, that despite its economic and social advantages over neoliberalism, 'in terms of ideological status and political prestige, the Rhine model is in retreat' (1993:169). A recent example of the triumph of neo-liberalism can be found in the criteria imposed by the European Union (EU) upon countries seeking to join the euro. Public investment and welfare spending programmes have been the main casualties of the fiscal prudence demanded by the EU. This is the main reason why Sweden, one of the few countries to still swim successfully against the neo-liberal tide, voted against joining the euro in 2003 for fear that its extensive welfare system would be diminished.

Lash and Urry (1987) call this current stage of development 'disorganised' capitalism. This label is however misleading, for capitalism has not become disorganised so much as it has been reorganised and depoliticised. Capitalism is now regulated in the boardrooms of large corporations and via the undemocratic World Bank, World Trade Organisation, and International Monetary Fund, rather than in the elected political assembly. These new institutions of global governance, which taken together form an Economic Management Regime (EMR), have been growing rapidly in significance since the 1980s.

The model of capitalism adopted by this regime is the so-called 'Washington Consensus', or neo-liberalism by another name. Highly abstract models of the free market have been promoted by the EMR in the old Soviet bloc, Africa and Latin America; loans and aid programmes have been made dependent upon the neo-liberalisation of economies. The emphasis has, above all, been upon removing fiscal and political barriers to the movement of capital by western multinational corporations (MNCs). Such powerful companies can increasingly hold governments to ransom by threatening to remove investment if 'anti-market' legislation, such as higher taxation, trade union rights, or social welfare are pursued. A recent example of the deregulation of national economies at the expense of citizens' rights occurred in August 2003 when the Indian Supreme Court, under pressure from both local and global capitalists, declared that government workers have 'no fundamental, legal, moral or equitable right' to go on strike. Praful Bidwai (2003) estimates that three quarters of India's organised workforce will be affected by this legislation and argues that this illustrates 'how far Indian elite thinking has gone down the road of economic neo-liberalism'.

The EMR has, however, been uneven in its application of pure capitalist principles. In some areas, where powerful corporate interests are threatened, the EMR has allowed protectionism. High-technology industries are a good example, as patent rights on new inventions have been jealously guarded by MNCs. As Adam Smith observed, corporate interests are just as much a barrier to free trade as is an over-centralised government. Yet it is the interests of influential corporations rather that those of genuine competition that are served by the EMR. This is why defenders of the market, such as David Korten, can nonetheless mount strong attacks on depoliticised capitalism. Korten (1998) states:

we live in a world being pillaged by the institutions of global capitalism to enrich the few at the expense of the many. We must replace the global capitalist economy with democracies and market economies. In a healthy market economy enterprises are human-scale and predominately locally owned.

While it is true that the socially embedded market favoured by Korten would mark an improvement over the current dominance of large corporations, nonetheless, as the decline of the period of politically regulated capitalism demonstrated, any political community or model of citizenship that is rooted in market relations is vulnerable to the inevitable fluctuations of the free market economy. The fact that capitalism's uneasy truce with democratic citizenship during the postwar period was quickly abandoned once it no longer appeared to serve the interests of capitalism highlights the ongoing need to challenge the dysfunctions of capitalism at a more profound level. Marx remains the best starting point for such a challenge.

CONTRADICTIONS AND CRITIQUE

Marx for and against capitalism

While Marx is capitalism's most insightful critic, he nonetheless saw capitalism as a necessary step forward for humankind. The emergence of industrial capitalism meant that human beings could look forward to a post-scarcity society where everyone's material needs would be met, thereby giving them the opportunity to develop their true creative potential through work, science, art and critical thought. This is because capitalism has 'created more massive and more colossal production forces than have all preceding generations together'. The restless dynamic of capitalism was also crucial in stripping away the narrow mindedness of previous social forms, rescuing in the process 'a considerable part of the population from rural idiocy'. Capitalism has 'pitilessly torn asunder the motley feudal ties that bound man to his "natural superiors", and has left remaining no other nexus between man and man than naked self-interest, than callous "cash payment"' (Marx and Engels 1985:85, 84, 82).

Human kind is forced then to face up to the material reality of its essence, stripped bare of any comforting illusions. The essence of human beings as creative actors who express themselves through labour is, however, perverted by the inherent contradictions of capitalism. Of crucial significance to Marx's critique is the observation that the 'naked, shameless, direct, brutal exploitation' (1985:82) of the many by the few leads to large-scale inequalities of wealth, power and life chances. Moreover, even when basic subsistence may be assured, material inequalities become central to one's sense of well-being in a system where 'money is the alienated essence of man's work and existence; the essence dominates him and he worships it' (Marx 1964:37).

This point leads us to consider a second important insight into the human consequences of the capitalist mode of production. In

Capital, Marx shows how the commodification of all aspects of life and the obsession with the monetary value of things obscures the suffering that is an inevitable consequence of capitalism. Capitalists and workers alike are locked in an abstract relationship, which is dehumanising and alienating for both parties. Thus human relationships are reduced to naked self-interest where 'the only force bringing them together, and putting them into relation with each other, is the selfishness, the gain and the private interest of each. Each pays heed to himself only, and no one worries about the others.' (Marx 1976:280) The superficiality of the values and ends promoted by capitalism ensures that though the capitalist may enjoy great material wealth, he or she is 'just as enslaved by the relationship of capitalism as is his opposite pole, the worker' (Marx 1976:990). As Kolakowski comments, 'alienation is nothing but a process in which man deprives himself of what he truly is, his own humanity' (1978:265).

This alienation has profound social and political implications. Ties of community and citizenship, which require bonds of affection and mutual obligation much deeper than those generated by a purely economic contract between individuals, are undermined in a system based upon the right to property which 'leads every man to see in other men, not the realisation, but rather the limitation of his own liberty' (Marx, in Waldron 1987:146). The modern state is a barrier rather than a potential solution to the problems of capitalism because the community it claims to protect is an abstract one which masks the state's primary role as a defender of class interest. By treating human beings as abstract agents, whose relationships are conceived of as contracts in the market, capitalism not only ignores individuals' concrete interests as members of a social class, it also denies other aspects of their identities, such as gender, ethnicity and religion, which are crucial to their sense of self. This, I would argue, means that any challenge to these abstractions constitutes a challenge to the very logic of capitalism. Struggles for the emancipation of women, or for gay or disability rights, for example, are as crucial as working-class struggles in exposing the contradictions of a market system that would treat all individuals as abstract economic entities, whose only value is as faceless consumers.

Marxism has rightly been criticised for its scientific delusions, its dismissal of the importance of morality and its romantic portrayal of the working class as the inevitable harbinger of a better society. Nevertheless, the deeply humanistic insights of Marx discussed above remain powerful tools of analysis that help us to uncover the essentially pathological nature of capitalism. Marx shows that the Weberian notion that capitalism is the economic expression of human rationality obscures the decidedly irrational consequences of capitalism in practice (see Sayer 1991). Of pressing concern are the severe levels of inequality across the globe and the consequence of a profit motive that pays little heed to human need or environmental considerations.

Inequality and global risk

One of the promises made by proponents of global capitalism is that, if left alone, market forces will create enough wealth for all. This doctrine was expressed in Reagan and Thatcher's infamous philosophy of 'trickle-down economics' which asserted that if we allow the rich to get even richer we all benefit from the investments they make and the jobs they create. The evidence overwhelmingly suggests, however, that as capitalism has become freed from democratic restraint inequality and poverty have grown rapidly. As a 2002 OECD report showed, the differences in income levels between rich and poor in developed industrial countries actually increased between the mid 1970s and mid 1990s. States which have embraced neo-liberalism most firmly, like the USA and Britain, not surprisingly saw the biggest growth in inequality (Henning 2002). Of even greater significance have been the appalling levels of poverty found in 'developing' countries.

In July 2003 the United Nations Development Program published its annual report on human development (see Madrick 2003). The report makes distressing reading. Fifty-four nations out of the 175 examined in the report are poorer now than they were in 1990. The report estimates that in excess of 1 billion people live in extreme poverty, lacking adequate access to the most basic of resources, such as food, water and shelter. Nearly 3 billion live on less than the equivalent of $2 a day. Many of the poorest countries, such as those in sub-Saharan Africa, have been targeted by the EMR for neo-liberalisation. The policy of structural adjustment, basically the indiscriminate application of market forces, has however clearly been a disaster for such countries. Capitalism has a tendency to abstract such human tragedies from their social context and this is why the EMR has consistently argued, in face of a strong body of evidence to the contrary, that the problem is not global capitalism but bad governance. This is to ignore how such inequality is rooted in the colonial past of many countries, especially in Africa. Today such inequality is perpetuated by the EMR allowing protectionist policies, in agricultural goods and textiles for example, which defend the interests of western countries and corporations. Another key factor in explaining the structured inequality experienced by the poorest countries is the appalling levels of debt many owe to capitalist organisations such as the IMF. Between 1990 and 1997 for example, a period of relative boom in the world economy, developing countries repaid more in debt than they received in new loans from the EMR (Danaher 2001:22–3).

Optimistic claims about the merits and benefits of globalisation, which can be defined as the growing interdependence of peoples, cultures and economies, clearly then mask a growing polarisation both within and between countries. Globalisation is in some aspects, however, far from being a myth. The communication-technology revolution has, in a sense, made the world a smaller and more interconnected place. The growing awareness of the suffering caused by global inequality, facilitated mainly by the widespread availability of television and the Internet, has created some opportunities for the anti-capitalism movement to at least expose some of the failures of the EMR neo-liberal agenda.

There is of course a strong moral case to be made for the richest countries of the world to play a much more proactive role in tackling global poverty. The great technological strides made in recent decades mean that these problems could undoubtedly be solved if the political will existed. Even if one does not accept the argument that global capitalism is the root cause of inequality, it is clear that its simple-minded logic is the principal barrier to tackling the problem in a systematic and planned fashion. However, from the point of view of western states, the globalisation of risk, linked as it is to inequality, has created a more pressing reason than morality for seeking more effective mechanisms of global governance than the institutions of the EMR. Wealthy states are increasingly finding that many of the problems they face are global in their impact and cannot be tackled by one state, however powerful, acting alone. Arguments of morality have merged with arguments of self-preservation because global problems such as migration, illegal drug trade, war and environmental damage are all interconnected, are rooted in inequality, and are transnational in their effects (see Faulks 1999:189–94). The illegal drug trade, for example, which accounts for 10 per cent of total global trade, can in large part be explained by protectionism by bodies like the European Union's Common Agricultural Policy, which, by flying in the face of genuine competition, have restricted imports from the Third World and thus have indirectly encouraged farmers in countries such as Pakistan to seek the much higher profit margins associated with the production of illicit drugs.

The institutions of global capital have often been implicated more directly in the creation and intensification of global risks. An example is the damaging consequences the actions of MNCs have had for the environment. To take just one illustration, nearly 90 per cent of global pesticide sales in 1994 were made by just 20 MNCs. These powerful companies have encouraged the excessive use of dangerous chemicals in farming which can destroy the long-term fertility of land and has major consequences for animal and human health (Elliot 1998:123).

Because in a capitalist system exchange value always takes priority over use value, natural resources are useful only in as far as they can be manufactured into a product that can be sold for money. As Danaher observes:

A tree has no value standing; it is only when the tree gets killed and turned into plywood and hot tubs that it generates market value. A fish swimming has no value; it is only when the fish is killed and marketed as a commodity that it generates value. Thus destroying nature is generic to the market economy. (2001:59)

Where the EMR has tried to restrict ecological damage, it has attempted to use the bizarre logic of the market. Thus for example, under the 1997 Kyoto agreement, pollution quotas were given to each participating country who could, if they so chose, sell all or part of their quota to the highest bidder. Global risks require democratic governance, operating at both a local and global level, precisely because the short-termism of a system that reduces all things to their monetary value is ill-equipped to deal with the long-term consequences of widespread inequality and environmental damage. As the next section will explore, however, capitalism is necessarily opposed to the principles and values of democracy.

Capitalism and democracy

Capitalism and democracy are seen by defenders of the new world order as two sides of the same coin (Fukuyama 1992). Korten (1998), however, captures much more accurately the true nature of the relationship:

Contrary to its claims, capitalism's relationship to democracy and the market economy is much the same as the relationship of a cancer to the body whose life energies it expropriates. Cancer is a pathology that occurs when an otherwise healthy cell forgets that it is part of the body and begins to pursue its own unlimited growth without regard to the consequences for the whole. The growth of the cancerous cells deprives the healthy cells of nourishment and ultimately kills both the body and itself. Capitalism does much the same to the societies it infests.

Capitalism is the antithesis of democracy in several ways. First, capitalism inherently presupposes and, indeed, celebrates inequality. Democracy, in contrast, has its moral foundations in the idea of equal citizenship for all citizens. Societies which base their economies on capitalist principles inevitably limit the scope of citizenship because economic inequalities necessary skew political resources, influence and power towards the wealthy. As Hertz notes, in countries like the USA 'access to elected political office ... is now almost exclusively the privilege of the seriously rich' (2002:120).

Second, capitalism's conception of human relationships in abstract, contractual terms and its emphasis upon values such as competition, selfishness, materialism and consumerism are directly opposed to the ethics of democratic citizenship, which include cooperation, civic responsibility, morality and political participation. In a capitalist system it is impossible to generate the kinds of extensive obligations between citizens necessary to a deep sense of citizenship where the needs of the community are seen as preconditions to the development of self. Declining rates of political participation in most industrial countries, most obviously demonstrated by falling turnout at elections, is largely down to the emphasis these societies now place upon consumerism rather than citizenship.

Third, capitalism demands freedom from democratic interference, even where its relentless pursuit of money is at odds with the wider needs of the community. Capitalism is therefore parasitic in its relationship to democracy. An excellent example is the bizarre activities of the world's stock markets, where brokers spend billions every day speculating on the ups and downs of currencies, transactions that have nothing to do with the real economy and everything to do with greed. Such 'casino capitalism' can have huge effects on elected governments. In 1992, for example, John Major's Conservative government spent billions trying unsuccessfully to protect the British pound against currency speculators and this led to Britain's withdrawal from the European exchange-rate mechanism.

Fourth, capitalist corporations are not averse to investing in dictatorships, which systematically torture and kill their own citizens. Companies with household names have happily done business with figures such as Marcos in the Philippines, Pinochet in Chile and the Saudi royal family. It is clear then that capitalism is no friend of democracy, for it pays little heed to the protection of human rights or indeed the needs of anyone beyond a small elite.

CONCLUSION

My aim in this chapter has been to outline the main features of capitalism, show how it has developed over time and highlight some of the problems it poses for democratic and environmentally sustainable governance. Other chapters in this volume have the rather more difficult task of conceptualising ways to resolve these problems. I will restrict myself here to just a brief comment on the anti-capitalism movement.

As I have argued, Marx's diagnosis of the ills of capitalism remains profound and is central to building a left alternative. His speculative cure in the form of a proletarian revolution seems an unlikely way forward however. Although the negative effects of capitalism have become more apparent in recent years, thanks in part to the efforts of anti-capitalist protestors, the prospects for an alternative remain unclear. This is because anti-capitalism remains a highly incoherent and divided movement, containing as it does anarchist, socialist, libertarian and green elements.

While anti-capitalist protestors share a common enemy, they are less certain about what would replace capitalism and how such a transformation can best be achieved. Callinicos (2001:118–19) may be right to see the incoherence of anti-capitalism as a potential strength, allowing as it does the articulation of a variety of fresh alternatives to the status quo. We should not, however, let such optimistim blind us to the undemocractic aspects of the movement and, in particular, to those elements which advocate the use of violence as a form of resistance. Using violence can only damage the movement by playing into the hands of political elites who wish to label all anti-capitalists as extremist. It will weaken the case against capitalism by alienating ordinary citizens from its cause and, given the power of the state, the movement cannot in any case hope to defeat capitalism by the use of force.

The anti-capitalism movement, if it is to move beyond mere protest politics, will need to connect more successfully with mainstream politics. Traditional parties of the centre left, such as the British Labour Party and German SPD, have in recent years sought an accommodation with capitalism through their advocacy of a business friendly, 'Third Way', approach to governance (Callinicos 2001). Nevertheless, given the electoral support that such parties can still command, they remain important in challenging the worst excesses of capitalism. The challenge for the myriad of social movements that seek to transcend capitalism is therefore to seek to build common purpose with traditional political parties and in the process seek whenever possible to radicalise them in ways which more profoundly challenge the corrosive logic of capitalism.

GUIDE TO FURTHER READING

Saunders (1995) provides a concise, sociological overview of capitalism and a spirited defence of its achievements. Nozick (1974) is a more philosophically grounded attempt to link the free market to individual freedom. For an interesting comparison between the contrasting neo-liberal and Rhine models of capitalism, see Albert (1993). Marx and Engels' *The Communist Manifesto* remains the classic critique of capitalism and is still very readable. For more up to date critiques of capitalism, Sklair (2002) is a very thorough if slightly dry account of the pitfalls of global capitalism, while Hertz (2002) is a livelier but slightly flowery exploration of the consequences of capitalism for democracy and politics. On the anti-capitalism movement, see the useful, if variable, collection of essays edited by Bircham and Charlton (2001).

NOTES

1. The Luddites were disaffected croppers, weavers and knitters who between 1811 and 1817 vented their feelings against new labour-saving machines by smashing them and burning the factories that housed them. The government responded strongly, using troops to break the demonstrations and hanging seven Luddites at York in 1813.
2. In 1819 some 60,000 people gathered in St Peter's Field, Manchester to protest against rising unemployment and to listen to a speech by the radical Henry Hunt. Despite the peaceful nature of the protest, local

magistrates responded by unleashing the army upon those assembled. The result was eleven people dead and 400 injured. The Conservative government congratulated the magistrates upon the decisiveness of their action and embarked upon a series of repressive reforms.

3. Inequality that is inherent to, and which results from, the unstable and uncertain patterns of investment and profitability of the capitalist system.

4. A series of reform acts in the mid to late nineteenth century gradually extended the vote to the working class. Women, though, did not achieve parity of voting rights until 1928.

REFERENCES

Albert, M. (1993) *Capitalism against Capitalism* (London: Whurr).

Bidwai, P. (2003) 'A Blow to Citizenship Rights', <www.flonnet.com/fl207/stories/2003082900692700.htm>.

Bircham, E. and Charlton J. (eds) (2001) *Anti-Capitalism: A Guide to the Movement* (London: Bookmarks).

Callinicos, A. (2001) *Against the Third Way* (Cambridge: Polity Press).

Danaher, K. (2001) *10 Reasons to Abolish the IMF and World Bank* (New York: Seven Stories).

Dicken, P. (1998) *Global Shift: Transforming the World Economy* (London: Paul Chapman).

Elliott, L. (1998) *The Global Politics of the Environment* (Basingstoke: Macmillan).

Faulks, K. (1998) *Citizenship in Modern Britain* (Edinburgh: Edinburgh University Press).

—— (1999) *Political Sociology: A Critical Introduction* (Edinburgh: Edinburgh University Press).

Fukuyama, F. (1992) *The End of History and the Last Man* (London: Hamilton).

Gray, J. (1998) *False Dawn: The Delusions of Global Capitalism* (London: Granta).

Henning, D. (2002) 'OECD Study Shows Growing Gulf between Rich and Poor', <www.wsws.org/articles/2002/sep2002/oecd-s2.shtml>.

Hertz, N. (2002) *The Silent Takeover: Global Capitalism and the Death of Democracy* (London: Random House).

Kolakowski, L. (1978) *Main Currents of Marxism: Volume One* (Oxford: Oxford University Press).

Korten, D. (1998) 'Life After Capitalism' <www.pcdf.org/I998/capitalism.htm>.

Lash, S. and Urry, J. (1987) *The End of Organized Capitalism* (Cambridge: Polity Press).

Madrick, J. (2003) 'Grim Facts on Global Poverty', *New York Times*, 7 August.

Marshall, T.H. ([1950] 1992) 'Citizenship and Social Class', in T.H. Marshall and T. Bottomore *Citizenship and Social Class* (London: Pluto Press).

Marx, K. (1964) *Early Writings* (New York: McGraw-Hill).

—— (1976) *Capital, Vol. 1* (Harmondsworth: Penguin).

Marx, K. and Engels, F. (1985) *The Communist Manifesto* (Harmondsworth: Penguin).
Nozick, R. (1974) *Anarchy, State and Utopia* (Oxford: Blackwell).
Saunders, P. (1995) *Capitalism: A Social Audit* (Buckingham: Open University Press).
Sayer, D. (1991) *Capitalism and Modernity: An Excursus on Marx and Weber* (London: Routledge).
Sklair, L. (2002) *Globalization: Capitalism and its Alternatives* (Oxford: Oxford University Press).
Smith, A. (1976) *The Wealth of Nations* (Oxford: Clarendon Press).
Waldron, J. (1987) *Nonsense upon Stilts* (London: Methuen).

3
Class

Peter McLaverty

Class has played a vital role in the work of socialist theorists over the years. In the nineteenth and early twentieth centuries, when socialist or social democratic parties were created in many parts of Europe, the relationship of those parties to the working class, and the role they saw class struggle playing in the achievement of their goals, was a defining feature of individual parties (Sassoon 1997). However, the role that class should play in understanding capitalist society and in achieving radical social change has been debated since at least the nineteenth century. The debates continue today.

Many of the debates concern the adequacy of the approach to class which is to be found within the broad Marxist tradition. In this chapter, therefore, I will outline the theory of social class developed by Karl Marx. Marx's depiction of class in capitalist society and his theory of the role of class struggle in the transformation of capitalism into socialism will be discussed in detail. Marx's argument that capitalist society is dividing into two mutually antagonistic classes, the bourgeoisie and the proletariat, will be considered. In particular, I will investigate the view that the central agency in the transformation of capitalism into socialism is the working class which, in moving from being a class in itself to becoming a class for itself, will inaugurate the classless socialist or communist society. I will suggest that the relationship between class in itself and class for itself, as applied to the working class in capitalist society, is problematic. Criticisms of the Marxist approach will be outlined, including the argument that in capitalist society there are not two main classes but at least three. The problem of the 'middle class' in Marxist analysis will be assessed. Arguments that class in advanced capitalist society is crosscut by divisions such as race, ethnicity and gender will be considered.

I will conclude by suggesting that class remains crucially important in analysing the modern world. However, I will also suggest that all ideas of the inevitability of working-class unity and of the working class necessarily carrying out a mission have to be rejected. The importance of subjectivity in politics needs to be recognised in the development of progressive politics.

THE CLASSICAL MARXIST APPROACH

For Marx, class was the motive force of societal change. He saw class as an economic category which has wider political and social consequences. Once primitive communism had ended, history became the history of class struggle (Marx and Engels 1998). Classes, Marx argued, are antagonistic. Class struggle is inevitable in class societies. This provides the basis for a theory of how societies have changed historically. Change has been due to conflicts between a declining dominant or ruling class and an emerging dominant or ruling class. Until capitalism, one minority class was replaced as the ruling class by another minority class. What is unique about capitalism is that for the first time in history the vast majority (the working class) is in a position to displace a minority ruling class and create the conditions for the achievement of the classless socialist or communist society.

Marx's main focus was on capitalism, which he argued was splitting into two mutually antagonistic classes: the capitalist class (or bourgeoisie) and the working class (or proletariat). The bourgeoisie owns and controls the means of production, such as factories and offices and the machinery used in production; the working class live by offering their labour power for sale. Capitalists make profits by exploiting the working class; that is, the workers create a value – surplus value – which is greater than the value of their labour power and which is appropriated by the capitalist in the form of profit. Workers experience alienation – the purpose of their work is determined by others and what they produce becomes an alien force which comes to control them in the form of capital. Workers are also politically oppressed through the workings of the state. Conflict between capitalists and workers is inevitable and takes a number of forms. It can be latent, as well as manifest.

Marx accepted that in the actual capitalist societies which he studied the class structure was complex, with intermediate strata and groups clouding the emerging picture. He saw the division of capitalism into two mutually antagonistic classes as a tendency, and fully recognised, for example, the continued existence of the petty-bourgeoisie in the capitalist societies of his day. However, Marx regarded any overlapping strata between the capitalist class and the working class as 'immaterial for our analysis'. This was because:

> We have seen that the continual tendency and law of development of capitalist production is to separate the means of production more and more from labour, and to concentrate the scattered means of production more and more in large groups, thereby transforming labour into wage labour and the means of production into capital. (Marx 1909:1031)

As he explained the underlying trends of class structure in capitalist society, is it accurate to say that Marx argued that working-class revolution and the achievement of socialism or communism was inevitable? Support for the view that he did so is to be found in works like *The Communist Manifesto* (Marx and Engels 1998), where he wrote about capitalism producing its own grave diggers, set out a schema in which the working class would become organised, first in trade unions and then in political parties (or a political party), and saw working-class revolution on the horizon. However, throughout his writings, Marx argued for the need for working-class political organisation and for socialists to work to this end. Had he regarded such political organisation as inevitable, there would have been little point in his arguing that this was a task that had to be consciously completed. In this sense, it seems fair to question whether Marx's assertions in *The Communist Manifesto* of the inevitability of working-class political organisation and the achievement of socialism should be seen as polemical excess. That he did not regard working-class revolution as inevitable is strongly suggested by the distinction he made between a 'class in itself' and a 'class for itself' in *The Poverty of Philosophy* (Marx 1975). For Marx, the working class was a 'class in itself' simply because of the position in the capitalist mode of production which members of the class shared. However, Marx argued that the members of the working class also had an overriding collective interest in transforming capitalism into socialism. If the members of the working class became aware of this interest and worked to fulfil it, then the working class would become a 'class for itself'. The move from one position to the other was seen as something that had to be actively achieved, as a result of conscious political class struggle and action by the working class, and was not viewed as inevitable.

Marx's general position seemed to be based on the following analysis: Classes exist due to their relationship to the means of production. Interests flow from those class positions but class members may not be aware of them; they may experience 'false consciousness'. Socialists have to engage in struggle to help the majority of working-class people become aware of their real interests. However, Marx argued that the working-class experience of capitalism would tend to increase awareness of their class interests (class consciousness) and to undermine false consciousness.

PROBLEMS WITH MARX'S APPROACH

Intermediate groups

The question of class consciousness is crucial to Marx's analysis. Yet this part of his theory, in particular, has faced major criticisms. In order to discuss this issue, it is worthwhile considering Marx's categorisation of classes in capitalism in slightly more detail. One of the main criticisms of Marx's approach is that there are not only two major classes (capitalists and workers) in capitalist society and that capitalist society is not moving towards this position. There is also a class (or there are classes) in between, 'the middle class' (or middle classes) – comprising middle managers, specialised workers and professionals, along with the traditional petty-bourgeoisie – whose relationship to the means of production, and position in the labour process, is not the same as that of workers or capitalists. This class (or these classes) is not being squeezed out of existence and is, indeed, in some arguments, growing. In a tradition which can be traced back to the work of Max Weber, class in capitalist society is not seen as essentially dichotomous but as based around three (or more) divisions (see, for example, Marshall et al. 1988, Goldthorpe 1997).

Many efforts have been made by those working in the Marxist tradition to accommodate this middle group. I will outline only two positions, as there is not enough space to deal with all the variations. While the two positions to be considered are in no way regarded as representative of the Marxist approaches, they do bring to light an important issue in the Marxist analysis of class which I want to highlight and consider. The two approaches are those of Nicos Poulantzas and Eric Olin Wright.

Poulantzas's analysis of class starts from exploitation in the capitalist economy. In classical Marxist terms, Poulantzas (1975) sees exploitation in capitalism as based around the extraction of surplus value by capitalists from workers. For Poulantzas, productive workers are those who directly create surplus value. They constitute the working class. Those who own the means of production and exploit the working class make up the capitalist class. All those in intermediate positions between these two classes comprise the petty-bourgeoisie. On this definition, all workers who are concerned with the realisation or distribution of surplus value and those who work in non-profit-making organisations, whatever work they do, are not working class. Routine office workers, sales assistants, manual workers employed by non-profit-making state bodies, along with middle managers, professional workers and those who own and work their own businesses are all part of the petty-bourgeoisie. In this position, far from comprising the vast majority of the populations of capitalist societies, the working class makes up a minority in such societies. The political implications of this analysis are stark. While they have an interest in ending their exploitation and in seeing the achievement of socialism, *on their own* the working class are not in a position to do so. However, that does not mean that socialism has ceased to be an historical possibility. The interests of the members of the petty-bourgeoisie are not straightforward. They share aspects of their position with the working class (such as economic insecurity, low incomes, inadequate access to essential services, the power of big business) though their interests are not identical. Poulantzas, therefore, called for the development of alliances between the working class and at least certain elements of the petty-bourgeoisie. In such alliances, those aspects which the members of the petty-bourgeoisie share with members of the working class would be stressed.

There have been many criticisms of Poulantzas's approach to class, most of which spring from his definition of the working class. There are debates about whether Marx thought the working class in capitalism only comprised those who directly produced surplus value or whether, rather than the production of surplus value being the defining feature of working-class membership, the crucial element was non-ownership of the means of production. There is evidence that in the *Grundrisse* (1973) Marx saw exploitation in broader terms than those used by Poulantzas and certainly included workers concerned with the realisation of surplus value, and not just those who directly produce surplus value, in his understanding of the working class. However, the point that I want to raise, and to consider after outlining Eric Wright's work on class in the 1970s and 1980s, is the link that

Poulantzas (and Wright) makes between class position, political interests and political action.

In the 1970s, Eric Olin Wright (1975) developed the idea of contradictory class locations. In this argument, middle managers, professionals, the self-employed and other 'non-workers' – what might be termed the members of the middle group, or intermediary strata, between workers and capitalists – are both exploiters and exploited. Questions of control, over and in the labour process, are crucial in this approach. In a later work, and as a refinement of his earlier position, Wright (1985, see also 1989) argued that people can have four types of assets in the capitalist labour process: labour-power assets, skill assets, organisation assets and capital assets. In this later approach, Wright no longer argues that work autonomy is a central element in the development of contradictory class positions. The possession of skills and expertise, as well as position in organisational hierarchies, is seen as important in the amended approach. Wright's aim is to map out as accurately as possible the objective contours of class in advanced capitalist society. In addition, however, Wright is trying to establish the political interests that spring from people's objective class positions. He assumes that once a group's objective class position has been accurately assessed, they have interests which spring from their position and which can also be objectively evaluated. Wright therefore argues that while those who own only labour-power assets have an interest in the achievement of socialism, those who own organisation assets can be seen as having an interest in the achievement of a system in which managers will be dominant. Similarly, professionals and others with skill assets will want to see a society in which those with skills are in dominant positions.

While the conclusions Wright reaches from his class analysis are not identical to those of Poulantzas, I want to suggest that the efforts of both writers to try to determine objective interests (including, crucially, political interests) from objective class position may raise more problems than they solve. Can you just read off the interests of a group (including their political interests) once you have correctly analysed their class position? The issue of consciousness is central to this analysis. It may be true that in an *objective* sense members of the working class do have an interest in building a socialist society. I accept there are very good reasons for thinking so. However, if the majority of working-class people do not *subjectively* accept this, where does the objective analysis leave us? (Of course, I am not alone in questioning the link between class position, class interests and political action. See, for example, Pickvance 1977; Lockwood 1981; Hindess 1987; Pahl 1989; and Crompton 1998.)

Other dimensions of inequality

Related to this criticism is a point concerning the importance of class in the development of political consciousness and whether social classes are homogeneous groups. Two points are crucial in this respect: are there divisions within the experience of those that make up the different classes and are there other aspects of people's lives which may be as important as, if not more important than, their class position?

Even if one accepts that class is primary in determining people's political interests, do all of those that make up a particular class in reality share exactly the same interests? To an extent this will depend on how broadly or narrowly classes are defined. If one adopts a narrow definition of class there is less likelihood that people will see their interests as diverging. However, Marx adopted broad definitions of class, including the definition of the working class, which he based around the non-ownership of the means of production in capitalist society. If one adopts this definition, do all of those that comprise the working class share the same interests? Let us take the example of routine office workers in Britain. It has been argued that in the 1960s and 1970s the positions of male and female routine office workers were very different. Most male workers of this kind were able to gain promotion to supervisory positions, while most female routine office workers were not (Crompton and Sanderson 1990:109–33). It might be argued that objectively the long-term interests of the routine office workers remained the same (working to replace capitalism with socialism). However, it could also be argued that their short-term interests were very different. Is it reasonable to expect long-term interests to take precedence over short-term interests?

But there is a more fundamental challenge to the primacy of class which questions whether class is the main determinant of people's interests in present-day society. As feminists have long argued, people's interests cannot simply be reduced to their class position. We have seen how gender may impact on class interest, at least in the short term, simply because some groups of males and females may face different 'class trajectories', at certain times in history. However, such divisions may not be a temporary historical factor, which simply makes it difficult for members of the working class to recognise their essential unity of position and interests. Rather, it is

argued that women, *as women*, have particular interests, whi
across class divisions (see Bryson 1999, 2003). There are, of c
differences within the feminist analysis. However, even within
the socialist feminist approach, it is argued that modern capitalist
societies are not only class societies but are also male-dominated
societies. Women have overwhelming responsibility for the domestic
sphere, as well as taking on the caring roles in society and being
concentrated in low-paid jobs. Women have an interest in ending
male domination, it is argued, and that is true of all women, whatever
their class position.

This argument basically relates to whether social oppressions of
various kinds are as important as class exploitation in understanding
capitalist society and the ways in which it might and should be
transformed. (See the later chapter by Mary Davis on oppression.)
Just as feminist writers argue for the importance of gender divisions
within society, so do others argue that oppressions based around race
and ethnicity, like those of gender, crosscut class divisions (Solomos
and Black 1995). Racial oppression does not simply affect those from
a particular class, within a racial group, but impacts on the whole
racial group. Again, even if one does not accept that race or ethnicity
is more important than class in defining present-day society and in
determining people's interests, the argument would be that it stands
alongside class in these areas. And is it not at least possible, if not
inevitable, that people's interests as women or as members of an
ethnic minority group will sometimes clash with their class interests?
In a similar way people's interests as members of an ethnic minority
group may be crosscut by their gender interests and vice versa (see
Bryson 1999, 2003). Present-day society is crosscut by a number of
social divisions, it is argued, and, in this situation, it is not clear that
class retains the central importance accorded to it in the past.

Developments since Marx's time

Another criticism of the Marxist view of class and its political
consequences relates to historical changes. I will concentrate on the
argument of one writer who takes this line: G.A. Cohen. Cohen
(2000:107–15) argues that the Marxist view of socialist revolution, in
which class was crucial, was based on four factors, none of which, he
argues, any longer holds true. The four interconnected elements were:
the working class represent the majority of society; they produce the
wealth of society; they are the exploited in society; they are the needy
people in society (Cohen 2000:107). As a result, in this approach the

working class had little to lose in taking a gamble on revolution. This, Cohen argues, is no longer true; indeed, he maintains that, most important of all, people in advanced capitalist society know that these elements no longer form an accurate depiction of the position of the working class. He contends that even if objectively most people in advanced capitalist societies live by offering their labour power for sale, politically this does not have revolutionary implications. He also rejects arguments that, because on a world scale the working class still comprises the vast majority, traditional views of socialist revolution should not be dismissed. He contends, rather, that the chances of real unity being forged between workers in advanced capitalist societies and those in 'developing countries' are slim, and that the workers in developing countries are in a weak position politically. Moreover, the poor in advanced capitalist societies, he argues, tend not to be workers but rather those who cannot gain entry to the labour market or are excluded from it. One does not have to accept Cohen's argument in its entirety to be in sympathy with the major point that comes out of his analysis: class and its consequences have to be analysed historically, and what may have had relevance in one period may no longer do so in another (or may need serious revision).

Cohen also contends that given environmental constraints it will be impossible to transcend issues of distributive justice in the way that Marx argued. Ethical issues, particularly those of distributive, or social, justice, must remain central to the socialist position, Cohen argues. This does not make class politics, or the influence of class on politics, irrelevant, even in the advanced capitalist societies. For I would argue that the inequalities which are found in societies have a class basis (in relation to Britain, see Beynon 1999, and for the USA and Britain see Edgell 1993:106–10). Whatever divisions there may be among those who live by offering their labour power for sale in advanced capitalist societies, it is people who are in that position who face the greatest insecurity, who rely most on public services and state welfare, rather than private services and welfare, and who suffer from a socially unjust system. None of which is to deny that over the years the standard of living of workers in the advanced capitalist societies has generally substantially improved, as Cohen argues. Nor is the argument a denial of the importance of gender, race or ethnic divisions in society. However, whatever oppressions women or black people and those in minority ethnic groups may share, *as members of such groups* working-class members will face additional issues which other members of the groups will not face.

Moreover, the working-class members of the groups will share those issues with other members of the working class.

The rising standard of living of the majority of working-class people in the advanced capitalist societies links into Cohen's point about socialism, and the revolutionary transformation it involves, representing a gamble. When the majority of workers were poor it could be clearly argued that they had little to lose by taking the gamble of socialism. That may no longer be the case. Whatever limitations capitalism has as a social system, for the majority in the advanced capitalist societies it has brought certain freedoms, a better standard of living and quality of life. (For the position in Britain after 1945 see Glynn and Booth 1996:188–215.) If working-class people are to be convinced of the desirability of consciously working for a much more egalitarian and democratic society which is based on the common ownership of the means of production (which is how I would define socialism) then they must be convinced that such a society is achievable and would represent an improvement on the capitalism under which they live. (To avoid misunderstanding, I should make it clear that I am not arguing that capitalist societies no longer face periodic economic crises; nor am I arguing that capitalism is now able to meet everyone's human needs. Still less am I arguing that the inequalities that exist within and between societies in the modern world are no longer important.)

Class consciousness and collective action

The difficulties in achieving the type of working-class consciousness which has been outlined in this chapter are reflected in the work of Claus Offe and Helmut Wiesenthal (1980). For Offe and Wiesenthal, the capitalist class and the working class are in very different positions within capitalist society and, as a result, face different issues in trying to engage in collective action. The interests of capitalists, they argue, are clear and easily understood by individual capitalists. The accumulation of capital and the achievement of profit distinguish the interests of the capitalist. Whether the capitalist is furthering his or her interests is determined by signals from the market. The state is dependent on the investment decisions of capitalists for the successful functioning of the economy, which means that the state is dependent upon capitalists to invest and will therefore try to create the favourable conditions in which this can happen. Moreover, the interests of capitalists are accepted as legitimate within the wider society. For labour, or the working class, however, the situation is very different. Workers have a number of short-term and long-term interests (including, for example, higher wages, job satisfaction, health, leisure time, continuity of employment) and it is not self-evident which should be given priority or whether the priority should be the same for all workers. Therefore, Offe and Wiesenthal (1980:74–6, 87) argue that workers can only determine the priority of their interests and the action they should take in furtherance of those interests through debate and discussion, or what they term dialogical patterns of collective action. Or at least, Offe and Wiesenthal argue, the dialogical pattern is likely to play some part in the way that organisations of the working class operate. For capitalists, however, what Offe and Wiesenthal call an instrumental-monological approach is possible, as a result of the greater simplicity and the generally accepted nature of their interests.

The approach to collective action advanced by Offe and Wiesenthal gives important insights into the operation of class in capitalist society. Not only does their analysis help to explain the problems involved in achieving working-class unity and in the working class becoming a class for itself but their work also helps us to understand why the unity of the capitalist class is more easily achieved than that of the working class. Moreover, their stress on dialogical patterns of working-class collective action serves to show the importance of democracy for working-class organisation.

PROGRESSIVE POLITICS IN THE TWENTY-FIRST CENTURY

The relationship between class and progressive politics is far from straightforward. Adam Przeworski (1985) has argued that the logic of electoral politics leads social democratic parties to appeal to groups in their populations other than the traditional working class. In order to win elections, social democratic parties have to gain the support of groups other than the workers and this necessarily, Przeworski argues, reduces the socialist content of the parties' electoral programmes. The logical conclusion of this analysis might be the type of politics associated with the so-called 'Third Way' and supported by a number of social democratic governments (see Giddens 2001). In order to win elections and maintain support, the parties behind such governments, and the governments themselves, aim to develop good relations with business and to operate in a way that transcends class politics. While internationalism (see the later chapter on working-class internationalism) has been an important element of the socialist tradition, since the nineteenth century the focus of socialist politics has largely been within specific nation-states. Over the past twenty-five years or so, however, academic interest has focused on changes connected with the concept of globalisation (for example, Hay and Marsh 2001). Radical politics is still often based around the nation-state. However, in recent years, there have been a number of developments which have been placed, perhaps misleadingly, under the generic heading of anti-globalisation (and are also sometimes placed, perhaps equally misleadingly, under the heading anti-capitalist; see for example, Epstein 2001; Bircham and Charlton 2001).

These developments mark a move away from traditional radical politics and raise important questions about the relationship between class and radical politics in the twenty-first century. Since the late 1980s, meetings of international organisations (such as the World Bank, the IMF, the World Economic Forum, the G8) have faced large-scale protests. Loose coalitions opposing the exercise of global corporate and political power have been constructed. While these coalitions certainly include organisations and individuals representing workers who argue for the centrality of class struggle in the achievement of social change, the coalitions are not driven by a clear class analysis or a commitment to the primacy of class politics. The groups and individuals engaged in the coalitions are disparate and a number of views exist about the best way of promoting social change and about the aims of social change. Similarly the World Social Forum and the regional social forums that have developed are not clearly and unambiguously groupings that accept the primacy of class politics. Such developments are potentially very significant, even if the ways in which they can contribute to major and sustainable social change are as yet unclear. The ways in which the coalitions and groupings should, and in the future will, relate to more traditional forms of class politics are also unclear. (For analyses of developments, groupings and prospects, the ongoing debates in *New Left Review* present a variety of approaches. See the articles collected in Mertes 2004.)

CONCLUSION

Crucial to the whole debate about the potential of the working class as a political actor is the question of class consciousness and the importance of subjectivity in politics. We cannot assume any longer, even if at one time we could, that the members of the working class will see politics in class terms. Contemporary politics, certainly in capitalist liberal democracies, will remain in large part a battle about how people make sense of their experiences in society and the interests that they see springing from their experiences. The view that people's political commitments can be worked out from their objective class position cannot be sustained. It is worth bearing in mind that this view was not exclusively one which was held by Marxists. Social democrats have also worked from this assumption. The view commonly held until recently was that working-class people in Britain would vote Labour, unless they were fooled out of doing so.

This is not to deny the importance of class in advanced capitalist society or to argue that it has lost its significance for understanding politics in capitalist society. But it is to deny that history is following a clear course and to recognise that the future is much more open than it was previously considered to be in much socialist thinking. And it is also to accept, along with E.P. Thompson (1963), that class is a process and that classes are made. The analysis being advanced here also involves accepting that just as classes can be made they can also be unmade. In other words, classes can stop being classes for themselves, though they remain classes in themselves. It would be premature to write off class as a mobilising force in advanced capitalist societies. But we do need, I think, to recognise the continuing importance of ethics to progressive politics and the importance of social justice to the socialist case. Ethics and social justice will not be transcended by developments in capitalism and will not become irrelevant. People have to be convinced of the desirability of socialism, not of its inevitability. Those on the wrong side of capitalism's inequalities will always be the main focus of progressive politics; and class certainly has not ceased to be a prime source of social inequality. But the support of people on the wrong side of capitalism's inequalities for progressive change, let alone their active commitment to and involvement in it, cannot be taken for granted.

GUIDE TO FURTHER READING

The literature on social class is vast, though much of it does not relate directly to the topics considered in this chapter. For a consideration of different ways of approaching class and a number of useful extracts from the literature on class see Joyce (1995). E.P. Thompson's major work (1963) remains a marvellous account of the creative activity of the working class in late eighteenth and early nineteenth-century England and develops an important approach to the understanding of class. An important work which shows the centrality of class and working-class action to Marx's theory and which examines the role of class in the broader Marxist tradition is Miliband (1976). Wood (1986) offers a rigorous defence of the centrality of social class in socialist analysis and criticises those who have moved away from a class analysis. Two influential critiques of Marx's approach (and of broader Marxist approaches) to class are Gorz (1982) and Hindess (1987). The work by Gorz is a critique of the Marxist approach to class and social change from a former Marxist who argues that social changes have rendered Marx's approach to class largely historically irrelevant. The work had a major impact on the debate among socialists after it was published. Hindess (1987) criticises the view that classes can be social actors and this criticism extends to all writers who adopt that approach, including those writing from a non-Marxist perspective.

REFERENCES

Beynon, H. (1999) 'A Classless Society?', in H. Beynon and P. Glavanis (eds) *Patterns of Social Inequality* (London: Longman).

Bircham, E. and Charlton, J. (eds) (2001) *Anti-Capitalism: A Guide to the Movement* (London: Bookmarks).

Bryson, V. (1999) *Feminist Debates: Issues of Theory and Political Practice* (Basingstoke: Macmillan).

—— (2003) *Feminist Political Theory: An Introduction* (Basingstoke: Macmillan).

Cohen, G.A. (2000) *If You're An Egalitarian How Come You're So Rich?* (Cambridge MA: Harvard University Press).

Crompton, R. (1998) *Class and Stratification: An Introduction to Current Debates* (Cambridge: Polity Press).

Crompton, R. and Sanderson, K. (1990) *Gendered Jobs and Social Change* (London: Unwin Hyman).

Edgell, S. (1993) *Class* (London: Routledge).

Epstein, B. (2001) 'Anarchism and the Anti-globalization Movement', *Monthly Review*, Vol. 14, No. 4.

Giddens, A. (ed.) (2001) *The Global Third Way Debate* (Cambridge: Polity Press).

Glynn, S. and Booth, A. (1996) *Modern Britain: An Economic and Social History* (London: Routledge).

Goldthorpe, J. (1997) 'The "Goldthorpe" Class Schema', in D. Rose and K. O'Reilly (eds) *Constructing Classes* (London: Office for National Statistics).

Gorz, A. (1982) *Farewell to the Working Class* (London: Pluto Press).

Hay, C. and Marsh, D. (2001) *Demystifying Globalization* (Basingstoke: Palgrave).

Hindess, B. (1987) *Politics and Class Analysis* (Oxford: Basil Blackwell).

Joyce, P. (ed.) (1995) *Class* (Oxford: Oxford University Press).

Lockwood, D. (1981) 'The Weakest Link in the Chain', in S. Simpson and I. Simpson (eds) *Research in the Sociology of Work: 1* (Greenwich Con: JAI Press).

Marshall, G., Newby, H., Rose, D. and Vogler, C. (1988) *Social Class in Modern Britain* (London: Hutchinson).

Marx, K. (1909) *Capital*, Vol. III (Chicago: Kerr and Co).

—— (1973) *Grundrisse* (Harmondsworth: Penguin).

—— (1975) *The Poverty of Philosophy* (Moscow: Progress Publishers).

Marx, K. and Engels, F. (1998) *The Communist Manifesto* (London: Verso).

Mertes, T. (2004) *A Movement of Movements* (London: Verso)

Miliband, R. (1976) *Marxism and Politics* (Oxford: Oxford University Press).

Offe, C. and Wiesenthal, H. (1980) 'Two Logics of Collective Action: theoretical notes on social class and organizational form', *Political Power and Social Theory*, Vol. 1.

Pahl, R. (1989) 'Is the Emperor Naked? Some questions on the adequacy of sociological theory in urban and regional research', *International Journal of Urban and Regional Research*, Vol. 13, No. 4.

Pickvance, C.G. (1977) 'From "Social Base" to "Social Force": some analytical issues in the study of social protest', in M. Harloe (ed.) *Captive Cities: Studies in the Political Economy of Cities and Regions* (London: Wiley).

Poulantzas, N. (1975) *Classes in Contemporary Capitalism* (London: New Left Books).

Przeworski, A. (1985) *Capitalism and Social Democracy* (Cambridge: Cambridge University Press).

Sassoon, D. (1997) *One Hundred Years of Socialism* (London: Fontana).

Solomos, J. and Black, L. (1995) *Race, Politics and Social Change* (London: Routledge).

Thompson, E.P. (1963) *The Making of the English Working Class* (London: Gollancz).

Wood, E.M. (1986) *The Retreat From Class* (London: Verso).

Wright, E.O. (1975) *Class, Crisis and the State* (London: New Left Books).

—— (1985) *Classes* (London: Verso).

—— (1989) 'A Generative Framework for the Analysis of Class Structure', in E.O. Wright (ed.) *The Debate on Classes* (London: Verso).

4
The State

Andrew Taylor

... the bourgeoisie has at last, since the establishment of Modern Industry and of the world-market, conquered for itself, in the modern representative State, exclusive political sway. The executive of the modern State is but a committee for managing the common affairs of the whole bourgeoisie. (Marx and Engels 1848:37)

INTRODUCTION

The 'third wave' of democratisation and the global triumph of capitalism at the end of the twentieth century made the modern representative state (MRS) a universal form. This chapter explores how Marx, Engels, Lenin and Gramsci theorised the MRS and, using their insights, argues that irrespective of national variations the MRS has a universal function: the maintenance of a class compromise.

Forty years ago Miliband complained that Marx and Engels' 'extremely complex and by no means unambiguous' work on the state had 'congealed into *the* Marxist theory of the state, or into *the* Marxist-Leninist theory of the state' (Miliband 1990:14–15). Complexity and ambiguity flows from the tension between theory, exemplified by *The Communist Manifesto* (1848) which set out Marx's basic view of the state from which he never departed, and the empirical, exemplified by *The Eighteenth Brumaire of Louis Napoleon* (1852). In their empirical work Marx and Engels encountered 'the innumerable intersecting forces, an infinite series of parallelograms of forces' (Engels 1890a:683) and 'without admitting it, Marx found himself compelled by events to accord to the capitalist state a large measure of autonomy, certainly larger than his theoretical preconceptions had prepared him for' (Elster 1985:386).

The extent of the state's autonomy from the bourgeoisie provoked a memorable, if futile, controversy. Miliband's *The State in Capitalist Society* (1969) began a debate with Poulantzas over state autonomy that generated more heat than light (Miliband 1969, 1970; Poulantzas 1969, 1976, 1980). This chapter sidesteps this important debate because it is irresolvable; autonomy depends on historical circumstances. The chapter regards the state as fundamentally coercive and serving the interests of the economically dominant. However, the MRS does not routinely govern by coercion and often pursues policies seemingly hostile to the interests of the economically dominant. In the MRS, power concentrates in the bureaucracy, but the institutions and processes of liberal democracy offer a defence against revolution.

BACK TO BASICS: THE STATE OF MARX

The Communist Manifesto's two basic precepts were that the state was coercive and that it served the interests of the economically dominant. However, of itself this explains little. Marx and Engels argued that the state can be an instrument of the economically dominant *and* be autonomous for two reasons: 'the bourgeois do not allow the state to interfere in their private interests and give it only as much power as is necessary for their own safety and the maintenance of competition and because the bourgeois in general act as citizens only to the extent that their private interests demand it' (Marx and Engels 1977:377). We must avoid the trap of arguing that whatever the state does *must* be in capital's long-term interests simply because capital survives: this *reductio ad absurdum* could only be disproved *via* a socialist revolution. Marx's work on the state contains elements which view 'politics as an autonomous phenomenon that is constrained by economics but not reducible to it' (Elster 1985:399).

Autonomy and dependence coexist and the state is independent only where estates had not fully formed into classes (Marx and Engels 1977:99). In the absence of crisis political power would not need to be held by the bourgeoisie, indeed it would be dangerous for it to do so. Autonomy

> is designed to capture precisely this in-between theoretical position: the state is not reducible to capitalist interests but neither is it entirely autonomous. At the same time, however, the thrust of the 'classical view' [1848] could be maintained by arguing that, in the end, capitalist interests generally prevail over those of the working class or the state. (Wetherly 1998:171)

The state is autonomous from, but reducible to, capital's interests (Marx and Engels 1977:99). Marx concluded: 'forms of state are to be grasped neither from themselves nor from the so-called general development of the human mind, but rather have their roots in the material conditions of life ... combine[d] under the name of "civil society"' (Marx 1859:181). The economic base does not 'act', but constrains the state. So, as Engels argued:

> if someone twists this into saying that the economic element is the *only* determining one, he transforms that proposition into a meaningless, abstract, senseless phrase. The economic situation is the basis, but the various elements of the superstructure ... also exercise their influence upon the course of the historical struggle and in many cases preponderate in determining their *form*. (1890a:682; and Marx 1852a:96)

He conceded that Marx and he placed too much emphasis on 'the *derivation* of political, juridical and other ideological notions [and actions] from basic economic facts ... in so doing we neglected ... the ways and means by which these notions, etc., come about' (Engels 1893:690). The state maintained accumulation and managed conflicts between fractions of capital, but capitalists 'do not have to act collectively in order to utilize [their] collective power' (Dowding 1996:74–5). Taxation was the price paid by capital to 'ensure that the state servants are a force available for their protection – the police; they willingly pay, and force the nation to pay high taxes so as to be able without danger to shift the sums they pay on to the workers' (Marx and Engels 1977:217). Capitalists seldom behave collectively because they do not need to. *The Critique of the Gotha Programme* (1875) argued that 'present day society' was capitalist, albeit at different levels of development, but '[the] "present day state" changes with a country's frontier. It is different in the Prusso-German Empire from what it is in Switzerland, and different in England from what it is in the United States' (Marx 1875:327). There is no 'capitalist state', only 'the state in capitalist society'. Marx stressed repeatedly the state's importance for capitalism's survival. The state bureaucracy is most closely attuned to capital's interests and its operations are largely hidden from public view and popular control (Marx 1871:285–6). The bureaucracy and its political directorate are indispensable to capital: 'the state enmeshes, controls, regulates, superintends and tutors civil society from its most comprehensive manifestations of life down to its most insignificant stirrings, from its most general modes of being to the private existence of individuals' (Marx 1852a:127). It is as a result of the contradiction 'between the particular and the common interests' that the common interest of capital 'assumes an independent form as the *state*, which is divorced from the real individual and collective interests' (Marx and Engels 1977:52). The state grows in scale and scope as capitalism develops in complexity, providing 'new material for state administration'; activities are 'snatched' from civil society and 'made an object of government activity' leading to the 'centralisation of governmental power' (Marx 1852a:169).

The Communist Manifesto had identified bourgeois rule with the MRS but the MRS was also 'a system for the conciliation and welfare of all classes'. This duality permeates Marx and Engels' work on the state, as do the limits capital places on the power of 'democratic' institutions (Marx 1852a:119, 130). Parliaments cannot unite state and civil society even though Marx did originally see universal suffrage as revolutionary (Marx 1852b and 1854). Power is siphoned away from 'popular' institutions and parliaments become infected with 'that peculiar malady ... parliamentary cretinism'. The legislative process, whose outputs are presented as being in the general interest, reflects the interests of the capitalists and is controlled by the executive. Political struggles within the state 'are merely the illusory forms' of class struggle (Marx 1852a:148, 168; Marx and Engels 1977:52). Representative government as a means of managing class struggle is the specific product of modern bourgeois society (Marx 1852a:151–2; see also Hindess 1980 and 1983).

With its emphasis on coercion, *The Civil War in France* (1871) extended the analysis of *The Eighteenth Brumaire*. The Paris Commune (1871) was important for Marx's thinking on the state because for the first time a bourgeoisie and a workers' state were in direct confrontation (Marx 1871:285). *The Civil War in France* emphasises the state's repressive functions, but Paris Communes are infrequent in the governance of capitalist societies, and the state does not *normally* rule by force even though the state *is* organised coercion. However, confronted by a 'threatening upheaval of the proletariat, [the bourgeoisie] used that State power mercilessly and ostentatiously as the national war-engine of capital against labour' (Marx 1871:286). The state, then, only reveals its true nature *in extremis*, when faced by a *'threatening upheaval of the proletariat'* but Marx was incorrect when he concluded 'Class rule is no longer able to disguise itself in a national uniform' (Marx 1871:306). Class rule has done exactly that. Capitalism and the MRS are inseparable and the MRS is most effective when not controlled openly by the bourgeoisie (Marx and

Engels 1977:216). If the state clearly and immediately acted in the interests of the bourgeoisie (or a fraction of it) its interventions would be condemned by those capitalists who did not benefit, and would also encourage the development of the proletariat's revolutionary consciousness (Marx 1852a:130).

Autonomy means the state acts in the *general* interests of capital. A direct correspondence between state and bourgeoisie would mean that an attack on either/both would be an attack on the capitalist *system*. It would be impossible to maintain the fictions of liberal democracy and of the autonomy of the political, the crucial 'firebreak' in the politics of capitalist societies. Marx argued that for capitalism to function and survive, and for the bourgeoisie 'to preserve its social power, its political power must be broken' (Marx 1852a:131). Even though the state remains the 'instrument' of capital, the state retains its autonomy and 'politics' appears separate from 'economics'. In the MRS the purpose of politics is the capture of state power, but the acquisition of state power does not confer power over capital (Marx 1852a:169). Engels argued that the state was indispensable because of capitalism's extensive division of labour which creates both different material interests and the need for coordination, but this coordination does not create a simple base–superstructure relationship (Engels 1890b:382). Autonomy broadens and deepens as capitalism develops because of the fragmentation of the bourgeoisie and because of its withdrawal from political involvement. The state thus develops and pursues its own interests (Marx 1852a:169). The state 'strives for as much independence as possible', and, once established, is 'endowed with a movement of its own'; but, like the 'free' market, this independent movement is not truly independent. Any movement is in reaction to, or a response to, change in the economic sphere, and any action by the state in any sphere will generate opposition and resistance, so producing further 'movement' (Engels 1890b:686).

If *capitalists* ruthlessly pursue their interests, *capitalism's* stability is endangered. Capitalists must therefore be compelled to behave in their own best long-term interests: 'They grumble at the government whenever it restricts their freedom, and at the same time demand that the government prevent the inevitable results of this freedom' (Marx 1843:199). Tension between the general and the specific explains why the state appears to act against the interests of the economically dominant. Technology amplifies capitalism's dynamism – or instability – and dealing with this instability is a major state task. State regulation of dynamism, Marx argued, serves the interests of capital in general, as well as specific capitals, but 'capital never becomes reconciled to such changes ...' (Marx 1887:451).

The cumulative effect is a permanent tendency to crisis, reflected in unemployment and the disappearance of entire industries (Marx 1894:194, 264). Every sphere of capital, and every capitalist, has an interest in the total productivity of labour but the *individual capitalist* has an interest in exploiting labour as fully as possible and investing as little as possible, even though this is not in the interests of *capitalism*. The only institution able to reconcile, at least temporarily, capitalism's contradictions is the state whose actions are resisted by individual capitalists and sectors of capital, and intervention 'is limited to exceptional co-operation in times of great stress and confusion' (Marx 1894:120). Capitalism's dynamism produces crises and the state exists to resolve crisis.

THE STATE AS (BLUNT) INSTRUMENT?

Lenin is often presented as having a crudely instrumental interpretation of the state. In fact, Lenin was deeply impressed by the ability of the MRS to manage class conflict, and in the advanced capitalist states revolution depended on massive exogenous shocks (particularly war) which would compel the state to reveal to the working class its true nature.

Lenin believed variations between states would fade and in the Imperialist epoch states would become authoritarian. By 1917 even the freest states had 'plunged headlong into the all-European dirty, bloody morass of military-bureaucratic institutions to which everything is subordinate and which trample everything under foot' (Lenin 1917a:45). Lenin saw the state as organised violence, 'a power which arose from society, but [which] places itself above it and alienates itself more and more from it. What does this power mainly consist of? It consists of *special bodies of armed men which have prisons, etc., at their command.*' The state grows alongside the working class and '[a] *standing army and police are the chief instruments of state power*' (Lenin 1917a:10). 'Mainly' and 'chief' imply that other non-coercive instruments are available to the state but their existence does not alter the state's fundamentally coercive nature. The state grows because of the threat and reality of class struggle. This state is not only coercive, it has little autonomy.

The state's reliance on repression depended, however, on the strength of the revolutionary working class. Capitalists 'acquired the habit of ruling the people without the use of force, and if they now resort to force, it shows that they have come to feel that the revolutionary movement is growing and that they cannot do other wise' (Lenin 1917b:139). Although fraudulent, democracy is best for capital:

> A democratic republic is the best possible political shell for capitalism, and, therefore, once capital has gained control of this very best shell ... it establishes its power so securely, so firmly, that *no* change, either of persons, of institutions, or of parties in the bourgeois-democratic republic, can shake it. (Lenin 1917a:15–16 original emphasis)

The MRS reveals the bourgeoisie at its most subtle and cunning. Thus: 'In those countries where democratic parliamentary culture is of long standing, the bourgeoisie has excellently learned to operate not only by means of violence, but also by means of deception, bribery, flattery' (Lenin 1919:235). Parliamentarianism is powerfully symbolic but politically powerless: 'To decide once every few years which member of the ruling class is to repress and crush the people through parliament – such is the real essence of bourgeois parliamentarianism' (Lenin 1917a:54). Nevertheless, like Marx, Lenin placed considerable emphasis on the utility of 'the "pig-sty" of bourgeois parliamentarianism' (Lenin 1917a:16, 51).

Lenin, like Marx, saw the state as dominated by bureaucracy. Even in countries with minimal states such as England, where bureaucratic control 'is far from being complete, even there the bureaucracy ... is not infrequently the master and not the servant of the people'. Under imperialism and monopoly capitalism these variations would fade and states would become bureaucratic (Lenin 1897:46). Power resides in the state executive: 'The centralised state power that is peculiar to bourgeois society came into being in the period of the fall of absolutism. Two institutions are most characteristic of this state machine: the bureaucracy and the standing army' (Lenin 1917a:34). As Marx predicted in *The Eighteenth Brumaire*, the growth of state power 'has been going on more slowly, *in more varied forms, on a much wider field*', but the final stage was 'the perfection and consolidation of the "executive power," its bureaucratic and military apparatus' (Lenin 1917a:37–8, emphasis added). Imperialism would,

Lenin believed, encourage the homogenisation of the state. *The State and Revolution* holds that 'the real business of the "state" is performed behind the scenes and is carried on by the departments, chancelleries and General Staffs. Parliament itself is given up to talk for the purposes of fooling the "common people"', and 'it is in the chancelleries and staffs that they "do" the business of the "state"' (Lenin 1917a:55–6). This facade could be shattered by war. 'There was freedom in England', Lenin wrote, 'because there was no revolutionary movement there. *But the war has changed everything.* In a country where for decades there was not a single instance of interference with the socialist press, a typically tsarist censorship was established and English prisons became crowded with socialists' (Lenin 1917b:139).

Lenin denied that state spending on welfare and infrastructure represented significant modifications of capitalism because these were 'paltry sums' compared to the total surplus value extracted, and were financed through taxation to which workers were the majority contributors. These policies were also in the self-interest of the bourgeoisie who benefited from a healthier and better educated workforce. Substantial state spending on welfare would not 'assail the foundations of its rule, it does not interfere with any substantial sources of revenue' and 'any attempt to touch capital, is invariably and absolutely vetoed in the most categorical fashion by the central government of the bourgeois state' (Lenin 1907:90–1).

Lenin agreed with Marx and Engels that autonomy was the product of the history of a country's bourgeoisie (Lenin 1915:151). The development of capitalism as a global system, however, made the universal growth of repressive bureaucracy inevitable as states clashed externally and were challenged internally by revolutionary movements. Imperialism marks the final emergence of the modern state, characterised by the 'unprecedented growth of its bureaucratic and military apparatus, in connection with the intensification of repressive measures against the proletariat both in the monarchical and in the freest republican countries' (Lenin 1917a:38). This seemed plausible when the world was at war, a war followed by the rise of fascism, but after 1939–45 there was no general 'intensification of repressive measures' and capitalism was maintained. The historical shift from liberal democracy to *repressive* liberal democracy, accompanied by the withering away of national variations as a result of war, imperialism, and the threat of revolution, did not take place. The state would be revealed in all its repressive majesty *only* if a revolutionary movement developed, but what if no revolutionary movement developed?

THE PASSIVE REVOLUTION AND TRASFORMISMO

Gramsci argued that a passive revolution occurs when capitalist hegemony is threatened. The passive revolution's purpose was to re-establish or maintain hegemony (Gramsci 1971:58 n.8, 104–5, 106–20, hereafter SPN). The result may be radical and far-reaching social, economic and political change, but this change comes from above, *via* the state and without mass mobilisation. The passive revolution seeks to fragment those who are challenging capitalist hegemony and prevent active revolution by using state power to create a political compromise (SPN:114). The concept of the passive revolution emerged from Gramsci's study of the Italian *Risorgimento* and Italy's unification under Piedmont which was achieved not by mass mobilisation but via revolution from above orchestrated by the Piedmontese ruling class who 'wished to "dominate" and not to "lead". Furthermore, they wanted their interests to dominate, rather than their persons' (SPN:104–5). An autonomous force – the Piedmontese state with its military, diplomatic and political resources – was at the disposal of those who wished Italy united in a particular way.

The passive revolution occurs, Gramsci argued, when problems have 'piled up' in a polity and cannot be resolved by the existing political process. The passive revolution was common in the twentieth century because of the concentration of interconnected crises – the 1914–18 war, the 1917 Bolshevik Revolution, the interwar depression, the rise of fascism, the 1939–45 war, the reconstruction of the international political economy, the Cold War, etc. – which required resolution via the involvement of the state. Permeating the long crisis of the last century was the threat posed by the organised working class and the emergence of mass democracy 'which objectively reflects the fact that a new social force has been constituted, and has a weight which can no longer be ignored, etc.' (SPN:106).

The passive revolution was a response to crisis but state intervention leads to further crises, hence the instability of any equilibrium. The passive revolution counterbalances mass mobilisation, but the existence of an organised working class and mass democracy necessitate *mass endorsement* of the status quo. The state, 'the organ of one particular group', must therefore present itself as a universally representative force. Gramsci defined the problem thus: 'can a rift between popular masses and ruling ideologies as serious as that which emerged after the war be "cured" by the simple exercise of force?' (SPN:276).

Gramsci's first conception of the state – *political society* – embraced both coercive instruments (police, armed services, judiciary, prisons, etc.) and the administrative machinery. The state depended on a monopoly of coercion; however, the state was not always coercive. Gramsci's equivalent of relative autonomy is the 'separation of powers', which underpinned political and economic liberalism, and concentrated effective power *away* from any institutions which threatened to extend popular control (SPN:245–6). The state engaged, therefore, in political and social engineering so 'the State must be conceived of as an "educator", in as much as it tends precisely to create a new type or level of civilisation' (SPN:246–7). This produced Gramsci's second, and broader, 'ethical' or 'cultural state' whose 'most important function is to raise the great mass of the population to a particular cultural and moral level, a level (or type) which corresponds to the needs of the productive forces for development, and hence to the interests of the ruling classes'. The most developed state – the MRS – is 'political society plus civil society', or *the integral state* (SPN:258, 263).

Faced by a serious threat 'the State as pure force is returned to', but the state strives to maintain the status quo by non-coercive methods (SPN:261). As conditions vary from country to country so does the state form; so, for example, the ethical state coupled with the 'night-watchman state' promoted 'protection and economic nationalism', while other versions took 'the "protection" of the working classes against the excesses of capitalism'. The regulatory state is 'the "state" as guardian of "fair play" and of the rules of the game' and Gramsci postulates 'the coercive element of the State withering away by degree, as ever-more conspicuous elements of regulated society (or ethical State or civil society) make their appearance' (SPN:262–3).

Central to the politics of the passive revolution is *trasformismo* (SPN:110, 112). *Trasformismo* describes the process whereby historic 'left' and 'right' parties – the liberal and conservative parties of the nineteenth century – merge into a party of order. This is encouraged by the emergence of socialist parties and the organised working class, but *trasformismo* is a powerful technique for managing class politics. As socialist parties grew in strength they became subject to *trasformismo*, to accommodation with, and incorporation into, the state. *Trasformismo* predicts the political trajectory of social democratic and left-of-centre parties in a passive revolution. *Trasformismo* describes 'the formation of an ever more extensive ruling class' and 'the gradual but continuous absorption ... even of those who come from antagonistic groups and seemed irreconcilably hostile' (SPN:58–9).

Power always moves away from parliament to the executive, change comes not from universal suffrage but from 'private organisms ... or of great civil servants unknown to the country at large, etc.' (SPN:261). Elections 'take away from "the man in the street" even that tiniest fraction of power of decision over the course of national life which he possesses' (SPN:193). The core executive 'not only formulates directives ... but at the same time creates the instruments by means of which the directives themselves will be "imposed", and by means of which it will verify their execution'. In modern states 'the greatest legislative power belongs to the State personnel ... who have at their disposal the legal coercive powers of the State' (SPN:266). Parliamentary democracy seduces rivals into the ranks of the ruling groups and is a plausible facade disguising the real power structure, whilst offering the prospect of reform. Liberal democratic states are the most effective state form for capital because they protect capital's dominance whilst permitting non-capitalist parties to form governments, thereby securing the consent of the governed (SPN:148). Passive revolution and *trasformismo* constitute the MRS's core political process, the negotiation of class compromise.

THE STATE AS CLASS COMPROMISE

This final section argues that the MRS's basic task is to manage class conflict. Its purpose is to present a general model of politics in capitalist society based on the passive revolution and *trasformismo*. Representative institutions are central to the MRS's management function and disguise the fact that some groups get what they want effortlessly 'because of the way society is structured' (Dowding 1996:71). The *non*-involvement of the bourgeoisie as a class in politics makes the MRS a powerful support for capitalism. Private ownership coupled with liberal democratic political institutions indicates the existence of a compromise between workers (who concede profit) and capitalists (who concede liberal democracy), a compromise which Marx saw as unstable. This political arrangement has, however, survived and prospered. The MRS can use coercion, but it is confined to specific segments of the working class and is of limited duration (Przeworski and Wallerstein 1982:215).[1]

A class compromise exists when, in the formula of Przeworski and Wallerstein: 'Workers consent to capitalism; capitalists consent to democracy' (1982:218). State autonomy is constrained by

> a relatively enduring set of relations between a set of actors understood in terms of the functional roles they occupy in society and in the economy. The system of relations is such that no single actor is necessary or sufficient for the continuance of the system, and if one or more actors fail to fulfil their roles there are strong incentives for others to take their place. (Dowding 1996:74)

Capitalism appears to operate under its own momentum which implies the state is unnecessary; but capitalism is based on irreconcilable conflict whose management requires the state's intervention. It has, however, withstood this conflict so that: 'Whenever class conflict happens to generate a threat to the reproduction of capital relations, some mechanism, most often thought to be the state, must come to the rescue by repressing, organizing ideological domination, or coopting' (Przeworski 1986:201). The mechanism whereby this is achieved is of some importance and is expressed in Figure 1 (adapted from Przeworski 1986:176–9).

Figure 1 expresses two phenomena; first, Marxism's presentation of how workers should behave under capitalism; and second, an explanation, focusing on the political process in the MRS, which explains why they behave as they do. Figure 1 assumes workers and capitalists are rational. Both seek to maximise the benefits of any activity whilst minimising costs. Activity should occur where the costs of activity are low and the chances of success are high. The rational-actor model is derived from capitalism's market logic and therefore can also be applied, via the base–superstructure relationship, to politics (Elster 1982:452–82; Carver and Thomas 1995). In the long run workers would be better off under socialism (S–S_1) than under capitalism (C–C_1); the vertical distance between S–S_1 and C–C_1 represents the workers' welfare gain.[2] At t_1 a majority of the working class decides to begin the transition to socialism (completed at S_4 at t_4) but this is immediately followed by a catastrophic fall in worker welfare, far below that which they would have enjoyed if they had not decided to move to socialism (t_2). Worker welfare reaches where it would have been without the decision to move to socialism at C_3, a level which would have been achieved without the dramatic fall in worker welfare at t_2. If workers continue to push towards socialism then worker welfare will be significantly greater at S_4 than at C_4 but securing this level of welfare comes only after substantial falls over a long period of time. Figure 1 gives no indication of the transition timescale but it is much longer than the electoral cycle.

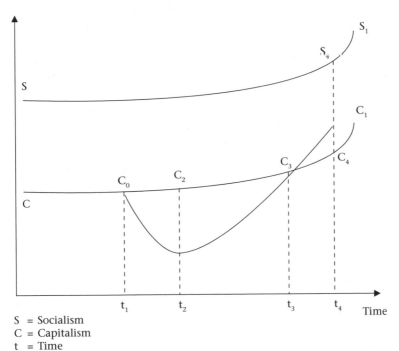

S = Socialism
C = Capitalism
t = Time

Figure 1   The Liberal Democratic State and the Politics of Class Compromise.

The electoral cycle protects capitalism by creating space for competing political strategies such as the passive revolution and *trasformismo*. Politicians will not secure (re)election if they mismanage the economy, and maintaining accumulation is not characteristic of the transition to socialism. The *costs* of moving from t_1 to t_4 outweigh the *benefits* gained between C_4 to S_4 and the move takes far longer than the electoral cycle. The disruption and turmoil of t_1–t_2 would result in electoral defeat (assuming that elections were permitted) and those forces – domestic and external – hostile to the transition would not roll over and accept history's verdict. Rational capitalists wishing to ensure their security would therefore promote liberal democracy. Figure 1 depends on a calculation of workers securing real and substantial gains between t_1 and t_4 compared to the impact of the costs of transition. Even if a majority of the population would be better off at S_4 compared to C_4, a majority would also be better off at C_4 than at C_0 (the start of the transition), so it is in the majority interest to remain on $C–C_1$ rather than expose themselves to the transition costs of $S–S_1$. It is rational for capitalists to ensure welfare increments to significant sections of the population *and* abdicate from politics. This could be – and is – reinforced by propaganda denigrating alternatives to capitalism.

Revolutionary activity would, given the state's coercive power, result in serious individual and collective costs for the working class, up to and including death, with, history suggests, little chance of success. Unlike voting, which entails minimum risk and commitment, revolutionary politics are confined to a tiny minority willing to accept the immediate costs in the expectation of long-term gain. By making the cost of revolutionary activity high, the state dramatically reduces the numbers involved. A secure MRS would tolerate revolutionary activities, because the revolutionary minority could be stigmatised and repressed at little overall cost. Compared to the costs of a socialist transition a rational actor would conclude that participation via voting and group activity is rational, involving lower personal costs and the likelihood of immediate gains.

The logic of collective action applies to liberal democratic politics but participation is vital for the MRS's legitimacy (Olson 1965). In an election with many millions of voters, the chance of one vote significantly affecting the outcome is 0, so a rational actor would not vote even though the personal costs were minimal. However, mass non-participation would weaken liberal democracy's credibility and legitimacy; participation is more likely when benefits will be, or are likely to be, secured at minimal cost. Participation must be maintained at a level sufficient to avoid vulnerability to a legitimation crisis and sufficient to convince actors that participation brings benefits. As participation produces benefits, an actor's sense of efficacy is maintained at a level sufficient to ensure minimal participation over time. An individual worker might reason that although his or her participation is unlikely to be effective, it is still worth acting to demonstrate support (e.g. for a trade union movement or social democratic party, or for a benefit such as a welfare state). Even if the party loses, there will be a subsequent election when the party might win; if the workers' party wins but disappoints its supporters when in government, it may be rational to continue to support that party in the light of the alternative(s).

Any compromise is unstable because the conditions in which it emerges are historically specific. There is, in addition, the problem of unforeseen or unintended consequences and, of course, the compromise may fail. The state is therefore permanently active:

> Neither the workers' consent to capitalism nor the capitalists' consent to democracy constitutes consensus ... A compromise holds if and only if it is continually in the best interests of workers and capitalists and only if it is repeatedly remade. A compromise is not a commitment for some indefinite or even limited future; it is an outcome of strategies chosen today which today appear optimal. (Przeworski and Wallerstein 1982:218)

Capitalism's survival cannot be guaranteed by the functioning of capitalism, and if capitalists behaved solely as capitalists the results would be disastrous for capitalism, especially when the working class begin to mobilise and socialism becomes a political project. Hence the functional requirement for an institution – the state – *outside* of, but *related* to, the economy whose purpose is system maintenance using repression, ideological domination, or co-option. In relation to Figure 1, the state acts to prevent the working class moving from $C-C_1$, so the focal point of liberal democratic politics is $C-C_0$ and avoiding any situation where $S-S_1$ becomes more attractive. This activity must be replicated over time to maintain the trajectory of $C-C_1$ and corresponds to *trasformismo*.

The liberal democratic electoral cycle protects capitalism without the need for the bourgeoisie to be active in politics and creates space for strategies such as social democracy:

> Between the capitalist path and the socialist one there is a valley that must be traversed if workers move at any time toward socialism. If such conditions exist and if workers are interested in a continual improvement of their material welfare, then the descent will not be undertaken or, if it is undertaken, will not be completed by workers under democratic conditions. (Przeworski 1986:176–7)

The MRS's task is to make this descent as unthinkable and/or unattractive as possible. It must operate in all three dimensions of power but most crucially in the third dimension which corresponds to hegemony (Lukes 1974:24). The MRS is the 'very best shell' for capitalism because its purpose is to secure class compromise. 'The state', Przeworski concludes, 'must enforce the compliance of both classes with the terms of each compromise and protect those segments of each class that enter into a compromise from non-cooperative behaviour of their fellow class members' (1986:202).

'Pro-business' conservative parties pursue policies seemingly not in capital's immediate interests; social democratic parties pursue policies not in the immediate interests of labour; but there can only be pro-business parties in liberal democracies. Irrespective of which party forms the government, the state responds to capital's interests because the state depends on continued accumulation, but capital also requires the state to carry out general functions. This is invariably described as maintaining 'business confidence'. As Robert Reich noted, 'it's always our "credibility" with Wall Street. It is repeatedly said that we must reduce the deficit because Wall Street needs to be reassured, calmed, convinced of our wise intentions ... Who fretted about Wall Street's feelings when Reagan and Bush racked up the biggest debt in American history?' (Reich 1998:65). Reich, President Clinton's first-term Secretary of Labor, was not advocating socialism but a programme of infrastructural investment to improve the competitiveness of US capital which was therefore in capital's long-term, general interest. Increased public spending was not, however, in Wall Street's interests. This 'anticipated reaction' reflects the structural power of capital (Ward 1987:593–610). Stock markets are the most powerful part of capital because other fractions cannot, except in the most extreme circumstances, act collectively. Stock markets are concerned with the system's dynamism and '[w]hat matters is which firm is doing well now, and if it does badly soon, investment can easily be shifted' (Dowding 1996:76).[3] What concerns the state is not the viability of *individual* capitals but capital as a *system*.

Capital can, and will, adapt to the environment in which it finds itself, even a social democratic government committed to redistribution, because to do so is in its interests (Przeworski and Wallerstein 1988:11–29). State policies are designed to sustain the capitalist system and are seldom the product of a state facing a *revolutionary* working class; states are 'an expression of a class compromise in the immediate interests of both capitalists and workers' (Przeworski 1986:202). Autonomy derives from the tension between capital's individual and collective interests which means that 'the state at any given time is not simply the instrument of the current generation of capitalists, but a means to the survival of capitalism as a system. It is in principle ready to sacrifice not only individual capitalists, but even short-term interests of the class as a whole' (Elster 1985:410).

CONCLUSION

Marx's basic precepts on the state are straightforward, but much Marxist work on the state is obscurantist and concerned with unresolvable (and pointless) debates over autonomy. Capitalism works best and is most secure when the bourgeoisie abdicates from politics; what needs to be explained is not the state's dependence on capital but the nature of autonomy. This chapter has argued first, that the state is coercive; second, that coercion is not a secure political base; and third, that the state is autonomous. It concentrates on the politics of the MRS which is the one most appropriate to capitalism. The MRS manages class conflict; the rise of organised labour, mass electoral democracy, and the concentration of power in the executive means that it does so by organising class compromise.

A Marxist analysis of the state is not economically determinist. If there were unity between base and superstructure it would be pointless to analyse the state. Capitalism is inherently crisis-prone but the MRS is designed to strive for crisis resolution via class compromise. This developed during the long crisis of the twentieth century and took the form of the passive revolution and *trasformismo*. The MRS ensures continued accumulation at the cost of individual capitalists or fractions of capital. Accumulation cannot be guaranteed solely by the operation of capitalism because capital is fragmented and incapable of guaranteeing its general interest. The result is the creation, failure and recreation of class compromise. There are many ways for the state to maintain accumulation but the MRS is the best long-term political framework for capitalism.

Exploring the politics of class compromise is an empirical task because of the variety of forms generated, and it is futile, as well as profoundly un-Marxist, to encase this variety in a sterile theoretical straitjacket. As Engels insisted, we should focus on historical cases, otherwise we shall produce 'the most amazing rubbish' (Engels 1893:683).

GUIDE TO FURTHER READING

Marx's most extensive analyses of the state can be found in *The Eighteenth Brumaire of Louis Bonaparte* (1852) and *The Civil War in France* (1871). *Marx and Engels: Selected Works in One Volume* (1970) contains both texts as well as a wide selection of other relevant writings. *The State and Revolution* (1917) sets out Lenin's analysis of the state as capitalism's 'best possible shell' while Selections from the Prison Notebooks (1971) includes many of Gramsci's writings on the passive revolution and *trasformismo*. This volume also contains a useful introduction. There is a huge amount of work analysing Marxism and the state. Though often difficult, Jessop's books (1982; 2002) are indispensable. Articles by Ward, on structural power, and by Przeworski and Wallerstein (1982; 1988) and Przeworski (1986), show how theory can be applied to empirical cases.

NOTES

1. Can the politics of class compromise occur in the absence of an *organised* working class? My answer would be yes. The most important factor is the *emergence* of a working class which is *believed* to have the potential for autonomous action which would trigger a passive revolution and *trasformismo*. The extent and radicalism of the passive revolution would depend on the development and consciousness of the working class, but states react to the presence of a working class whose presence is strongly associated with the growth of liberal democracy (Rueschmeyer, Stephens and Stephens 1992).
2. The assumption that workers would be better off under socialism was implicitly held by capitalists and states who have devoted huge resources to crushing, discrediting and neutralising any socialist 'threat'.
3. An omission in this chapter is how the state as class compromise relates to issues of state security and its role in the international state system. The relationship between security, national interests, and autonomy is complex but of increasing importance in a globalising world (Burnham 1998:190–201).

REFERENCES

Burnham, P. (1998) 'The Communist Manifesto as International Relations Theory', in M. Cowling (ed.) *The Communist Manifesto: New Interpretations*.

Carver, T. and Thomas, P. (eds) (1995) *Rational Choice Marxism* (London: Macmillan).

Cowling, M. (ed.) (1998) *The Communist Manifesto: New Interpretations* (Edinburgh: Edinburgh University Press).

Dowding, D. (1996) *Power* (Milton Keynes: Open University Press).

Elster, J. (1982) 'Marxism, Functionalism, and Game Theory', *Theory and Society*, Vol. 11, No. 4.

—— (1985) *Making Sense of Marx* (Cambridge: Cambridge University Press).

Engels, F. (1890a) 'F. Engels to J. Bloch, 21 September 1890', in *MESW*.

—— (1890b) 'F. Engels to C. Schmidt, 27 October 1890', in *MESW*.

—— (1893) 'F. Engels to F. Mehring, 14 July 1893', in *MESW*.

Fernbach, D. (ed.) (1973) *Marx: Surveys From Exile* (Harmondsworth. Penguin).

Gramsci, A. (1971) *Selections from the Prison Notebooks*, edited by Quinton Hoare and Geoffrey Nowell Smith (London: Lawrence and Wishart).

Hindess, B. (1980) 'Marxism and Parliamentary Democracy', in A. Hunt (ed.) *Marxism and Democracy* (London: Lawrence and Wishart).

—— (1983) *Parliamentary Democracy and Socialist Politics* (London: Routledge and Kegan Paul).

Jessop, B. (1982) *The Capitalist State: Marxist Theories and Methods* (Oxford: Martin Robertson).

—— (2002) *The Future of the Capitalist State* (Cambridge: Polity Press).

Lenin, V.I. (1897) 'The Tasks of the Russian Social-Democrats', in Lenin (1969).

—— (1907) 'The Agrarian Programme of Social Democracy in the First Russian Revolution', in Lenin (1969).

—— (1915) 'English Pacifism and English Dislike of Theory', in Lenin (1969).

—— (1916) 'Imperialism and the Split in the Labour Movement', in Lenin (1969).

—— (1917a) *The State and Revolution. The Marxist Teaching on the State and the Tasks of the Proletariat in the Revolution* (Peking: Foreign Languages Press 1973).

—— (1917b) 'All Russian April Conference', in Lenin (1969).

—— (1918), *The Proletarian Revolution and the Renegade Kautsky*, in V.I. Lenin, *Selected Works* (Moscow: Progress Publishers 1977).

—— (1919) 'Tasks of the Third International', in Lenin (1969).

—— (1969) *British Labour and British Imperialism* (London: Lawrence and Wishart).

Lukes, S. (1974) *Power: A Radical View* (London: Macmillan).

Marx, K. (1843) 'Critical Marginal Notes on the Article by a Prussian', in K. Marx and F. Engels *Collected Works*, Vol. 13 (London: Lawrence and Wishart).

—— (1852a) *The Eighteenth Brumaire of Louis Bonaparte*, in *MESW*.

—— (1852b) 'The Chartists' (10 August), in Fernbach (1973),

—— (1854) 'The British Constitution' (2 March), in Fernbach (1973).

—— (1859) *Preface to A Contribution to the Critique of Political Economy*, in *MESW*.

—— (1871) *The Civil War in France*, in *MESW*.

—— (1875) *The Critique of the Gotha Programme*, in *MESW*.

—— (1887) *Capital: A Critique of Political Economy. Volume One: The Process of Production of Capital* (London: Lawrence and Wishart).

—— (1894) *Capital: A Critique of Political Economy. Volume Three: The Process of Capitalist Production as a Whole* (London: Lawrence and Wishart).

MESW (1970) *Marx and Engels: Selected Works in One Volume* (London: Lawrence and Wishart).

Marx, K. and Engels, F. (1848) *The Communist Manifesto*, in *MESW*.

—— (1977) *The German Ideology* (Moscow: Progress Publishers).

Miliband, R. (1969) *The State in Capitalist Society: The Analysis of the Western System of Power* (London: Weidenfeld and Nicolson).

—— (1970) 'The Capitalist State – Reply to Nicos Poulantzas', *New Left Review*, No. 59.

—— (1990) 'Marx and the State', in B. Jessop (ed.) *Karl Marx's Social and Political Thought. Vol. III: The State, Politics and Revolution* (London: Routledge).

Olson, M. (1965) *The Logic of Collective Action: Public Goods and the Theory of Groups* (Cambridge, Mass.: Harvard University Press).

Poulantzas, N. (1969) 'The Problem of the Capitalist State', *New Left Review*, No. 58.

—— (1976) 'The Capitalist State – A Reply to Miliband and Laclau', *New Left Review*, No. 95.

—— (1980) *State, Power, Socialism* (London: Verso).

Przeworski, A. (1986) *Capitalism and Social Democracy* (Cambridge: Cambridge University Press).

Przeworski, A. and Wallerstein, M. (1982) 'The Structure of Class Conflict in Democratic Capitalist States', *American Political Science Review*, Vol. 76, No. 2.

—— (1988) 'Structural Dependence of the State on Capital', *American Political Science Review*, Vol. 82, No. 1.

Reich, R.B. (1998) *Locked in the Cabinet* (New York: Vintage).

Rueschmeyer, D., Stephens, E.H. and Stephens, J.D. (1992) *Capitalist Development and Democracy* (Cambridge: Polity Press).

Ward, H. (1987) 'Structural Power – A Contradiction in Terms?' *Political Studies*, Vol. 35, No. 4.

Wetherly, P. (1998) 'A Capitalist State? Marx's Ambiguous Legacy', in M. Cowling (ed.) *The Communist Manifesto: New Interpretations*.

5
Imperialism

Graham Harrison

The profound hypocrisy and inherent barbarism of bourgeois civilisation lies unveiled before our eyes, moving from its home, where it assumes respectable form, to the colonies, where it goes · naked. (Marx and Engels 1974:86)

How, then, might we define this troublesome word 'imperialism' and justify its use? Since the nineteenth century the term has gained such partisan and pejorative connotations that there are many who with some reason maintain that it would be altogether better to ban it from use ... The argument in support of its retention, however, is that the literature on imperialism constitutes a tradition of some importance in the analysis of international relations and that no better, alternative grammar exists to describe such a category of relations between the strong and the weak. By banning the word, we would risk cutting ourselves off from the richness of that literature and impoverishing our debate. (Smith 1981:5)

IMPERIALISM AS A CONCEPT:
AN AWKWARD PARTNER IN THE MARXIST LEXICON?

Imperialism[1] is a peculiar term within the general Marxist lexicon. It was not elaborated by Marx but has flourished throughout the twentieth century within Marxist theory (Owen and Sutcliffe 1972; Brewer 1990; Kemp 1967). It has meandered in and out of Marxist frameworks of analysis, and attached itself to many of the salient world events of the last century: the rise and fall of colonialism (Hobsbawm 1995), the 'thirty years war' between 1914 and 1945, the 'rise to globalism' of the United States, the rise and fall of development as a theoretical–political issue, and most recently the 'war against terrorism'. Running parallel to imperialism's persistence are attempts by non-Marxists to do away with the concept, and these attempts relate to a more general desire to render Marxism a theory for a bygone age. Nevertheless, imperialism and other Marxist concepts have not gone away, despite the best efforts of the orthodoxies in all social science disciplines. New, original and insightful work continues to be produced by scholars within the Marxist tradition, as other chapters in this book demonstrate.

Marxism is a tradition of analysis and critique. Even the abstractions of Marx's *Capital* are infused with metaphor and irony which evoke judgements of capitalism. For example, consider the following which, in my reading, is as close as Marx comes to an allusion to imperialism in the first volume of *Capital*:

> The discovery of gold and silver in America, the extirpation, enslavement, and entombment in mines of the aboriginal population, the beginning of the conquest and looting of the East Indies, the turning of Africa into a warren for the commercial hunting of black-skins, signalised the rosy dawn of the era of capitalist production. These idyllic proceedings are the chief moment of primitive accumulation. On their heels treads the commercial war of the European nations, with the globe for a theatre. (Marx [1867] 1999:376)

One can see irony and even plain sarcasm in the tract above and the quotation that opens this paper: bourgeois civilisation is nothing more than the emperor's new clothes, its respectability contingent, perhaps tenuous. This is not just a 'contradiction', it is a 'hypocrisy' – analytical and normative. Imperialism can be read as a concept that develops the moral suggestion from Marx's allusions to the intrinsically global nature of capital. Imperialism as a concept has failed to make a sufficiently clear and stable understanding of this 'double standard' – 'civilisation' and 'barbarism' or, to give it a modern nomenclature, development and underdevelopment – but it is the argument of this chapter that the Marxist tradition provides us with enough of a reason to continue with the term in this vein.

Imperialism was not a term used by Marx. Nevertheless it has proven to be an enduring part of the Marxist tradition of analysis, and it contains a strong connotation of political judgement. The concept of imperialism also persists because it provides a critical entrée into the analysis of a global system that is indisputably and extremely uneven in the distribution of wealth, property and power. Finally, we should also note the radical elasticity of the term. There is, in fact, no generally accepted cognition of what 'imperialism' is, whereas almost everyone agrees some basic object around which Marxist interpretations of the state or class revolve. We can readily get a sense of this by reviewing the principal contributions to the theorisation of imperialism, which is the task of the next section. Subsequently, we will consider imperialism's contribution to the notion of development before ending with a reflection on the relevance of imperialism to the study of our contemporary global system.

A BRIEF GENEALOGY OF IMPERIALISM

Imperialism is a concept that has endured turbulence equal to the histories it has attempted to describe and explain. Imperialism has not moved in dialectical fashion towards a synthesis or a higher level of understanding. Rather, it has lurched from one unresolved controversy to another, fallen in and out of intellectual fashion, fixed on certain historical events before falling away with no clear message to speak to a broader history. Thus, a straightforward description of different theories of imperialism will not achieve much more than a sense of imperialism's conceptual elasticity. A cursory genealogy of imperialism will involve a more *interpretive* endeavour which attempts to find a narrative embedded within the twists and turns of the imperialist *opus*.

Imperialism as the highest stage of capitalism

Lenin's pamphlet *Imperialism: The Highest Stage of Capitalism* remains the *locus classicus* of imperialism (Lenin [1916] 1975). Lenin makes a series of associations that tie capitalism as a social system to the rise of national rivalries on a global scale. His approach is one of immanence: there are properties intrinsic to capitalism that lead it, teleologically, to imperialism which is, as Lenin's historically pre-emptive phrase has it, the highest stage of capitalism. Lenin outlines five features of imperialism (Lenin [1916] 1975:106):

- The concentration of production into monopolies.
- The merging of bank and industrial capital.
- The export of capital becoming more important than the export of commodities.
- The formation of 'international capitalist combines'.
- The territorial division of the whole world.

In essence, imperialism is the process through which large national monopolies seek to export capital to all parts of the world, underpinned by a national state that works to secure the former's project. As such, rivalries between national monopolies become rivalries between nation-states. Imperialism creates capitalist expansion and a tendency towards war.

For Lenin, these features require that we understand capitalism as having entered a new stage; in fact in some passages it appears that Lenin believes that capitalism has been replaced by another social system based in monopoly (Lenin [1916] 1975:20, 105, 148). Lenin's analysis of monopoly capitalism/imperialism portrays a kind of capitalism, awkwardly defined also as a post-capitalism, in which the social relations of competition are bypassed and production is socialised into a small number of financial–industrial conglomerates, intertwined with powerful managerial states.

A key component of *The Highest Stage* concerns the effects of imperialism outside Europe. This is central to the concerns of this chapter because it goes to the notion of hypocrisy. Here, Lenin's thinking is in the first place that of a political activist and strategist, but he is equivocal in his conclusions. In fact, two different voices can be heard. Firstly, imperialism impoverishes and degrades non-capitalist societies; in fact, Lenin sounds like a dependency theorist:

> As long as capitalism remains what it is, surplus capital will be utilised not for the purpose of raising the standard of living of the masses in a given country, for this would mean a decline in the profits of the capitalists ... In these backward countries profits are usually high, for capital is scarce, the price of land is relatively low, raw materials are cheap. (Lenin [1916] 1975:73)

Secondly, imperialism is framed in a far more 'progressive' fashion:

> The export of capital affects and greatly accelerates the development of capitalism in those countries to which it is exported. While, therefore, the export of capital may tend to a certain extent to *arrest development in the capital exporting countries*, it can only do so by *expanding further development throughout the world*. (Lenin [1916] 1975:76)

Lenin establishes a global image: a critique of capitalism as an international system which produces a radical disjuncture between capital's 'Lockean heartlands' (van der Pijl 1998) and the spaces outwith these relatively small parts of the world which, nevertheless, also constitute the very being of capitalism. This disjuncture is the beginning of the recognition of capitalism's double standards: herein lies Lenin's contribution for our purposes, but it is limited by Lenin's failure to make serious reference to Marxist theory and his simplistic account of capitalism's political forms. Let us now look at a more explicitly Marxist attempt to understand imperialism.

Imperialism and primitive accumulation

Rosa Luxemburg wrote before Lenin (1913), but her impact on the concept of imperialism is more limited, and key aspects of her theorisation, concerning the realisation of surplus value, have been generally refuted (Brewer 1990:60–6). Nevertheless, Luxemburg's writings have experienced a gradual rehabilitation in the aftermath of Leninist orthodoxy and this is principally because of her attention to the impact of capitalism on non-capitalist modes of production and societies more generally. This was something that Lenin and most other 'classical' theorists of imperialism did only *en passant*. For Luxemburg, non-capitalist societies were *constitutive* of capitalism itself, not extraneous spheres waiting to be swept into the tide of 'real' history; not the functional effects of imperialist competition.

For Luxemburg, capitalism emerges out of a long and violent history of primitive accumulation[2] in feudal Europe, as Marx and others have described. But primitive accumulation – the dispossession of peasants and the increasing of absolute surplus value[3] – is not a 'birth pang' of capital, it is rather intrinsic to its functioning, more akin to a tendency than a stage. In other words, capital constantly seeks out non-capitalist societies to exploit, to dispossess and to crush, only to remake them into associations of 'free' labourers. Luxemburg takes Marx's account of primitive accumulation and argues that this is intrinsic to capitalism as a global system. Thus, she begins by quoting a famous passage from Marx: 'Sweating blood and filth with every pore from head to toe' characterises not only the birth of capital but also its progress in the world at every step (Luxemburg [1913] 1951:453).

It is the relationship between global capitalism and primitive accumulation that I want to highlight from Luxemburg. It provides an understanding of imperialism that contains more theoretical purchase than Lenin. For her, it is the social forms of capital and the sectors of the economy that matter: one region of Europe might exploit another, or one industry in England might seek markets in a particular country in the colonies.

Luxemburg also establishes a theory of *peripheralisation* within political economy; that is, the active construction of areas that serve the 'core' processes of capitalist development. She also provides a very insightful account of violence and capitalism through primitive accumulation:

> Accumulation can no more wait for and be content with, a natural internal disintegration of non-capitalist formations ... than it can wait for the natural increase of the working population. Force is the only solution open to capital: the accumulation of capital, seen as an historical process, employs *force as a permanent weapon*, not only as its genesis, but further on down to the present day. (in Brewer 1990:69, my emphasis)

The attention that Luxemburg pays to the violence of capitalism's expansion as a global system has given her writing a continued salience: 'Luxemburg's "primitive accumulation" theory of imperialism ... has a life of its own quite independent of errors of reasoning which partly lead to it' (Sutcliffe 2002:48).

Like Lenin, Luxemburg is highlighting a double standard or hypocrisy. Lenin's global distinction between strong and weak states is now coupled with Luxemburg's distinction between *progress* and *degradation*. Marx was often intrigued by the tension between capitalism's claims to progress and the violence and alienation of its ascendancy – 'drinking nectar from the skulls of the slain' (Marx in Marx and Engels 1979:217) in his evocative language – but Luxemburg allows us to think of this tension as a persistent tendency within global capitalism. Thus, to make a brief contemporary contextualisation, imperialism might highlight the integration of bourgeois ideologies of progress, globalisation, governance and development against processes of mass dispossession, child labour, resource wars and environmental degradation.

Lenin and Luxemburg are not the only writers to theorise imperialism within the Marxist tradition in the early twentieth century. (Other notable writers were Nikolai Bukharin and Karl Kautsky, with his concept of 'ultra-imperialism'; in addition to further reading, see Bromley 2003 and Shaw 1984.) Nevertheless, they do provide a sound point of departure in one important sense. They define two key disjunctures in the constitution of global capitalism that both relate to other classical works of imperialism and they give us two axes along which capitalism's double standards might be conceived:

1. The radically unequal constitution of a system of nation-states as a result of the historic processes of the emergence of capitalism and imperial projects in various parts of the world. This has produced a modern system of formal sovereign equality underpinned by a political economy which remains (albeit dynamically and in complex ways) clustered around certain capitalist cores.
2. The violent deconstruction and reconstruction of societies (more or less purposefully) as capital expands, deepens, or changes throughout global space. This has produced modern liberal bourgeois discourses of modernity, stability and rational instrumentalism which ideologise processes of violence, imposition, and dispossession.

Thus classical theories of imperialism make two important statements concerning the nature of the global political economy – points that endure beyond the times at which these theories were written. Many of the concerns that imperialist theory raised were, in fact, carried over into the post-Second World War period under the general rubric of 'development'.

IMPERIALISM AND THE DISCOVERY OF DEVELOPMENT

Early writers within the dependency 'school'[4] of development theory explicitly take Lenin as their starting point. Paul Baran's work on monopoly capitalism (Baran 1957) follows Lenin's argument that capitalism has attained a monopoly form, but the international repercussions of this form are given more clarity and set in contrast to some passages in Lenin's *Imperialism*. Baran is writing about the rise of transnational corporations in America in the post-Second World War period and the repercussions of foreign direct investment in the post-colonial world. Baran's innovative work fed into the rise of dependency theory which constituted the main radical critique to liberal development theory in the 1960s and 1970s. One of dependency theory's most eloquent representatives, Fernando Henrique Cardoso, starts with Lenin and interprets him as follows:

the consequence of imperialism with respect to dependent economies and nations ... was the integration of the latter into the international market. Inequality among nations and economies resulted from imperialism's development to the extent that import of raw materials and export of manufactured goods were the bases of the imperialist-colonial relationship. The reproduction and amplification of inequality between advanced economies and dependent economies developed as a by-product of the very process of capitalist growth. (Cardoso 1972:83)

In essence, what Cardoso is saying is that development in post-colonial countries is limited and conditioned by powerful economic forces that emanate from Europe and America. Dependency theory re-imagines imperialism as a form of global capitalism, based in the core states, 'underdeveloping' the peripheral states within a systemic global schema of surplus-value extraction. Sutcliffe defines this as a phase in the study of imperialism, involving 'a more complex, post-colonial dependency of the peripheral countries, in which foreign capital ... profit repatriation, [and] adverse changes in the terms of trade all play a role in confining, distorting or halting economic development and industrialisation' (Sutcliffe 1972:172). Foster-Carter pithily summarises this as a 'gigantic and systematic rip-off' (1993:107).

The ascendance of radical dependency theory transforms imperialism in some important ways:

- A focus on the form of capitalism in developed states is replaced by an interest in the effects of imperialism in the Third World.
- The equivocal nature of capitalist development – as historically progressive but destructive and anarchic – is lost to a more determined judgement concerning underdevelopment.
- A framework of world-systems and states is firmly established.
- Most focus is placed on structures of trade and surplus extraction rather than production and wage labour.

One gets the sense, in retrospect, that dependency theory made a flawed theorisation of an important development: the entry of post-colonial states into a global political economy historically shaped by the west. The inequalities that worked to limit the possibilities of formal sovereignty (captured in the term 'neo-colonialism' – political independence attenuated by ongoing economic subservience) led radical development theory to identify global structures and to argue that these structures were enduring and immutable in the absence of some form of profound rupture (Amin 1990). As such, radical development theory was grappling with the unequal constitution of nation-states mentioned earlier in the section on Lenin. Its weaknesses derive from its inability to understand the social processes of capitalist accumulation which – for better or worse – provide the enabling condition for all examples of 'development' in modern history. This weakness is one that Warren addresses in his powerful revision of imperialism.

Bill Warren argued directly against the reformulation of imperialism made by dependency theory. For Warren, imperialism was not the progenitor of underdevelopment but the pioneer of capitalism (Warren 1980). Claiming himself a place in a classical Marxist tradition, Warren argued that imperialism has produced both industrialisation (Warren 1973) and a national bourgeoisie that could use newly independent states to promote accumulation within national societies. Warren effectively reclaimed the double-edged nature of capitalist expansion expressed in Marx's journalistic writings and in the concept of primitive accumulation used by Marx and Luxemburg: colonialism might have been a brutish project but it established the social conditions for the rise of national bourgeois projects in the Third World which might subsequently champion economic growth and capitalist development. Historically posed, imperialism was not the last stage of capitalism but a prelude to a truly global capitalism that would then enable the possibility of socialism.

Let us return to the theme of hypocrisy. Radical development theory represents an ongoing attempt to understand the double standards of sovereignty/self-determination and the history of capitalism as a 'combined and uneven' social system. Although less strong concerning the social nature of accumulation, dependency theory does provide important insights. In this sense, one might define development as a concept that attempts to judge the social effects of accumulation. Does capitalist accumulation produce an improvement in general well-being? (Seers 1973). If capitalist growth leads to a massive concentration of wealth within a small and insular class which employs state power to suppress the mass of the population, it has failed its developmental mandate; if capitalism produces an increase in incomes and employment and finally a state with institutionalised accountability to its citizenry, then we might speak of capitalist development. In Cramer's words:

> As Marx put it, primitive accumulation is to political economy what original sin is to theology. And the study of the political economy of development ... surely needs to be the study of ... primitive accumulation and its varieties, points of susceptibility to progress, and the formation of and relations among particular classes. (2002:324)

'Development' in this sense is a concept that attempts to hold global capitalism accountable. Where the expansion of capitalism fails to prove itself a globally progressive system, causing extreme social disruption, impoverishment, new forms of violence and so on, we can identify the hypocrisy in declarations of progress and development through market expansion.

Let us draw together the key points from our excursion through imperialist theory:

- Lenin's work suggests a complex of national rivalries that establish a system of states in competition with one another and dominating other states outside the heartlands of capital.
- Luxemburg establishes the intrinsic tendency towards violence and expropriation within capitalism's global laws of motion.
- Dependency theories alert us to the limited extent to which formal sovereignty matters in a global political economy based on the massive conglomerations of capital in the west (or parts of it).
- Finally, development can be used as a metaphor to critique the universalist and progressivist images of capital as an international social form.

I bring these out essentially to justify my starting point: capitalism as a global system needs to be theorised as an integrated but differentiated system, or as a combined and uneven social entity (Rosenberg 1996). Marx understood this in his analyses of India, although he hardly developed this understanding in his written work. Nevertheless, the quotation that begins this chapter reveals a key property that should be at the centre of all Marxist work: critique. The notion of double standards alludes to the properties of global capitalism, but in a way that attacks the latter; imperialism remains the most appropriate theoretical point of departure from which to launch this attack.

RECONSTRUCTING IMPERIALISM

So, how might we rethink imperialism as a contemporary theory of capitalism's global double standards? Let us start with Halliday's (2002:80) argument for the enduring pertinence of imperialism:

- The inexorable expansion of capitalism as a socio-economic system on a world scale.
- The necessarily competitive, expansionist, and warlike character of developed capitalist states.
- The unequal nature of capitalist expansion, and the reproduction on a world scale of socio-economic inequalities.
- The creation on a world scale of structures of inequality of power and wealth not only in the economic, but also in the social, political, legal and cultural spheres.
- The generation, through the very process of capitalist expansion, of movements of resistance, of anti-imperialism.

These five points relate closely to the discussion in previous sections, and make a persuasive argument to persist with the concept of imperialism when making sense of global politics. By way of conclusion, we can make a few remarks to demonstrate the utility of imperialism as a concept in understanding what are probably the two main themes in contemporary politics: globalisation and international terrorism.

Globalisation concerns the increasing integration of national societies and the formation of global social activities, usually making reference to a changing or denuded national state capacity (Harrison 2002). By and large, globalisation is seen in liberal terms: networks, equalisation, mutual interdependence, and a general sense of progress that derives from expanding and deepening market relations. Surely, imperialism should be the official conceptual opposite of globalisation articulated in this sense? There are nevertheless plenty of aspects to 'globalisation' that scream out for a more critical concept: the allocation of massive power to unaccountable international organisations such as the World Bank and the IMF; the enduring protectionism of developed capitalist states, many aspects of which directly disadvantage post-colonial economies; the socially deleterious effects of integration into the global economy in many circumstances; the enduring global debt regime; new forms of globalised ecological destruction; and the increasing vulnerability of economies and people whose lives are profoundly conditioned by the footloose and turbulent flows of finance. Globalisation cannot take these phenomena as seriously as it should because it is derived from a liberal and progressive world vision; imperialism can represent these phenomena as part of the way the world has been historically structured by a capitalist 'heartland' to produce inequalities, interventions, and forms of exploitation.

International terrorism has, of course, become the main issue of international politics since September 2001. The 'war against terrorism', announced by George W. Bush soon after, has infused a broad range of political relations. There is a moral case to be made for a war against terrorism, but this is not to say anything specific about the nature of this war or about how literally we should take the word 'war'. It is now clear that the war against terrorism is principally a new power-projection strategy effected by the US and based on its massive military superiority. The US military had a budget for the fiscal year 2002 of $396 billion, including a $40 billion approval by Congress in late 2001; it went to war in two countries in two years, and has other states on its list; it has expanded its permanent military presence in the wake of intervention. The massive rise in American power-projection is one of the most striking aspects of the 'war against terrorism' and it leads us to one of the core concepts of imperialism: the radical inequality between states. Unsurprisingly, some have referred to the current period as one of 'hyperimperialism'.

But, one should not be excessively blinded by the sheer preponderance of military power and technology. Each intervention also involves issues of accumulation and the (attempted) reordering of geopolitical relations to ensure a global economic agenda developed within the current US administration. One can see this in the 'pipeline politics' of Central Asia (Klare 2001; Rashid 2001) and of course in the oil politics of the Middle East (RUPE 2003). There is no space to deal with these in detail here, but I do insist on the point that these interventions were produced as acts of both power-projection and strategic economic thinking. This is not to determine these interventions according to some fully worked through economic 'logic', but it would be equally fanciful to imagine the US, with the largest and most highly globalised economy, intervening in such resource-strategic regions without a consideration of future oil-market trends, the influence of American oil companies, the economic rivalries with other developed capitalist regions, and the future of the dollar as an international currency.

In sum, we live in a world where massive inequalities of power between states are intertwined with the combined and uneven development of capitalism. This has led to the persistence of massive inequality, war and insecurity. Although imperialism as a concept has not been fully developed and clarified, imperialism as a *process* has not disappeared with perestroika and globalisation. If imperialism is here to stay, it would be folly to abandon the concept.

GUIDE TO FURTHER READING

It is worth reading Lenin ([1916] 1975) – a pamphlet with as much political rhetoric as theoretical analysis. Rosa Luxemburg's book ([1913] 1951) is not an easy read! The best general survey of imperialist theory is Brewer (1990), although it is now a little dated. Others worth looking at are Fieldhouse (1967), which looks at classical political economy and historical tracts concerning imperialism and empire; Kemp (1967) makes an engaged review, but this book has weathered time less well than Brewer; Owen and Sutcliffe (1972) provide a collection of interesting engagements with imperialist theory. The extent to which imperialism was alluded to by Marx, and whether Marx perceived of European expansion as historically progressive or not, have been subject to some debate. See Warren (1980) and especially Larrain (1991) for reflections on this theme. Two important writers mentioned only briefly in this chapter, but recommended reading for those interested in the full imperialism opus, are Bukharin (1972) and Kautsky (1970). Two other good collections are Radice (1975) and Rhodes (1970). After a lull in the 1980s and early 1990s, imperialism is being used in academic writing once more. See, for example, Biel (2000), Halliday (2002), Callinicos et al. (1994), *Review of African Political Economy* (2003) Vol. 30, No. 95, and *Radical History Review* (1993) No. 57, Fall.

NOTES

1. 'Imperialism' is, unless explicitly noted otherwise, used here as a reference to a theoretical term, not a historical project or process.

2. Primitive accumulation is the process through which capitalist social relations are established, principally by separating peasant farmers from their land. In doing this, property-less workers are compelled to earn wages from the owners of property. As a historic process, the divorcing of farmers from their land has been accompanied by large doses of state compulsion and violence (see Bottomore 1991:444–5).
3. Absolute surplus is the extraction of value from labour without making improvements to productivity. In other words, 'squeezing' more value from workers under existing conditions of production.
4. Dependency theory is a theory of Third World 'underdevelopment' based on the premise of the existence of a developed capitalist 'core' extracting surplus from a Third World 'periphery'.

REFERENCES

Amin, S. (1990) *Delinking: Towards a Polycentric World* (London: Zed Press).

Baran, P. (1957) *The Political Economy of Growth* (New York: Monthly Review Press).

Biel, R. (2000) *The New Imperialism: Crisis and Contradictions in North/South Relations* (London: Zed Press).

Bottomore, T. (ed.) (1991) *A Dictionary of Marxist Thought* (Oxford: Blackwell).

Brewer, A. (1990) *Marxist Theories of Imperialism* (London: Routledge and Kegan Paul).

Bromley, S. (2003) 'Reflections on Empire, *Imperialism*, and United States Hegemony', *Historical Materialism,* Vol. 11, No. 3.

Bukharin, N. (1972) *Imperialism and the World Economy* (London: Merlin Press).

Callinicos, A., Rees, J., Harman, C., Hayes, M., (eds) (1994) *Marxism and the New Imperialism* (London: Bookmarks).

Cardoso, F. (1972) 'Dependency and Development in Latin America', *New Left Review,* No. 74.

Cramer, C. (2002) 'Review of Bates', *Journal of Modern African Studies,* Vol. 40, No. 2.

Fieldhouse, D.K. (1967) *The Theory of Capitalist Imperialism* (London: Longman).

Foster-Carter, A. (1993) 'The Sociology of Development', in M. Haralambos (ed.) *Sociology: New Directions* (Ormskirk: Causeway Press).

Halliday, F. (2002) 'The Pertinence of Imperialism', in M. Rupert and H. Smith (eds) *Historical Materialism and Globalization* (London: Routledge).

Harrison, G. (2002) 'Globalisation', in G. Blakeley and V. Bryson (eds) *Contemporary Political Concepts: A Critical Introduction* (London: Pluto Press).

Hobsbawm, E. (1995) *The Age of Empire* (London: Weidenfeld and Nicholson).

Kautsky, K. (1970) 'Ultra-imperialism', *New Left Review,* No. 59.

Kemp, T. (1967) *Theories of Imperialism* (London: Dennis Dobson).

Klare, M. (2001) *Resource Wars: The New Landscape of Global Conflict* (New York: Metropolitan).

Larrain, J. (1991) 'Classical Political Economists and Marx on Colonialism and "Backward" Nations', *World Development*, Vol. 19, Nos 2/3.

Lenin, V.I. ([1916] 1975) *Imperialism: The Highest Stage of Capitalism* (Peking: Foreign Language Press).

Luxemburg, R. ([1913] 1951) *The Accumulation of Capital* (London: Routledge and Kegan Paul).

Marx, K. ([1867] 1999) *Capital*, Vol. I (Oxford: Oxford University Press).

Marx, K. and Engels, F. (1974) *On Colonialism* (Moscow: Progress Publishers).

—— (1979) *Collected Works* (London: Lawrence and Wishart).

Owen, R. and Sutcliffe, B. (eds) (1972) *Studies in the Theory of Imperialism* (London: Longman).

Radice, H. (ed.) (1975) *International Firms and Modern Imperialism* (Harmondsworth: Penguin).

Rashid, A. (2001) *Taliban: Islam, Oil, and the Great Game in Central Asia* (London: I. B. Taurus).

Research Unit for Political Economy, RUPE (2003) 'Behind the War on Iraq', *Monthly Review*, Vol. 55, No. 1.

Rhodes, R. (ed.) (1970) *Imperialism and Underdevelopment* (New York: Monthly Review Press).

Rosenberg, J. (1996) 'Isaac Deutscher and the Lost History of International Relations', *New Left Review*, No. 215.

Seers, D. (1973) 'What are we Trying to Measure?', *Journal of Development Studies*, Vol. 8, No. 3.

Shaw, M. (1984) 'War, Imperialism, and the State System: a critique of orthodox Marxism for the 1980s', in M. Shaw (ed.) *War, State and Society* (London: Macmillan).

Smith, T. (1981) *The Pattern of Imperialism: The United States, Great Britain and the late-industrialising World since 1815* (Cambridge: Cambridge University Press).

Sutcliffe, B. (1972) 'Imperialism and Industrialisation in the Third World', in R.Owen and B. Sutcliffe (eds) *Studies in the Theory of Imperialism*.

—— (2002) 'How Many Capitalisms? Historical materialism in the debates about imperialism and globalization', in M. Rupert and H. Smith (eds) *Historical Materialism and Globalization* (London: Routledge).

van der Pijl, K. (1998) *Transnational Classes and International Relations* (London: Routledge).

Warren, B. (1973) 'Imperialism and Capitalist Industrialization', *New Left Review*, No. 81.

—— (1980) *Imperialism: Pioneer of Capitalism* (London: Verso).

6
The Division of Labour

Renzo Llorente

It would be hard to overstate the importance that the left has attached to the division of labour throughout much of its history. Indeed, Marx himself once stated that 'the division of labour ... is in a certain respect the category of categories of political economy' (1988:267), while most radical thinkers of the nineteenth century – socialists, communists and anarchists alike – made the transformation of the division of labour a centrepiece of their proposals for radical social reform. Such figures as Robert Owen (1991), Wilhelm Weitling (Schäfer 1982), Peter Kropotkin (1972) and Michael Bakunin (1972) all condemned the existing division of labour for what they perceived to be its adverse impact on workers' welfare, as well as its baneful repercussions for the condition of society as a whole. While, to be sure, the condemnation found in these theorists' writings seldom progressed beyond fragmentary, discontinuous indictments, Marx and Engels succeeded in giving a relatively systematic expression to this criticism, elaborating what in effect amounts to a multifaceted *critique* of the division of labour.

Yet interest in the division of labour has hardly been limited to left-wing social theorists. 'For the classical economists', writes Ugo Pagano, 'the problem of stating how the division of labour was organised and how it should be organised for improving social welfare was a crucial problem in economic analysis' (1985:122). What Pagano says of 'the classical economists' (for example, Adam Smith, David Ricardo, James Mill) is likewise applicable to many of the classical sociologists as well, in as much as Comte, Spencer, Durkheim and Weber, for example, all saw fit to address the question of the division of labour in some detail. In short, then, if radical social critics once regarded a transformation of the division of labour as one of their major priorities in establishing the bases for the creation of a more just society, this was in part because the division of labour was a central topic in *all* strains of social theory and analysis.

The concern with the division of labour evident in different varieties of classical social theory is, however, notably absent from contemporary normative social and political philosophy, which tends to take present work roles and patterns of occupational specialisation more or less for granted. Against this trend, I shall argue that the critique of extreme specialisation developed by the classical radical theorists continues to remain highly relevant today. First, however, we shall have to consider and assess the critique itself. Accordingly, after briefly addressing some terminological and conceptual considerations, I go on to discuss the work of Adam Smith and Émile Durkheim, for left-wing criticism of the division of labour has been directed largely at the views that were first systematically articulated and defended by these two thinkers. Following my discussion of Smith and Durkheim, I turn to Marx and Engels, whose analysis of the division of labour may be said to represent the great counterstatement, or retort, to the perspectives deriving from the work of Smith and Durkheim. The chapter then concludes by suggesting that the classical left analysis of the division of labour remains important and instructive today, especially insofar as it affords us some of the resources with which to conceptualise and justify a *right to meaningful work*.

CONCEPTUALISING THE DIVISION OF LABOUR

The 'division of labour' is, without question, one of the primordial concepts of social theory. Indeed, a full millennium before Plato was to elaborate his vision of the ideal state on the basis of this concept (in the *Republic*), the Hindu *Rig Veda* had already identified the division of labour as one of the elemental principles of social structuration (Adiseshiah 1977:10). Still, despite this longstanding awareness and appreciation of the division of labour's centrality in social life and its relationship to numerous other essential social practices and institutions, the fact is that the division of labour remains, as one commentator puts it, 'a particularly amorphous concept in the theory of social organization', and its analysis 'one of the most neglected areas of investigation in sociology and economics' (Clemente 1972:31).

For our purposes – which is to say, for the purposes of understanding the classical left analysis and critique of the division of labour – 'division of labour' should be understood as referring to forms of occupational specialisation or specialisation of work roles, with their attendant functional differentiation. Note that I am not equating the division of labour with mere functional differentiation as such. The latter refers to the outcome (or process) of subdividing one task, function or process into several constituent – or 'partial' from the standpoint of the originally unified, integrated task – operations, which are subsequently carried out as discrete, functionally autonomous activities. In contrast, the division of labour proper denotes the combination of this functional differentiation *and* the organisation of the resulting operations as exclusive occupational roles.

But are there, over and above this very general consideration, any criteria that yield useful distinctions among different levels or categories of occupational specialisation, *distinctions*, that is, *which are both descriptively reliable and normatively significant*? One distinction that seems to fit the bill is the distinction, first introduced by Marx (Groenewegen 1987) between the 'social' and 'manufacturing' divisions of labour (this distinction is explained in section three below). This is also true of a related distinction, namely the contrast between the *social* and *technical* division of labour, which in its narrowest sense corresponds, roughly, to the distinction between task fractionalisation and worker specialisation within the production process, on the one hand, and occupational specialisation within society as a whole, on the other. Despite its inexactness, this latter distinction, which derives from – though is not identical to – the distinction established by Marx (as we'll see below), has since been embraced and employed by Marxists and non-Marxists alike, and continues to enjoy widespread currency today.

We shall return to Marx's analysis of the division of labour, and the considerations bearing on the distinctions that I have mentioned, below. Before doing so, it will be useful to review Adam Smith's treatment of the division of labour, for much of the left's subsequent criticism of the division of labour consists of a response, either directly or indirectly, to Smith-like celebrations of the division of labour.

CELEBRATING THE DIVISION OF LABOUR:
ADAM SMITH AND ÉMILE DURKHEIM

Smith commences Book One of the *Wealth of Nations*, first published in 1776, with a tribute to the division of labour: 'The greatest improvement in the productive powers of labour, and the greater part of the skill, dexterity, and judgement with which it is any where directed, or applied, seem to have been the effects of the division of labour' (1937:3). As this quotation, and the first few chapters of the *Wealth of Nations*, make clear, Smith's central concern is the relation between the division of labour and increasing productivity.

This is not the place to assess Smith's account of the division of labour's contribution to productivity, which I have sought to do elsewhere (Llorente 1998a). More important for our present purposes is Smith's view of the effect that the division of labour has on the personal capacities of those whose work is determined by it. The passage containing the main statement of Smith's view is worth quoting at length:

> In the progress of the division of labour, the employment of the far greater part of those who live by labour, that is, of the great body of the people, comes to be confined to a few very simple operations, frequently to one or two. But the understandings of the greater part of men are necessarily formed by their ordinary employments. The man whose whole life is spent in performing a few simple operations, of which the effects too are, perhaps, always the same, or very nearly the same, has no occasion to exert his understanding, or to exercise his invention in finding out expedients for removing difficulties which never occur. He naturally loses, therefore, the habit of such exertion, and generally becomes as stupid and ignorant as it is possible for a human creature to become. The torpor of his mind renders him, not only incapable of relishing or bearing a part in any rational conversation, but of conceiving any generous, noble, or tender sentiment, and consequently of forming any just judgement concerning many even of the ordinary duties of private life. (Smith 1937:734–5)

Smith holds, then, that extreme specialisation normally entails, indeed is almost proportional to, an attenuation or contraction of the (highly) specialised worker's cognitive, social and physical capabilities. In other words, Smith contends – consistent with his commitment to a kind of 'occupational determinism' – that many patterns of microspecialisation, particularly in industry, increase the disutility of work for the worker. Acknowledgement of these various evils, however, does not lead Smith to deplore, let alone condemn, extreme specialisation, for the increased productivity that the division of labour yields tends to generate 'that universal opulence' that eventually even 'extends itself to the lowest ranks of the people' (Smith 1937:11).

If Smith's exaltation of the division of labour was inspired by its contribution to productivity and economic well-being, Émile Durkheim would celebrate the division of labour for its contribution to social cohesion and individual autonomy – the very goods which, according to Smith, increasing specialisation generally tends to undermine. Although Durkheim's treatise on the division of labour, *The Division of Labour in Society*, was published in 1893, it is worth mentioning prior to a discussion of Marx and Engels' work, since, as is the case with Smith's writings, it provides the most systematic exposition of some of the basic theses disputed by Marx and Engels in their criticism of the division of labour.[1]

Durkheim's interest in the division of labour derives mainly from the role of occupational specialisation in the creation of what he terms 'social solidarity'. According to Durkheim, the division of labour constitutes the fundamental source of social cohesion, or solidarity, in modern, highly differentiated societies, having supplanted the ensemble of shared beliefs, norms, values and so on (the 'collective consciousness') that serves as the basis of individuals' bond with the collective in less developed, more homogeneous societies (Durkheim 1984).

The most striking difference between Durkheim and Smith, as regards the division of labour, concerns their respective views regarding the impact of specialisation on *autonomy*. In *The Division of Labour in Society*, Durkheim argues that extremely advanced occupational specialisation actually promotes individual autonomy,[2] notwithstanding Smith's claims to the contrary. Whereas Smith contends that, where advanced specialisation of work roles obtains, a thoroughgoing erosion of the conditions for autonomy is the norm and their enhancement the exception, Durkheim holds that just the opposite is true, that an autonomy-inhibiting stultification arises only in 'abnormal' states (which he identifies with 'pathological' forms of the division of labour; see Durkheim 1984:291–328).

Despite its approval of what would seem to be even highly advanced instances of the division of labour, Durkheim's account does include an acknowledgement of, and a warning against, the disutilities of excessive specialisation. Furthermore, Durkheim's emphasis on the need for some collective regulation of occupational specialisation underscores the indispensability of planning in order to prevent the characteristic disutilities of many extreme specialisations (for example lack of stimulation, the absence of autonomy, the elimination of any scope for the worker's creativity). All the same, *The Division of Labour in Society* gives these concerns short shrift, while generally underestimating the *increasing marginal disutility of the division of labour* in occupations that provide little scope for autonomy in the first place. It is precisely misconceptions of this sort that Marx's critique is intended to challenge and remedy.

THE MARXIAN CRITIQUE OF THE DIVISION OF LABOUR

As noted earlier, the left critique of the division of labour reaches its culmination in Marx and Engels' works, and particularly in the writings of Marx, who probably attaches more importance, and pays more attention, to the division of labour than any other radical critic.[3] The result of Marx's sustained engagement with the topic of the division of labour was the most comprehensive, and sophisticated, 'critique of the division of labour' of the many to emerge over the course of the eighteenth and nineteenth centuries. Hence it is hardly surprising that the influence of Marx's views on the division of labour has far surpassed that of any other radical social critic.[4]

The essence of Marx's critique of the division of labour lies in his distinction, mentioned at the outset, between the 'social division of labour' (or 'division of labour in society') and the division of labour 'in manufacture' or, alternatively, 'within the workshop'. It is this distinction which inspires the now familiar contrast between the 'social' and 'technical' divisions of labour, though the two are not in fact identical. Rather, the manufacturing division of labour is best understood as one possible species or instance of the technical division of labour.

What exactly is the 'manufacturing division of labour'? As Marx uses the term, 'manufacturing division of labour' refers to 'a specifically capitalist form of the process of social production', originating in the 'dissection of handicraft activity into its separate components' (1977:486), which begins with the passage from handicraft production to manufacture within the framework of early capitalism. Specifically, it consists in 'the breaking down of the particular labour which produces a definite commodity into a series of simple and co-ordinated operations divided up amongst different workers' (Marx 1971:268), and the resulting pattern of microspecialisation in production created by this extreme fractionalisation of tasks.

Marx contrasts the manufacturing division of labour with the 'social division of labour'. Among the most important criteria for distinguishing the social division of labour from the manufacturing division of labour, we can, following Andrew Sayer (1995:66–70),[5] identify the following. An important first distinction concerns the *mode of regulation*. As Marx writes in *The Poverty of Philosophy*: 'While inside the modern workshop the division of labour is meticulously regulated by the authority of the employer, modern society has no other rule, no other authority for the distribution of labour than free competition' (1976:184). A second important criterion of differentiation concerns the *basis of ownership and/or control*: 'The division of labour within manufacture', writes Marx, 'presupposes a concentration of the means of production in the hands of one capitalist; the division of labour within society presupposes a dispersal of those means among many independent producers of commodities' (1977:476). A third distinction, perhaps the most crucial as regards Marx's specific critique of the division of labour, pertains to *the range of an agent's activity, or status of his contribution*, within the production process: whereas the division of labour in manufacture consists, as I just noted, in the decomposition of commodity production into extremely simplified operations, each of which is permanently allocated to an individual worker, 'the division of labour within society outside the workshop' should be understood 'as *separation of occupations*' (Marx 1971:268).

Bearing in mind this contrast – which serves both normative and descriptive purposes, as will become clear – it should be emphasised that Marx's strictures against the division of labour are aimed principally, and almost exclusively, at the *manufacturing* division of labour: it is the 'evil' (Marx 1988:306) elements and consequences of *this* division of labour which elicit his condemnation. Specifically, Marx condemns the manufacturing division of labour for two kinds of systematic effects that are (allegedly) attributable to it. For convenience I will term these two effects *human impoverishment* – a shorthand expression for *cognitive, psychological* and *characterological* impoverishment – and *socio-economic disempowerment*.[6]

The first, and probably more decisive, criticism, the charge of human impoverishment, holds that, by restricting occupational functions to monotonous, highly simplified, circumscribed and repetitive tasks allowing little discretion and subject to constant close supervision, the manufacturing division of labour's fractionalisation of operations develops but one capacity in the worker and *thereby* impedes the development of most other capacities, faculties, abilities and so on. That is, workers whose occupational functions are determined by the manufacturing division of labour become *specialists* in the most extreme sense of developing but one capacity alone, and to the irremediable detriment of all other capacities, for by converting 'a partial task into the life-long destiny of a man', the division of labour 'everywhere lays the foundation for that specialisation, that development in a man of one single faculty at the expense of all others' (Marx 1977:459, 474).

The second basis for Marx's condemnation concerns the effects of socio-economic disempowerment. It is a twofold question, for Marx evokes the impact of such disempowerment on both individual agents and the class aggregate. As for the first, three different sources of this disempowerment can be identified, though all derive from the general contraction of occupational functions, and two of them specifically from the phenomenon of *de-skilling*, by which I mean a reduction in the number, variety and complexity of the skills involved in the performance of an occupational routine. With regard to the latter, Marx argues that, with the occupational assignments resulting from de-skilling, 'it is only the most simple, most monotonous, and most easily acquired knack that is required' of a worker (Marx and Engels 1964:14). This development of but one, or at best a few, most elementary skills deprives workers of the economic power that they would command were they to possess at least some special skills whose acquisition required extensive training or apprenticeship. An additional way in which de-skilling gives rise, according to Marx, to socio-economic disempowerment derives from workers' habituation to nearly skill-less work roles. Finally, the rigorous compartmentalisation and segregation of operations that is a typical component of the manufacturing division of labour also produces individual socio-economic disempowerment since these practices deprive workers of anything beyond the most partial understanding of the production process.

As already noted, Marx's condemnation of the division of labour in manufacture is also a response to the effect of *collective* socio-economic disempowerment, namely the disenfranchisement of workers, the proletariat, as a class. For in addition to underscoring the manufacturing division of labour's socio-economic impact on individual workers, Marx also links it to systematically asymmetrical purchases on power deriving from class membership. For example, by dividing tasks into discrete, minute, nearly skill-less microspecialisations and segregating their operatives, the manufacturing division of labour substantially enhances capitalist employers' ability to regulate, monitor and *control* workers' performance.

Marx's proposed remedy for the ills just described is, quite simply, the eradication of the manufacturing division of labour, a goal that is made attainable, so he suggests in *Capital*, by the increasingly sophisticated and automatic machinery of modern industry. As I have argued elsewhere (Llorente 1998a), it is primarily *this* kind or pattern of specialisation that Marx condemns and whose 'abolition' he urges – and not, as a pervasive misconception would have it, specialisation as such – although it is also true that Marx more generally advocates, and thought possible, the transcendence of the division between 'mental' labour and 'manual' labour (Rattansi 1982).

Compressed as it is, the preceding summary should provide some idea of how Marx's account of the division of labour amounts to a refutation of some of the basic theses defended by Smith and Durkheim, while at the same time developing their most important critical insights concerning the ramifications of extreme specialisation. Specifically, Marx refutes Smith in so far as he manages to show that, after a certain point, increasing specialisation constitutes a hindrance rather than an aid to greater productivity and economic efficiency, and he refutes the Durkheimian view by showing the various ways in which advanced microspecialisations tend to erode personal autonomy, while inhibiting and undermining certain forms of social cohesion (the latter theme is especially important in Marx's *1844 Manuscripts*). At the same time, in important respects Marx's critique involves a development of themes or ideas already present, but insufficiently explored, in Smith and in the sort of view that Durkheim would later defend, namely, the detriment to human welfare caused by specific patterns of occupational specialisation, on the one hand, and the need to regulate the division of labour, lest it proceed in ruinous directions, on the other.

In any event, while some aspects of Marx's critique of the division of labour are no doubt open to criticism (Llorente 1998a), I believe that its merits are such that the critique not only retains much of its relevance and validity today, but constitutes a vital resource for contemporary socialist theory. For one thing, recent research tends to validate the premise of a strong occupational determinism that informs Marx's critique of the division of labour. As Melvin Kohn and Carmi Schooler have demonstrated (1983), occupational conditions and experiences – especially the closeness of supervision on the job, the extent of work routinisation, and the substantive complexity of a job – do indeed exert a substantial, enduring impact on various facets of psychological and cognitive functioning, even 'off the job'. It is also true that contemporary psychological and sociological research tends to bear out some of Marx's assumptions and conclusions concerning the debilitating effects of the manufacturing division of labour in particular (Lane 1991). Finally, the critique still deserves our attention for the simple reason that the 'manufacturing' division of labour in Marx's sense survives and in large measure still defines the organisation of production in many enterprises today.

TOWARDS THE RIGHT TO MEANINGFUL WORK

As noted at the outset, contemporary social thought, that is, late twentieth- and early twenty-first-century social and political theory, displays little interest in the problem of the division of labour, and takes present patterns of occupational specialisation more or less for granted. It is reasonable to ask, then, if anything remains of the left's thematisation and critique of the division of labour. In my view, there are two ways in which *some* of the concerns that gave rise to the 'classical', so to speak, progressive critique of the division of labour continue to inform social theory, as well as popular consciousness. First of all, there is a concern with the gender-, race- and ethnicity-based disparities with respect to both occupational opportunities and patterns of distribution among different occupations. Second, there has been a growing critical awareness of the grossly asymmetrical, gendered division of labour that characterises the allocation of domestic duties in most families, even if progress in eliminating the injustices of the traditional household division of labour has been extremely modest, to say the least (for data and analyses regarding gender and the division of labour, see Bradley 1989; Jaggar 1988; and Young 1981).

Without question, both of these concerns with the division of labour are vitally important. Achieving genuine equality of access to occupations regardless of gender, race, ethnicity, age, etc. would represent immense progress, while the traditional household division of labour is, of course, one of the cornerstones of patriarchy. On the other hand, Iris Young has plausibly argued that analysis of the 'gender division of labour' is essential for 'understanding the economic structure and relations of domination of a social formation as a whole' (1981:56). Yet notice that these concerns do not address what was in fact the *essential* objective for the classical left analysis and critique of the division of labour: the transformation of *occupations and work roles themselves* such that all would be inherently attractive or, to the extent that this is not entirely possible, provision for the equal allocation of (and liability for) toilsome work. In other words, the classical left theorists sought not to remove unequal access to jobs of unequal value, although presumably all of them would have favoured such measures, but to remove the occupational inequalities themselves; their aim was not to establish equal opportunity for occupations of extremely varying degrees of desirability (within hierarchies of domination and subordination), but to render all jobs interesting and satisfying, and if possible conducive to self-realisation. (Or, put somewhat differently, they demanded equal opportunity *within* different occupations, as opposed to equal opportunity *for* different, very unequal – in terms of opportunities for exercising autonomy and intelligence, the range of satisfactions available, etc. – occupations.)

Is there, then, any sense in which the orientation of Marx and the other radical theorists that I have mentioned remains relevant and alive today? As it turns out, we do find a contemporary sequel to their project in the *right to meaningful work* defended by a number of philosophers and political theorists (for example Schwartz 1982 and Nielsen 1985; cf. Pateman 1970), which we should conceive of as the right to a job which is interesting, requires the exercise of intelligence and initiative, and allows for considerable worker autonomy as well as participation in decision-making bearing on the work process (Arneson 1987:522).

To be sure, the postulation of this right has been subjected to vigorous criticism. While a detailed discussion of the various objections is beyond the scope of this chapter (see Llorente 2002 for some criticism), it is important to mention two of the basic lines of such criticism, for they appear to be the main reasons for the general neglect of the division of labour in normative political and social theory today (even among those whose sympathies may lie with the ideal of a classless society). The more practical line of criticism holds that the sheer complexity of the division of labour in modern, industrially advanced societies makes any attempt to render all occupations 'meaningful' impracticable, since the cost in economic efficiency would be unacceptably high (since, on the one hand, the necessary 'upgrading', so to speak, of many occupations would be very costly and, on the other, it is at least implicitly assumed that more 'meaningfully' structured jobs would, in many sectors, be less efficient in the sense of diminished total productivity). The more philosophical objection, or reservation, concerns the ideal of meaningful work itself. According to this objection, the defence of a right to meaningful work involves a species of 'perfectionism', since, in Richard Arneson's words, it 'elevates one particular category of good, intrinsic job satisfaction, and arbitrarily privileges that good and those people who favour it over other equally desirable goods and equally wise fans of those other goods' (1987:524–5). In other words, insistence on the value of meaningful work to all people is in effect to dictate one conception of the good that all people ought to embrace, regardless of their actual preferences.

While both of these criticisms touch on important questions and raise basic issues, they are hardly as decisive as some may believe. As for the more 'philosophical' objection, one can plausibly argue, in light of the relevant studies (Kohn and Schooler 1983; cf. Lane 1991), that something like a right to meaningful work is entailed by a commitment to the protection of certain determinate preconditions for self-development; and to insist on this sort of protection hardly amounts to prescribing a specific conception of the good. As for the more 'practical' objection, if we assume, reasonably enough, that it would not prove particularly costly to implement, to borrow Robert Lane's formulation (1991), *a right to participate in decision-making affecting one's work*, a measure which would achieve in part some of the basic aims of a right to meaningful work – for example, promotion of effective autonomy and provision of the conditions for developing self-esteem – then there would seem to be some grounds for believing that the cost of establishing a right to meaningful work might not be so prohibitive after all.

It is of course difficult to know whether advocacy of a right to meaningful work can be politically effective in the short term. It is clear, however, that those who condemn the kinds of occupational injustices noted above ought to support and promote the goal of establishing such a right. Until this goal is reached, the classical left critique of the division of labour will rightly continue to provide inspiration and orientation for emancipatory social theory.

GUIDE TO FURTHER READING

For a reconstruction and evaluation of the classical left-wing critique of the division of labour, see Llorente (1998a). Typical expressions of this critique can be found in Marx (1976; 1977) and Engels (1972). For a comprehensive account and analysis of Marx's views on the division of labour, see Rattansi (1982). Braverman (1974) develops a modern Marxist critique of the division of labour, while Young (1981) proposes 'gender division of labour' as the central concept of a 'feminist historical materialism'. For an account of the normative

Marxist conception of work, see Elster (1989). Kohn and Schooler (1983) present a systematic, empirically-based analysis of the effect of various occupational conditions on personality; the policy implications (including 'the right to participate in the decisions affecting one's work') of their studies and related research are discussed by Lane (1991). For a formidable philosophical challenge to a right to 'meaningful work', see Arneson (1987).

NOTES

1. It is sometimes claimed that Durkheim has in mind social differentiation as such, and is not referring to *occupational specialisation* in particular (if at all), in *The Division of Labour in Society*. This interpretation is, however, quite mistaken, as is evident from Durkheim's discussion of what he terms 'pathological' forms of the division of labour.
2. Specifically, the division of labour fosters individual autonomy, on Durkheim's view, by i) providing both the means for, and inducement to, the exercise of autonomy; ii) promoting individualism; iii) dissolving autonomy-inhibiting power structures of diverse sorts; and iv) decisively contributing to the atrophy of the 'collective consciousness'. See Llorente (1998a).
3. This section is based on, and includes material from, Llorente (1998b).
4. If I refer to Marx alone here and in what follows (despite citing from some jointly written works), it is because Engels' remarks on the division of labour are, aside from the jointly authored works, invariably brief and convey nothing of the systematic analysis that Marx brings to the subject.
5. Actually, Sayer's criteria are intended to distinguish the *technical* division of labour from the social division of labour. However, since the manufacturing division of labour constitutes one species of the technical division of labour, the criteria serve to differentiate the former from the social division of labour as well.
6. This is not to deny the presence of other lines of criticism. My claim is merely that the criticisms I identify are Marx's principal grounds for assailing the division of labour, and more or less the only ones found in the later texts (which is also to say, the only grounds that are a constant over the course of his theoretical development). Furthermore, the charges of human impoverishment and socio-economic disempowerment are, I think, more cogently elaborated than the other lines of criticism.

REFERENCES

Adiseshiah, M.S. (1977) *Some Thoughts on Adam Smith's Theory of the Division of Labour* (Trivandrum, India: Department of Publications, University of Kerala).

Arneson, R. (1987) 'Meaningful Work and Market Socialism', *Ethics*, Vol. 97, No. 3.

Bakunin, M. (1972) 'Revolutionary Catechism', in Sam Dolgoff (ed.) *Bakunin on Anarchy* (New York: Alfred A. Knopf).

Bradley, H. (1989) *Men's Work, Women's Work: A Sociological History of the Sexual Division of Labor in Employment* (Minneapolis: University of Minnesota Press).

Braverman, H. (1974) *Labor and Monopoly Capital* (New York: Monthly Review Press).

Clemente, F. (1972) 'The Measurement Problem in the Analysis of an Ecological Concept: The Division of Labor', *Pacific Sociological Review*, Vol. 15, No. 1.

Durkheim, E. (1984) *The Division of Labor in Society*, translated by W.D. Halls (New York: The Free Press).

Elster, J. (1989) 'Self-Realisation in Work and Politics: The Marxist Conception of the Good Life', in J. Elster and K.O. Moene (eds) *Alternatives to Capitalism* (Cambridge: Cambridge University Press).

Engels, F. (1972) *Anti-Dühring: Herr Eugen Dühring's Revolution in Science*, translated by. E. Burns and edited by C.P. Dutt (New York: International Publishers).

Groenewegen, P. (1987) 'Division of Labour', in J. Eatwell, M. Milgate and P. Newman (eds) *The New Palgrave: A Dictionary of Economics*, Vol. 1 (New York: Stockton Press).

Jaggar, A.M. (1988) *Feminist Politics and Human Nature* (Totowa, New Jersey: Rowman and Littlefield Publishers, Inc.).

Kohn, M.L. and C. Schooler (1983) *Work and Personality: An Inquiry Into the Impact of Social Stratification* (Norwood, New Jersey: Ablex Publishing Corporation).

Kropotkin, P.A. (1972) *The Conquest of Bread*, edited by P. Avrich (Harmondsworth: Penguin).

Lane, R.E. (1991) *The Market Experience* (Cambridge: Cambridge University Press).

Llorente, R. (1998a) *The Division of Labor Revisited*, Ph.D. diss., State University of New York at Stony Brook.

—— (1998b) 'Marx's Critique of the Division of Labor: A Reconstruction and Defense', *Nature, Society, and Thought*, Vol. 11, No. 4.

—— (2002) 'Egalitarian Welfarism and the Right to Meaningful Work', in José Manuel Bermudo Ávila (ed.) *Retos de la razón práctica* (Barcelona: Publicacions de La Universitat de Barcelona).

Marx, K. (1964) *Economic and Philosophical Manuscripts*, in *Early Writings*, translated and edited by T.B. Bottomore (New York: McGraw-Hill).

—— (1971) *Theories of Surplus-Value*, Vol. 3, translated by J. Cohen and S.W. Ryazanskaya and edited by S.W. Ryazanskaya (Moscow: Progress Publishers).

—— (1976) *The Poverty of Philosophy*, translated by Harry Quelch, in K. Marx and F. Engels *Collected Works*, Vol. 6 (New York: International Publishers).

—— (1977) *Capital*, Vol. 1, translated by B. Fowkes (New York: Vintage).

—— (1988) *Economic Manuscripts of 1861–1863*, in K. Marx and F. Engels *Collected Works*, Vol. 30, translated by B. Fowkes (New York: International Publishers).

Marx, K. and Engels, F. (1964) *The Communist Manifesto* (New York: Monthly Review Press).

Nielsen, K. (1985) *Equality and Liberty* (Totowa, New Jersey: Rowman and Allanheld).

Owen, R. (1991) *A New View of Society and Other Writings*, edited by G. Claeys (Harmondsworth: Penguin).

Pagano, U. (1985) *Work and Welfare in Economic Theory* (Oxford: Basil Blackwell).

Pateman, C. (1970) *Participation and Democratic Theory* (Cambridge: Cambridge University Press).

Rattansi, A. (1982) *Marx and the Division of Labour* (London: Macmillan).

Sayer, A. (1995) *Radical Political Economy: A Critique* (Oxford, England and Cambridge, Mass.: Blackwell).

Schäfer, W. (1982) 'Collective Thinking From Below: Early Working-Class Thought Reconsidered', *Dialectical Anthropology*, Vol. 6, No. 3.

Schwartz, A. (1982) 'Meaningful Work', *Ethics*, Vol. 92, No. 4.

Smith, A. (1937) *The Wealth of Nations*, edited by. E. Cannan (New York: Modern Library).

Young, I. (1981) 'Beyond the Unhappy Marriage: A Critique of the Dual Systems Theory', in L. Sargent (ed.) *Women and Revolution* (Boston: South End Press).

7
Oppression

Mary Davis

The central argument of this chapter is that the perpetuation of non-class divisions based on race and sex is a key mechanism sustaining capitalist relations of production and thereby an important means of upholding class society. Women and black people, the unwitting agents in this process, have for centuries been the victims of unequal treatment. However, it will be demonstrated that the language and the concept of inequality do not fully express the nature of the relationship between class, race and sex. The term 'oppression' more accurately describes this relationship. In an etymological sense 'oppression' has come to refer to the unjust or cruel exercise of authority or power, but as a Marxist concept it has a more precise meaning and application, which this chapter will explore and develop.

EQUALITY, DIVERSITY AND OPPRESSION

Equality[1]

What is wrong with the equality paradigm? Today few 'progressive' people would deny the importance of equal rights; for women, for black people, for lesbians and gays, for those with disabilities and for many other groups. The concept of equality has a long pedigree linked with the development of capitalist society. In the struggle to end feudal and/or aristocratic domination, liberal constitutionalists advocated the notion of equality. Starting in seventeenth-century England, and boosted by the Enlightenment and the French Revolution at the end of the eighteenth century, the notion of equality became a largely unquestioned article of faith in the nineteenth and twentieth centuries. Initially it was a notion embracing men only, since only white men were perceived as citizens. 'Equality' began to embrace women and black people in the twentieth century. However, as Juliet Mitchell has pointed out, under capitalism the concept of equality has a very limited meaning – it can only refer to equality under the law; it is an abstract concept, saying nothing about the inherent and

111

pre-existing inequalities of those who are subject to its writ. Juridical equality 'does not apply to the economic inequities it is there to mask' (Mitchell 1987:29). This is not to deny the importance of the battles to obtain equality – without them women would still be voteless, and none but the sons of rich white males would be entitled to educational and countless other opportunities.

Despite the historic gains by workers, women and blacks in the struggle (under the banners of the labour movement, the women's liberation and black liberation movements) to push the liberal concept of equality to its furthest extent, the requirements of capitalism prescribe the inherent limitation of juridical equality. Ironically, this became clearer at the moment when it seemed that the notion of racial and sexual equality had penetrated mainstream thinking. In the 1970s and 1980s, the newly accepted wisdom of equal opportunity theory began to introduce an element of moral relativism into the debate, so that other aspects of discrimination based on age, sexuality, religion and physical ability were thrown into a competitive equal-rights melting point. In the UK, equal-opportunity units were established by most public and private sector employers and equal-opportunity policies were developed. The institutional champions of equal opportunities struggled for scarce resources in the Thatcher years of high unemployment. But despite the good intentions of these champions, the specificities of inequality remained misunderstood. Whilst some of the effects of unequal treatment were tackled, the analysis of the causes of structural discrimination, which had exercised the minds of liberationist theoreticians of the women's and black movements, was now left to wither. Pragmatism prevailed. As a result the 'unequal' became an undifferentiated mass to whom catch-all solutions were applied. These 'solutions' in turn entered into an unequal competition against each other. Hierarchies of disadvantage began to emerge which pitted 'the unequal' against each other.

Diversity

In the UK, the logic of this development has now been fully spelled out by the New Labour government (Department of Trade and Industry 2002): it is to jettison the collectivist approach (based on the common interests of 'disadvantaged' groups) to equality altogether. This can be seen in their plan to abolish the equality commissions (the Commission for Racial Equality, the Equal Opportunities Commission and the newly established Disability Rights Commission) and instead to create a new single overarching commission which may be coterminous with a Human Rights Commission. The theoretical approach underlying this is far more significant than the stated aim (which is to include groups hitherto outside the scope of the limited equality legislation). The real root of the policy change is a belief in the new postmodernist mantra of 'diversity', the motivation for which is expressed thus: 'People are increasingly looking for equal treatment that respects the many facets of their identities. Everyone's identity has multiple aspects, drawing for example on their gender, age, ethnicity, and religious affiliations among other characteristics' (Department of Trade and Industry 2002:9).

Thus at a stroke identity politics has ousted equality politics. The reason for this is, according to Anne Phillips, connected with the decline and fall of the socialist countries. This has removed the pressure to tackle economic and group inequality, replacing it instead with a new (neo-Victorian) emphasis on individual responsibility as the cornerstone of social policy. Equality now is seen as equality of opportunity to better oneself, mediated by a minimalist state whose role is 'to ensure that opportunities for self-advancement are available to every citizen' (Phillips 1999:13).

Despite its juridical limitations, the old concept of equal rights did at least recognise collective rather than individual solutions. Diversity politics encourages the opposite: it assumes that individual differences outweigh any group identity. Indeed we are invited to construct our own identities – a superficially attractive prospect designed to mask the reality of centuries of discrimination and oppression based on our most noticeable differences – our gender and our skin colour.

Oppression

Feminist and black liberationist theories posed a major challenge to the liberal conception of equality. However, as bell hooks (1987) has pointed out, the mainstream brand of feminism that demanded women's social equality with men internalised the traditional bourgeois juridical constraint. Hooks argues that equal-rights feminism benefited middle-class white women, whilst affecting black and working-class women only marginally, because the demand for equality fails to challenge, let alone change, the 'cultural basis of group oppression' (hooks 1987:63). She uses the term 'oppression' – an idiom which has been in widespread use since the 1960s by the more radical wings of the black and women's liberation movements. Rejecting the more liberal concepts of inequality, disadvantage and discrimination, women and black people in the 1970s and 1980s described themselves as oppressed groups and struggled to articulate the forms of their oppression and to challenge it, sometimes drawing upon Marxist categories and sometimes not. This has spawned a huge literature in which deep divisions have emerged as to the origins and nature of oppression. The great surprise and pity was the peripheral involvement of Marxists in the debate. Had the converse been the case it may have been that the separate spheres of the politics of class, race and gender may have combined in a more fruitful synergy – one that would have weathered the forthcoming storms of moral relativism and postmodernism.

By the 1980s there was far less interest in the language and theory of oppression. This was partly because some of the demands of the equal-rights agenda had been met, so that some (particularly women) were incorporated into 'the system', and partly because the individualism of the diversity approach was beginning to acquire a dominance (for the reasons discussed above). Despite the self-identity and campaigning of many other groups experiencing endemic societal discrimination (gays, lesbians, people with disabilities) in the last 20 to 30 years, the theoretical construct of oppression (as opposed to its looser use as a descriptive term) has been generally applied to women and black people alone. It denotes the historically entrenched way in which the freedom of women and black people has been limited by those with superior power (see Brittan and Maynard 1984).

I shall argue that although the earlier liberationist literature was correct to define women and black people as oppressed groups, there remains much unfinished business in establishing the usefulness of oppression as a theoretical construct. I contend that, understood in Marxist terms, oppression is central to understanding not only the status of women and black people, but the operation of class society in general.

MARXISM AND OPPRESSION

Marxist omissions

However, we have a problem. There are vital areas of social reality which Marxists (including Marx) have simply not addressed. If there is to be any renewal of Marxism, it is not simply a matter of going over old ground, but breaking the new. The most obvious omission centres around the realities of women and black people in society.

Despite the fact that Marxists frequently use the term oppression (it is as common a word in revolutionary parlance as class or struggle), Marxism has failed to develop a theory of oppression. It is clear that neither moral relativism nor the individualism of the diversity paradigm have much to offer the oppressed. This begs the question as to why Marxists need to understand oppression. It might be better to pose this question in reverse. Is it possible to understand the inner working of class society without such an understanding? Further, what kind of revolutionary practice (if any) would emerge without a consciousness of oppression? Although somewhat rhetorical, these questions help to concentrate the mind on the limitations both of equality theory in all its forms and of economism.[2] The former concerns itself with redressing the injustices suffered by the 'disadvantaged' and the latter relates to the immediate material needs of workers at the point of production. Important though such struggles are, neither can challenge, even if they wanted to, the root causes of both problems – namely, class exploitation. But class exploitation itself cannot be confronted let alone overthrown without an understanding of capitalist relations of production in a much wider sense. This entails looking further than the point of production itself, vital though this is. It necessitates an understanding of the way in which such relations operate in their economic, political and ideological/cultural settings and looking at how class rule is both maintained and reproduced. Oppression is a key factor in this.

The Marxist framework

A general conceptual framework has been laid in the works of Marx and Engels, which may be roughly summarised as follows. Women and black people, whilst not forming classes, are, as oppressed groups, intimately related to the class system in that all oppression is in itself based on class exploitation. But apart from some conceptual clues throughout much of Marx's writing, and the more direct contribution of Engels (1972), there is very little that deals systematically with the question of oppression and its form and function in class society to be found in classic Marxism. This is significant insofar as such an omission (and the failure of subsequent Marxists to rectify it) has meant that the experience of well over half the world's population has been only half understood. I say only half understood, because Marx's theory of class is relevant to those women and blacks (the majority) who sell their labour power for a wage. In other words, the perception of 'class' itself has to be stripped of its hitherto gender- and colour-blind construction. Class, however, is also relevant to those women, black and white, who, while not selling their labour power for a wage, indirectly contribute to the production of surplus value by producing and reproducing the labour force (I refer here to women's unpaid domestic labour). However, the position of women and black people in the class structure does not address the totality of their existence. Indeed without an understanding of the specifics of their oppressed status in society as whole, it is not possible to understand fully their position as the most exploited workers.

A theory of oppression can be extrapolated from the works of Marx and Engels (and to some extent from later classic Marxist theoreticians of the Second International period – for example Lenin, Bebel and Clara Zetkin[3]). However, without further development and concrete application, it is far from adequate. Indeed, the common (and lazy) way of doing this in the past was to extract selected quotes and then publish them as 'Marx, Engels and Lenin on the woman (or something else) question'. In fact of all the 'questions' to be examined in this way, or by subsequent Marxist writers, that of oppression has received the most scant attention. Apart from the vast corpus on Marxist political economy, there are tomes to be found on the Marxist view of ideology, nationality, religion, alienation, etc. There is, however, very little by comparison on oppression. This could mean one of two things: either that as a concept it is genuinely not very important, or that the predominantly white, male Marxist intelligentsia, in common with its generally colour-blind and gender-blind approach to politics, has simply chosen (in line with much of its practice) to ignore oppression in the sphere of theory. It is clear thus far that the latter explanation is to be preferred.

TOWARDS A MARXIST THEORY OF OPPRESSION

So, what is oppression? Is it the same as discrimination or disadvantage? At one level, of course, the search for a more precise use of abstract nouns is nothing more than a semantic quibble, but for our purposes these terms reveal important theoretical differences and are not interchangeable. Discrimination or disadvantage is experienced by many groups in society because of the difficulties they experience at some or all points of their lives in fitting in with the dominant norm. In this sense almost everybody experiences disadvantage – because they are too young or too old, because they are not 'handsome' or 'pretty', because they are too fat or too thin, etc. For others, like those with a disability, the discrimination is an ever-present feature of their lives. However, discrimination itself is not a *function* of class society even though it is an almost inevitable by-product of the inherent inequalities within all forms of class society. The term 'inequality' in itself is misleading, as much of the more radical anti-racist and feminist literature has shown. Redressing the phenomenal form of aspects of inequality by attempting to 'level the playing field', welcome though this is, does not address the essence of the problem which has its roots in the unequal division of wealth (and therefore power) in class society.

Oppression, however, although it may take the form of discriminating against the oppressed, stands in a different relationship to class society. It is the most important means of maintaining the class relations which support class exploitation and as such oppression is both a function of class society and a product of it. This is because oppression, unlike discrimination, is linked *materially* to the process of class exploitation as well as operating at a 'superstructural' level through oppressive ideologies which serve to maintain class rule by dividing the exploited. (This is particularly clear in the case of capitalism which will henceforth be used as the 'exemplar' of class society.) Such ideologies are not simply explained by 'false consciousness' operating as an invented infecting agent. They are themselves so rooted in the material world of production that they have become integral to it.

Let us now look at the way in which oppression operates at these two levels.

1. Class exploitation

At the material level, the historic subjugation of women and black people explains their augmented exploitation (super-exploitation) at the point of production. Historically an inbuilt inequality within the labour force, expressing itself through low wages and job segregation, it has reproduced itself as the normal process when workers sell their labour power. Its victims are the most easily identifiable workers – black people and women. At the level of sociological observation this fact – super-exploitation and job segregation based on gender and race – is not in doubt. All indices of wage rates nationally and internationally show that the wages of women and black people are lower than that of white males (see for example Equal Opportunities Commission 2001). This fact operates to the material advantage of the owners of the means of production – the capitalists for whom any increase in profit is dependent on an increase in the rate of exploitation. It is hence no accident that despite conventional morality about the sanctity of family life and the key role of women within it, the labour of women is often preferred to that of men because it 'attracts' lower wages.[4] Similarly, the transfer of production to the low-wage economies of the ex-colonies in Africa and Asia performs the same function for capitalism in its relentless pursuit of profit. Indeed, the function of slavery in establishing the conditions for the take-off of industrial capitalism in Britain in the late eighteenth century provides the most telling example of the historic de-humanisation of black people who became commodities in themselves (for a fuller elaboration of this point, see Williams 1964 and Davis 1993). The legacy of this, together with the aggressive imperialism of the late nineteenth century, provides the foundations for the continued super-exploitation of black people today *within* the imperialist nations as well as in the neo-colonial world.

Hence there is a material basis historically and at present for our suggestion that women and black people, for different reasons, have been used and are used as a source of cheap labour and that this fact has been integral to the operation of class exploitation. Women in particular are historic victims of job segregation and have continuously performed undervalued and sometimes unnoticed jobs outside the home. It is simply not the case that they have been used as a 'reserve army' of labour; their presence within the labour force has been constant. Whilst the fact of super-exploitation is not controversial, the significance we attach to it is more so, and 'raises' the status of women and black people beyond that of discrimination. Their role within capitalist relations of production as super-exploited workers is woven into the very fabric of these relations and is not a chance or transitory phenomenon. It is here that we must extend the analysis founded on historical materialism to more fully understand it.

The *fact* of class exploitation (and super-exploitation) as the central pillar of the capitalist mode of production does not in itself explain how the relations of production are maintained and reproduced. This can only be understood by examining factors which exist outside the economic relations of production through the operations of ideologies, whose function it is to maintain (whether consciously or not) class relations in a more general sense. There is a huge range of literature on the meaning of ideology, attempting to interpret the already voluminous writings of Marx and Engels on the subject (some of the most useful – and comprehensible! – contributions are Marx and Engels 1965; Althusser 1965 and 1971; Barrett 1986; Larrain 1983; McCarney 1980; Parekh 1982). The interesting point about the theoretical discussion of ideology is just that: it is entirely theoretical, with only rare references to a specific ideology and the way that it functions. What concerns us here though is something specific, namely the identification of ideologies which maintain the historic subservience of women and black people – in other words, the ideologies of oppression. But first it is necessary to say something about the role of ideology in general.

2. Ideologies of oppression

We have already noted the particular and super-exploited place of women and black workers within class society. It seems that the specific ideologies supporting this – racism and sexism – have operated so insidiously and so successfully over centuries in the concealment of contradictions that the ideologies have passed unnamed and unnoticed even into this century. Indeed a gender-blind and colour-blind approach to class politics has, until relatively recently, permeated even the most class-conscious sections of the labour movement.

As ideologies, racism and sexism can be seen to have a direct material connection to the maintenance of capitalist relations of production in two important ways. Firstly, they are related to the very real need of capital to maintain profit by pushing the value of labour power to its lowest possible limit. Secondly, the ideologies of racism and sexism are the chief non-coercive means of preventing the unity of the working class and thereby facilitating the perpetuation of the domination of the minority class over the majority. Hence these ideologies, unlike for example liberalism or nationalism, appear as an almost pure reflection of the material needs of the exploiting class. They perform a very obvious function in the maintenance of the existing relations of production.

This may seem to be a very crude and deterministic interpretation of ideology, failing to do justice to the sophistication of its lived form. It is true that other ideologies like religion are much harder to analyse from a historical materialist standpoint. They seem to have a life and history of their own, unrelated to the mode of production, and this has given rise to a major debate among western Marxists who get round the problem by one of two means. First, by suggesting that ideology is in itself a material force giving rise to its separate study as a means of representation which interacts with the economic base. Or, second, in an attempt to avoid economic determinism, the suggestion is made that ideology has a 'relative autonomy' within the superstructure but is connected to the economic base by being determined by it 'in the last instance'.

However, we do not appear to need the 'relative autonomy' waiver clause when analysing racism and sexism. That is not to say that as ideologies they do not have their own histories or that their form is at all times strictly determined by the economic base. Nevertheless, it is clear that their form and function as ideologies have a very direct relationship with the economic base, more so than most other ideologies (other than economic ideologies themselves, especially that of the 'free' market and the 'free' sale of labour). It is perhaps for this very reason that the ideological form of oppression has remained hidden. The subjugation of women and black people has been historically connected with class society for so long that it has become the accepted natural order of things. The oppressive ideologies sustaining subservience are so culturally rooted that they have passed beyond naked statements of class rule and entered into the very fabric of our lives, including language itself (for an excellent discussion of this point, see Barrett 1986, Chapter 3). As such, these ideologies have become universalised and hence disembodied from their class origins. They have thus fulfilled the ultimate goal of ideology – namely to represent the interests of the dominant class as the interests of society as a whole. How else are we to explain the permeation of racist and sexist ideas within the working class and even within the socialist movement? Perhaps the same could be said of all ideologies, but this misses the very direct function of oppressive ideologies, the force of which in the capitalist epoch is dependent on their ability to disunite the working class. It is of course true that women and black people do not constitute a class, but this fact, while explaining that not all women and blacks are exploited, should not obscure the fact of their oppression based on race and gender. This is the real meaning of the oft-quoted statement that all oppression is based on class exploitation.

Racism and sexism as material and ideological facts are central to the maintenance of capitalist and pre-capitalist class relations. However, this is not to put a narrow economistic interpretation on their force. They are not simply mechanisms for keeping black and women workers in a subordinate position since, as oppressive ideologies, they cut across class boundaries and depend, as all ideologies do, on their universalism. Hence they impinge on the lives of all black people and women regardless of class and determine society's perception of race and gender. They operate historically in varying degrees and forms through both the coercive and the ideological apparatuses of the state. It is not my place here to examine the ways in which these ideologies are produced and reproduced – there is a vast literature on this. I only want to re-state the critical importance of one aspect of oppressive ideologies and oppression in general for us today. That is, its specific function in relation to the definition of the working class.

Class

The point made earlier about women and black people not constituting a class has often obscured the relationship of these two huge groups to the class structure. Seen as non-class entities, socialist political practice has often assigned women and black people (along with other groups) to the newly invented category of 'new social forces'. At best this has been a well-meaning attempt to avoid class reductionism and to respect the autonomy of black and women's liberation groups, but at worst it represents a failure of Marxist theoreticians to confront reality. In practice such a failure has meant that no credible alternative has been posited to that of 'identity politics'. After all, if the oppressed and (disadvantaged) exist outside classes (that is, outside society), then the logic must be an increasingly atomised self-organisation based on self-identity. This is not to deny the importance of autonomy and self-organisation as a necessary complement to class politics. 'Identity politics', however, is founded upon a conscious rejection of class and is seen by its postmodernist advocates as a substitute for it. Although 'analytical Marxists' like Erik Wright eschew postmodernist identity politics, their comprehension of women's oppression is surprisingly detached from class analysis. Wright is one of the few male Marxists of today who engages with, let alone mentions, feminism. He regards both Marxism and feminism as emancipatory theories 'built around the critical analysis of oppression – class oppression and gender oppression', although in his view feminists, unlike socialists, are silent on the emancipatory project. This displays confusion as to the relationship between oppression and class exploitation and in so doing misses the critical point as to the role of oppression and oppressive ideologies as a material force in maintaining capitalist relations of production. In his attempt to 'distinguish class and gender as two dimensions of social relations which interact', Wright falls into the idealist trap of presuming that gender is only tangentially related to class (Wright 1994:212, 220). He makes no mention of race.

The debates during the 1980s about the composition of the working class missed a crucial point, namely that the working class is not all white and male. This is not simply a rhetorical point. If we take the so-called 'broad' definition of the working class, that is to say all who sell their labour power for a wage (as opposed to the narrower definition: those who are *directly* engaged in the production of surplus value), then it is clear that the vast mass of women and black people are workers.[5] Indeed all projections show that the proportion of 'economically active' women is set to rise despite the often high rates of male unemployment. Whilst the same cannot be said for black people in the western capitalist world, the prevalence of racial discrimination means that there is little likelihood of them owning capital or joining any intermediate self-employed strata. Marx anticipated that society would, because of changes in the means of production, become increasingly polarised into two classes. Indeed this is the main change that has taken place in the composition of the working class, albeit masked by the decline in the proportion of those workers involved directly in the production of surplus value. The ranks of the working class have been renewed and replenished by women workers in the only growth sector of the national economy in Britain, the service industries. The decline in industrial production in the 'developed' capitalist world, which has accounted for the decline in the traditional proletariat (usually white male workers), has occurred partly because of the utilisation of new technology, but partly because of the domination of production by transnational corporations who choose to invest in low-wage economies where the rate of exploitation is highest. This, in global terms, means the substitution of white male labour by cheaper black labour in the neo-colonial world. (This is accompanied by the appearance of 'core' and 'peripheral' workers in the capitalist heartlands, a factor which has affected all workers, but the declining 'core' has served to displace white males whilst at the same time confirming the disadvantaged status of the disproportionately high numbers of women and blacks in the periphery.)

This means that the relationship between class exploitation and oppression has become in our day a very tangible issue for class politics, provided we jettison traditional gender- and race-blind preconceptions about the nature of the working class. It does not mean that oppression is thus subsumed by class exploitation but it does mean that the traditional call by socialists for the unity of the working class has to be understood in a different way. Unity cannot be built by refusing to recognise differences. The argument here is that the most crucial divisions within the working class are based on race and gender oppression and that these have to be recognised as ideological practices in themselves if they are to be overcome. It is the *fact* of oppression which determines the super-exploitation of women and black people as *workers* as well as their inequality as citizens.

A class analysis of the two major oppressed groups is thus vital for the understanding of the nature of the working class today. This avoids the twin problem of not assigning half of the population of this country (and the majority of the population of the world) to any class whatsoever and of failing to notice the realities of today's class structure and the specific status of oppressed groups within it. This is not a class reductionist argument – it does not mean that the oppressed form a class, rather that they belong to a class and the overwhelming majority of them are workers. While it is true that class interests may divide the oppressed, this is probably less important now than in the nineteenth century because of the relentless tendency of capital to sweep intermediate strata, small producers and the petty-bourgeoisie into the ranks of wage/salary earners. This 'broadening' of the working class creates its own problems for socialists, namely the existence of strata within the working class and the consequent lack of perception of class consciousness among those whose exploitation is more masked, or who have less access to collective struggle and organisation. But lack of class consciousness should not be confused with an objective analysis of class position.

CONCLUSION

The ruling ideology renews itself by stealing our emancipatory concerns (and sometimes our language too), by turning them to the continued advantage of capital. In its anxiety to reverse the 'social exclusion' of those groups hitherto 'hidden from history', the ideology of diversity has attempted to appropriate the connotation of equality by divesting it of its radical meaning. It has, in addition, secured its divisive goal in its insatiable desire to maintain the relations of production by not only continuing to cultivate race and gender divisions within the working class, but now by dividing oppressed groups from each other and within themselves. For example, the term 'black' – a political term used to express the unity of all who experienced racism – is now questioned by the diversity culture which encourages the choice of multiple identities on ethnic and religious grounds. Among women, the incorporation of go-getting 'glass-ceiling' women into public life masks the reality of the lack of progress of the majority.

It is precisely because the connection between class exploitation and oppression has been imperfectly understood that intellectual enquiry has been forced into separate spheres. On the one hand 'mainstream' socialist literature still unconsciously constructs the history and development of the working class and labour movement through a white and male lens, and on the other hand the literature of the oppressed ploughs its own furrow as a separate entity filling the intellectual space and in some cases making important and creative discoveries. This is not to suggest that the latter should be subsumed in the former, but rather that at the level of theory it is now imperative for some degree of integration to prevail within a historical materialist framework. Without this, Marxism as a means of interpreting and changing the world will have failed to live up to the challenge of the twenty-first century, not because Marx was wrong but because the Marxists of today, having become so cautious of theoretical world outlooks, have retreated into their myriad specialisms and in so doing are failing to grasp what is new or to understand the interconnections between class, race and gender. Much more work needs to be done on a less abstract level to demonstrate the ways in which class exploitation is dependent upon racist and sexist divisions. By the same token, the argument that racist and sexist divisions are rooted in class society must also be renewed. Furthermore, we need to distinguish the differences and specificities of racism and sexism. But the crucial issue is to understand that racist and sexist oppressions are not chance phenomena, used at whim to bolster the relations of production; they are integral to the maintenance of those relations and as such have to be understood and challenged by all whose aspiration is the ending of class society.

GUIDE TO FURTHER READING

Anne Phillips (1999) provides a good introduction to the changing terrain of equality politics in the context of today's economic and political climate, while her 1987 edited volume includes a very useful collection of essays on some of the key debates in feminist theory in the 1970s and 1980s. Michelle Barrett (1986) presented an early and as yet unrivalled attempt to integrate Marxism and feminism. Engels (1972, written in 1884) remains the foundation for the Marxist analysis of women's oppression. Although best known for her women's suffrage work, Sylvia Pankhurst pioneered the attempt to integrate in a practical way the issues of class and gender oppression (see Davis 1999). Leiman (1993) provides a Marxist analysis of American racism. Kalbir (1999) traces the course of black and anti-racist politics in Britain since the 1940s.

NOTES

1. For related discussion, see Brendan Evans' chapter, below.
2. See Lenin (1964) for a definition of economism and a discussion of its limitations.
3. See Bebel (1904, first published in 1878, and also published as *Woman in the Past, Present and Future*); Zetkin (1984); and the collection of Lenin's writings on women (in Lenin 1977). Zetkin was the leader of the German Socialist Party's Women section and was also chair of the Women's Bureau of the Second International (see the collection in Zetkin 1984).
4. See Marx (1970) for useful insights from early nineteenth-century millowners on why they preferred to use the labour of married women with dependent children.
5. This is not to underestimate the difficulties involved in the 'broad' definition – most notably the managerial strata, who, whilst selling their labour power for a wage (salary), are functionally linked to the maintenance of the process of exploitation.

REFERENCES

Althusser, L. (1965) *For Marx* (London: Allen Lane 1965).
—— (1971) *Lenin and Philosophy and Other Essays* (London: New Left Books).
Barrett, M. ([1980] 1986) *Women's Oppression Today: The Marxist/Feminist Encounter* (London: Verso).
Bebel, A. (1904) *Woman under Socialism*, translated by D. de Leon (New York: New York Labour Press).
Brittan, A. and Maynard, M. (1984) *Sexism, Racism and Oppression* (Oxford: Blackwell).
Davis, M. (1993) *Comrade or Brother? The History of the British Labour Movement 1789–1951* (London: Pluto Press).
—— (1999) *Sylvia Pankhurst: A Life in Radical Politics* (London: Pluto Press).
Department of Trade and Industry (2002) *Equality and Diversity: Making it happen – Consultation on future structures for equality institutions* (London).
Engels, F. (1972) *The Origin of the Family, Private Property and the State* (London: Lawrence and Wishart).
Equal Opportunities Commission (2001) *The Gender Pay Gap* (Manchester).

hooks, b. (1987) 'Feminism: A Movement to End Sexist Oppression', in A. Phillips (ed.) *Feminism and Equality*.

Kalbir, S. (1999) *The Changing Pattern of Black Politics in Britain* (London: Pluto Press).

Larrain, J. (1983) *Marxism and Ideology* (London: Macmillan).

Leiman, M. (1993) *The Political Economy of Racism* (London: Pluto Press).

Lenin, V. (1964) *What Is To Be Done?* (Moscow: Progress Publishers).

—— (1977) *On the Emancipation of Women* (Moscow: Progress Publishers).

Marx, K. (1970) *Capital*, Vol. 1 (London: Lawrence and Wishart).

Marx, K. and Engels, F. (1965) *The German Ideology* (London: Lawrence and Wishart).

McCarney, J. (1980) *The Real World of Ideology* (London: Gregg Revivals).

Mitchell, J. (1987) 'Women and Equality', in A. Phillips (ed.) *Feminism and Equality*.

Parekh, B. (1982) *Marx's Theory of Ideology* (London: Croom Helm).

Phillips, A. (1999) *Which Equalities Matter?* (Oxford: Blackwell).

—— (ed.) (1987) *Feminism and Equality* (Oxford: Basil Blackwell).

Williams, E. (1964) *Capitalism and Slavery* (London: Deutsch).

Wright, E. (1994) *Interrogating Inequality* (London: Verso).

Zetkin, C. (1984) *Selected Writings*, edited by P. Foner (New York: International Publishers).

8
Production and Reproduction

Valerie Bryson

My starting point in this chapter is the classic Marxist theory of historical materialism: the idea that the basis of human society, the key to understanding its history and future potential, lies in the production and reproduction of material life. While accepting the value of this approach, I also use feminist theory to argue that 'malestream' theorists have interpreted production and reproduction in unhelpfully narrow ways to produce an analysis which is not only male based but also male biased. I argue in favour of an expanded notion of (re)production that includes the socially necessary work disproportionately performed by women; I conclude that without such an expansion we can neither understand existing society nor develop effective strategies for changing it.

BACK TO BASICS

According to the classic Marxist position, the first cooperative act of production formed the basis of the earliest primitive society and the beginnings of human history: 'life involves before everything else eating and drinking, a habitation, clothing and many other things. The first historical act is thus the production of the means to satisfy these needs, the production of material life itself' (Marx and Engels 1982:48). Unlike the instinctive activity of animals, such production is conscious and planned, and it changes over time, setting in motion the complex processes of economic, social, political and ideological development that constitute human history. The extent to which Marx's materialist conception of history implies a particular anthropological view of man and a theory of technological or economic determinism was and is a matter of intense political and scholarly debate. However, at a general level, it seems clear that Marx believed that social and political analysis must start by looking at how people produce rather than at their laws or beliefs – an approach which Tom Rockmore has recently summarised as: 'It's the economy, stupid' (Rockmore 2002:116). This materialist perspective

127

also means that any possibility of changing society is always limited by existing socio-economic conditions, so that radicals cannot always change society as they would like: 'Men make their own history, but they do not make it just as they please; they do not make it under circumstances chosen by themselves, but under circumstances directly encountered, given and transmitted from the past' (Marx and Engels 1968:97).

As long as this perspective is not accepted too rigidly or simplistically, it seems to provide a sensible starting point for understanding how societies have evolved and how they might develop in the future. However, its potential insights have been limited by a very narrow understanding of what we mean by the production and reproduction of material life. Marxists have largely ignored the ways in which biological reproduction, domestic work, sexuality and caring activities have been organised, treating these either as 'natural' and outside of human history, or as by-products of productive activity which have no dynamic of their own. This means that mainstream Marxism has told only half the story of human development, and that it has effectively replicated the public/private distinction of liberal thought, with its exclusion or marginalisation of activities predominantly associated with women. As a result, its understanding of human history and potential has been seriously flawed. This chapter argues that the Marxist concepts of production and reproduction should be extended to allow for a more comprehensive analysis.

TERMINOLOGY

An initial problem stems from the range of ways in which both Marx and later Marxist writers have used the terms *production* and *reproduction*. 'Production' is sometimes treated quite loosely, to refer to any purposeful activity which contributes to the satisfaction of human needs. However, this has not normally been interpreted to include the work involved in reproducing the species:

> All the labour that goes into the production of life, including the labour of giving birth to a child, is not seen as the conscious interaction of a human being *with* nature, that is, a truly human activity, but rather as an activity *of* nature, which produces plants and animals unconsciously and has no control over this process. (Mies 1998:45)

The exclusion from analysis of much 'women's work' is reinforced when 'production' is given a more precise economic meaning. Marxist economic theory argues that, under the historically specific conditions of capitalism, the only form of work that is technically 'productive' is paid work exchanged in the labour market for money and from which surplus value[1] is extracted. From this perspective, unpaid work done in the home is not productive and it does not have a value (see Himmelweit 1991; Jackson 1999; Grant 1993). This does not mean that such work is unimportant, for the 'productive' label is not inherent in the activity, only in its relationship to the money economy. Although in principle Marxist economic analysis makes this clear, there may be a subconscious equation of 'productive' with 'important' and of monetary value with human value; certainly, mainstream Marxists have shown little interest in analysing the changing nature of the unpaid work that is largely done by women or its complex relationship with the money economy.

At first sight, the concept of reproduction, which also has origins in original Marxism, seems more fruitful. In *The German Ideology*, Marx and Engels included biological reproduction as part of the material basis of society, referring to 'The production of life, both of one's own in labour and of fresh life in procreation' (Marx and Engels 1982:50). Although Marx never explored the implications of this, Engels did so in *The Origin of the Family, Private Property and the State*:

> According to the materialist conception, the determining factor in history is, in the final instance, the production and reproduction of immediate life. This, again, is of a twofold character. On the one side, the production of the means of subsistence, of food, clothing and shelter and the tools necessary for that production; on the other side, the production of human beings themselves, the propagation of the species. The social institutions under which the people of a particular historical epoch and a particular country live are conditioned by both kinds of production: by the stage of development of labour on the one hand and of the family on the other. (Engels 1978:4)

This implies that the way in which biological reproduction is organised may be independent of production in the wider sense, and indeed Engels argued that in the earliest stages of human society sexual relationships had evolved from unregulated promiscuity to the egalitarian 'pairing family'. However, he believed that the independent evolution of the family ceased at this early stage, when it became entirely dependent on conditions of production, narrowly understood. More specifically, he argued that in Europe the introduction of private property gave men a motive to dominate women (because they wanted to pass property to their known heirs), and that this 'world historical defeat of the female sex' would only be overcome in a future socialist society, as sexual relationships would then be free from notions of ownership and domestic work would be collectivised. From this perspective, conditions of reproduction had no independent dynamic, the oppression of women was a by-product of class society that would disappear with it, working women had no separate interests, and they should therefore join with men in the struggle against capitalism. Indeed, Engels argued that, unlike bourgeois women, working-class women were no longer oppressed as women, as they were in paid employment and their marriage did not involve property ownership. This left no way of recognising, let alone contesting, women's sex-specific exploitation in the workplace and the exploitation of their labour in the home, while Engels dismissed the problem of domestic violence in half a sentence as a 'left-over' from the introduction of monogamy (Engels 1978:65, 83).

Such an analysis is clearly inadequate. As with the concept of 'production', problems also arise from the confusing range of ways in which 'reproduction' is used in Marxist theory. Although sometimes equated with the biological processes of procreation, the term is also used by Marxists to refer to the broader reproduction of the labour force on a daily as well as a generational basis, by meeting a range of material and emotional needs (Mandel 1983). It is also used of the processes through which the economy 'reproduces itself', yielding inputs for future production and consumption. Social relations too have to be 'reproduced'. Such shifting meanings make it difficult to maintain a distinction between production and reproduction, and there is a danger that different levels of analysis become conflated and confused (see Jackson 1999 and Elster 1986).

In this chapter, I will attempt to bypass such confusions by using the term '(re)production' to refer to the work (physical and emotional) which is more or less directly linked to the generational reproduction and maintenance of the population and the care of those unable to look after themselves. Such work includes biological reproduction but is not confined to it; it is very disproportionately performed by women. Treating this (re)production as part of the material basis of society allows us to see it as part of economic life and human history rather than as simply 'natural' or a by-product of production. We can then see that particular conditions of (re)production may facilitate or restrict opportunities for creating a more equitable society; they may also be sites of economic, political and ideological struggle. This does not mean that we can make a universal and clear distinction between productive and (re)productive labour; rather, the shifting boundaries between productive and (re)productive work is one variable to explore. Other variables include developments in contraception and reproductive technology, the availability of labour-saving devices, the extent to which (re)productive work is shared with men, and whether it is provided collectively or by private individuals. Such an expanded notion of the material basis of society is important if we are to understand how society functions and how to develop effective strategies for change.

(RE)PRODUCTION AND EARLY MARXIST THOUGHT

As discussed above, Marx and Engels failed to acknowledge the importance of (re)productive work and oppression in the home. By the end of the nineteenth century, however, influential European Marxists such as August Bebel and Clara Zetkin in Germany and Lenin and Trotsky in Russia were writing about oppression in personal life and the 'double burden' of paid and domestic work experienced by many women. However, their orthodox Marxist approach provided no scope for analysing rather than documenting women's situation; they assumed that oppression would be ended in a socialist society and failed to explore the possibility that it might have its own dynamic, based in conditions of (re)productive life.

Ideas about the importance of the family and personal relationships were developed considerably further by Alexandra Kollontai, a leading Bolshevik and member of Lenin's first cabinet (Holt 1977; Stites 1981). Kollontai insisted that the transformation of family and personal life was central to creating both equality between the sexes and the preconditions for socialism. She argued that the collectivisation of domestic work and childcare and the liberation of sexuality from ideas of ownership facilitated the development of the kind of collectivist morality needed for a socialist economy to flourish. As such, they were an integral part of the process of creating good socialist men and women, involving both real, material changes and ideological transformation: 'The new morality is created by a new economy, but we will not build a new economy without the support of a new morality' (quoted in Holt 1977:270).

The idea that changes in the material conditions of (re)production are a precondition for building socialism had clear implications for political practice and priorities, and Kollontai had a remarkable degree of success in forcing the party to take them seriously during her brief period in political office, when she attempted to mobilise and consult 'ordinary' women and to treat (re)productive work as a collective responsibility. However, in 1923 her ideas on the family were officially declared erroneous. Some of her ideas survived in a distorted form throughout the years of Stalinist dictatorship, as labour shortages meant that women were needed both as producers and reproducers, and were enabled to combine these roles through (poor quality) state childcare provision. However, women still faced tremendous burdens in combining paid and domestic work in a society in which even a tap in the kitchen was a luxury and men still refused to accept domestic responsibilities. By the 1980s, official policy increasingly stressed women's 'natural' role in the home and the need to liberate them from paid employment, and the collapse of communism saw a full-scale retreat from any notion of collective support for (re)productive work (Buckley 1989; Rosenberg 1989).

Kollontai's loose form of Marxism was very different from the simplistic determinism that dominated Marxist politics for the first half of the twentieth century. Nevertheless, debates around women's oppression also surfaced in the small American Communist Party during the 1930s, producing some sophisticated analyses of the politics of personal life and the role of domestic labour in the capitalist economy (Weigland 2001; Shaffer 1979). However, as with the contributions of Kollontai, this analysis had little impact on mainstream Marxist thought, and it is only recently that such radical ideas have been rediscovered. This meant that when the women's liberation movement erupted in the west in the 1960s, women who wanted to use Marxist theory to understand their own situation could find little guidance.

DEVELOPMENTS AND DEBATES SINCE THE 1960s

The impact of radical feminism

Although the writers discussed in the previous section differed in their priorities, they generally agreed that the achievement of both a socialist society and equality between the sexes would require changes in what I have called the social relations of (re)production. However, they did not question the sexual division of labour that underlay these relations, and seemed to have assumed that collectivised childcare and housework would still be the responsibility of women. Nor did they explore in any detail the implications of changes in medical and contraceptive knowledge, or in the technology of housework, which could potentially change the conditions of biological reproduction and domestic labour.

These Marxist writers were attempting to extend man-made theory to the understanding of women's situation. As such, their approach was very different from the radical feminist theory which developed from the 1960s, partly in response to women's bad experiences in left-wing organisations, in which men's idea of an equitable division of labour was all too often 'you make the tea while I make the revolution', and in which 'women's issues' were treated as at best trivial and at worst a bourgeois distraction, designed to divide the working class. Radical feminists claimed that women's own experiences should be the starting point for theory, that these experiences showed that the fundamental power structure in society was the oppression of women by men, and that this oppression was not confined to economic or political life. Many such feminists claimed that male power both stemmed from and was maintained by 'private' family and sexual relationships, and by the ever-present threat of sexual violence and men's control over women's reproductive capacities. The radical feminist concept of *patriarchy* became central to such analysis. This claimed that men's patriarchal power over women is so universal, so complete and so all-pervasive that it is accepted as 'natural'. However, once it is labelled, we can see its recurrent and patterned nature, and the ways in which its apparently unrelated manifestations in public and private life are in fact interconnected, reinforcing each other to produce a cumulative and ubiquitous system of domination and oppression (for the classic discussion of this concept, see Millett 1985, first published 1970).

Marxist feminist responses

Although some Marxist women have been been very critical of the concept of patriarchy and the sometimes inflated and simplistic claims that have been made in its name, radical feminism was clearly putting new issues on the agenda which many women felt to be important, but which had not been seriously addressed by Marxist theory. For many such women, the task was therefore to 'ask the feminist questions, but try to come up with some Marxist answers' (Mitchell 1971:99), and the last 30 years have seen the growth of a rich and rapidly evolving body of thought that has attempted to blend Marxist and feminist methods and concerns. However, few male Marxists have participated in these debates or considered the implications for their own theory.

A pioneering and influential attempt at using Marxist theory to address feminist concerns was made by Juliet Mitchell (Mitchell 1966, 1971, 1974). Rejecting crude economic determinism, she drew on developments in western Marxism which stressed the 'relative autonomy' of political and ideological struggle; she also built on attempts by writers such as Herbert Marcuse to synthesise Marxism and psychoanalysis, and to explore the role of sexuality and the workings of the unconscious in understanding social processes and change. Mitchell argued that women's situation was determined by four structures: not only the structure of production, traditionally analysed by Marxist theory, but also the interconnected and family-based structures of reproduction, sexuality and the socialisation of children. Although she said that these were ultimately determined by production, she argued that they also had a degree of independence. This meant that they could be addressed directly, and that each might at times play a leading political role. Mitchell therefore advocated autonomous women's organisations, as there would be no automatic dissolution of patriarchy without feminist struggle.

A problem with Mitchell's approach is that it seems to be based on an artificial distinction between economic and ideological struggles, so that the family and (re)productive work are not fully part of a materialist analysis (Wilson 1980). Similar problems arise from the related arguments about the importance of ideology that were developed by Michelle Barrett (Barrett [1980] 1988; Barrett and McIntosh 1982).

While the above analyses effectively counterposed economics and the family, other writers attempted to use orthodox Marxist economic concepts to analyse the importance of women's domestic work. The ensuing 'domestic labour debate' usefully drew attention to the economic importance of women's work in the home; it also helped show that other forms of unpaid work, particularly by Third World peasants and homeworkers, are an integral part of the international economy, central to the processes of capital accumulation (Mies 1998; for recent overviews of the debate, see Gardiner 1997 and Bubeck

1995). However, in seeking to reduce women's oppression to the needs of the capitalist economy the debate failed to ask why it is that domestic labour is overwhelmingly performed by *women*, or to consider whether men as well as capitalism might benefit from the unequal division of domestic labour. For some feminists, Marxism seemed to be setting the terms of the debate in a form that failed to address the issue of male power, and many therefore agreed with Heidi Hartmann's assessment of the 'unhappy marriage' of Marxism and feminism that 'either we need a healthier marriage or we need a divorce' (Hartmann 1986:2).

Hartmann argued that, far from all social arrangements being a product of class struggle and relations of production, there are *two* dynamic forces in history, which must be understood in terms of patriarchy as well as class. She claimed that, because men benefit from traditional arrangements, which provide them with 'a higher standard of living than women in terms of luxury consumption, leisure time and personalised services', men of all classes have at least a short-term material interest in maintaining women's oppression (Hartmann 1986:9). This interest predates capitalism and, although it is often reinforced by capitalism, it can sometimes also come into conflict with it, as men's interests lie in keeping women in the home but capitalism at times needs them in the workplace. This means that patriarchy cannot be reduced to the needs of capitalist class society, and that it could continue beyond it.

A problem with this 'dual systems' approach is that, although Hartmann claimed to have discovered the material basis of women's oppression in men's control over their labour power, this does not make patriarchy a *system* in the same sense as capitalism, as it does not have its equivalent of the drive to profit (see Pollert 1996). This means that, while it is logically necessary for capitalists to exploit their workforce (if they do not, they will go out of business), it is in principle at least possible for relationships between women and men to be non-oppressive. Iris Young has, however, argued that this possibility cannot be realised in capitalist society which, she says, is based upon an oppressive gender division of labour. From this perspective, patriarchy is built into the whole system of production, so that what we have is not two separate systems, but a unified system of capitalist patriarchy. Young does concede that it is logically possible for capitalism to function without patriarchy. However, she argued that if we treat the gender division of labour as part of the material basis of society, and analyse its changing nature in relation to production, we can see that '... a patriarchal capitalism in which women function as a secondary labour force is the only *historical* possibility' (Young 1986:62).

Young's analysis followed orthodox Marxism in seeing relations of production as the sources of women's oppression, but reconceptualised these to include the gender division of labour, which she insisted was central to the understanding of any economic system and hence basic to the whole of society. This approach informs Maria Mies' more recent analysis of 'capitalist-patriarchy' as 'an intrinsically interconnected system' in which the gender division of labour and exploitation of women's labour are central to the never-ending, worldwide process of capital accumulation (Mies 1998:38). Both she and Young identify pre-capitalist forms of patriarchy but, rather than seeing patriarchy as unchanging and autonomous, they see it as evolving with changes in production and class relations. Anna Pollert similarly argues that there is a 'fused system of gender and class relations' which can be analysed through the development of a feminist historical materialism, although she dislikes any use of the term 'patriarchy', which she says implies inappropriate theoretical claims (Pollert 1996:647; for related arguments see Ebert 1996).

The ideas discussed in this section represent important steps towards recognising both that 'women's work' is economically important and that women's oppression is central to the maintenance of capitalism, rather than a by-product of class society, as most earlier Marxists had concluded. From this reformulated perspective, the analysis of gender inequalities must understand that these are bound up with the economic system, and feminist politics cannot be separated from anti-capitalist struggle. At the same time, any economic analysis that ignores gender issues will be partial and flawed. For some writers, this means that we must look much more closely at conditions of (re)productive life.

The analysis of (re)production

An important early contribution in this area was made by Lise Vogel, who argued that the key to women's oppression lay in what she termed 'social reproduction', by which she understood the generational reproduction of the workforce and the way in which this was organised. She argued that capitalism had resolved the potential conflict between its drive to extract the maximum profit from women's labour and its need for a continuing supply of healthy workers by institutionalising women's financial dependency on men.

This oppressive dependency would, she said, only be resolved in a socialist society in which, because production would be for use rather than profit, the imperative to exploit women's labour would no longer be operative and childcare and domestic labour would be socialised (Vogel 1983).

A problem with this analysis is that women's oppression is again seen as a simple product of class society, and the possibility that it might also benefit men is ignored. The conventional Marxist framework which Vogel attempted to develop can also be criticised for seeing the biological processes of reproduction as an unchanging, natural, animal-like activity. In contrast, some recent writers have argued both that reproduction has a history and that this must be central to our understanding of human society.

Most notoriously, Shulamith Firestone's *Dialectic of Sex* ([1970] 1979) claimed to have rewritten Marx's materialist conception of history by substituting 'reproduction' for 'production', so that the 'sexual-reproductive organisation of society' was the key to economic, legal and political institutions and dominant belief systems. She also claimed both that women's oppression was rooted in their childbearing role and that modern reproductive technology had the potential to liberate them from this, by allowing babies to be grown to term outside of the womb. Firestone's analysis was clearly simplistic, and has found little support from either Marxists or feminists. A more sophisticated attempt to conceptualise human reproduction as a social process related to human consciousness was provided by Mary O'Brien, who argued that two key moments of human history were the first early discovery of paternity, and the development of modern contraceptive technology (O'Brien 1981).

Accepting the importance of such developments need not mean that wider social changes can be simply 'read off' from developments in reproductive knowledge and technology, for the impact of these is mediated in complex ways by their wider economic context and dominant beliefs (including religious beliefs), and also by existing inequalities between women and men. However, recent rapid developments in reproductive technology (such as the now well-established use of in-vitro fertilisation, developments in genetics which make it possible to select the characteristics of an unborn child, and the increasingly likely possibility of human cloning) throw into stark relief the importance of reproductive issues not only for the situation of women and the nature of family life, but for the very meaning of what it is to be human. Although they have not been explored by mainstream Marxists, these developments must be a central part of any materialist analysis of society.

Biological reproduction is, however, only one part of the socially necessary domestic and caring work that I have labelled '(re)production' but which some other writers refer to as 'social reproduction'. Here, Johanna Brenner has done some important work in extending Marxist methods to explore the complex and historically specific ways in which such work has been organised. For example, she argues that the nineteenth-century 'breadwinner settlement', through which working men were widely expected to be financially responsible for maintaining their wives at home, cannot be understood simply as a response to the needs of either capitalism or patriarchy. Rather, it represented a response to the practical needs of working people at a time when the physical maintenance of a family involved ceaseless toil. As such, it was both fought for by many male trade unionists and welcomed by many working-class women. Since then, changes in the material conditions of domestic work in the west have made it much easier for women to combine (re)productive work in the home with at least some paid employment. This means that the material basis for the settlement is no longer relevant, and fewer women are totally economically dependent on their husbands. However, as Brenner also says, the full and equal participation of women in the workplace would require a degree of capital outlay on parental leave and childcare provision that is unlikely to be forthcoming. She therefore argues both that social reproduction should become a more collective responsibility and that, because this would require a 'serious redistribution of wealth', we will only achieve this as part of a more general anti-capitalist struggle (Brenner 2000:309).

The physical and emotional care of others is another aspect of (re)productive work which is usually unrecognised by economists. Like housework, this is frequently provided without a wage by women in the home, although 'emotional housekeeping' often performs an important function in the workplace, and carework can be paid for as part of the money economy. Unlike housework, much of this work can never be automated, for it is inherently dependent on social interaction. As Diemut Bubeck has argued, this raises problems for Marx's vision of communism as a society of abundance, in which necessary work will be kept to a minimum (Bubeck 1995). If we are to set realistic goals for a society in which human needs are met, we must therefore include an assessment of how caring work is to be organised.

CONCLUSION

In 1903, Clara Zetkin wrote: '[Marx's] materialist concept of history has not supplied us with any ready-made formulas concerning the women's question, yet it has done something much more important: it has given us the correct unerring method to comprehend that question' (quoted in Foner 1984:93). To the extent that Marxism sees women's oppression as the historically specific product of particular societies rather than a necessary or natural feature of human society, she was indeed correct. However, as I have argued throughout this chapter, Marx's materialist method needs to be extended to include the (re)productive work that is overwhelmingly performed by women. Such an extension does not offer a simple solution or explanation for oppression, but it is a necessary starting point for analysis.

As many feminists have argued, there is a danger that the use of man-made categories will channel us away from women's experiences and into a framework in which our concerns cannot be expressed. I therefore think that the concept of 'patriarchy', used in a descriptive rather than explanatory sense, should be retained to inform materialist analysis; without this concept the ubiquitous and patterned nature of male power becomes invisible and male priorities continue to be the unquestioned norm (see Bryson 1999).

There remains an ongoing debate between those (including Mary Davis in this volume) who argue that sex oppression is functionally necessary for capitalism, and those, such as Ellen Meiksins Wood, who argue that although it may be very useful it is not strictly necessary (Wood 1995). However, even if it is logically possible to imagine a capitalist society in which men and women are equal, this is highly unlikely. Not only does women's oppression conveniently divide the working class, as Davis argues, but an analysis of women's (re)productive work indicates that the material preconditions for equality would have to include either payment for the domestic and caring work that is currently undertaken without financial reward or the provision of good, affordable childcare and the kind of employment conditions that would allow women and men to combine paid employment with (re)productive work. Such preconditions are unlikely to be met in a society based on the pursuit of profit rather than the satisfaction of human needs.

This does not mean that women's oppression can only be addressed when we have achieved socialism. On the contrary, it means that struggles over conditions of (re)production can be seen as central to more general economic change. If, therefore, women campaign for free access to safe, affordable abortion, or against sexual exploitation, or if they insist that men do their share of the housework, these can be seen as basic material demands as well as political and ideological struggles, for sexuality, reproduction and the family are all part of the real material conditions in which we produce and reproduce. At the same time, the analysis of (re)productive work shows that this is vitally important to the health and survival of any society, and that changing conditions of (re)production can both constitute limitations and create possibilities for its future development. Giving weight to these areas of human experience and activity is not simply a matter of justice for women, 'something for the girls' to be added after the important issues have been dealt with, but an essential prerequisite for effective political analysis and action.

GUIDE TO FURTHER READING

For more detailed discussion of developments in Marxist feminism from the nineteenth century to the present day, see Bryson (2003), and for an expanded version of arguments in this chapter see Bryson (2004). On the concepts of 'production' and 'reproduction' in Marxist thought, see Marx's 'Introduction' to his *Grundrisse*, and the entries by Fine and Himmelweit in Bottomore (1991). Sargent (1986) provides a now classic collection on the relationship between capitalism and patriarchy. Stevi Jackson (1999) provides a good discussion of the relationship between Marxism and feminism from the early 1970s, which unpicks the question of terminology well. I have found the collection of articles by Brenner (2000) particularly insightful.

NOTE

1. In simple terms, surplus value is created when workers produce more than they need to maintain themselves. Under capitalism, this surplus is appropriated as profit by the owners of the means of production.

REFERENCES

Barrett, M. ([1980] 1988) *Women's Oppression Today: The Marxist/Feminist Encounter* (London: Verso).

Barrett, M. and McIntosh, M. (1982) *The Anti-Social Family* (London: Verso).

Bottomore, T. (ed.) (1991) *A Dictionary of Marxist Thought* (Oxford: Blackwell).

Brenner, J. (2000) *Women and the Politics of Class* (New York: Monthly Review Press).

Bryson, V. (1999) '"Patriarchy": a concept too useful to lose', *Contemporary Politics*, Vol. 5, No. 4.

—— (2003) *Feminist Political Theory: An Introduction* (Basingstoke: Palgrave).

—— (2004) 'Marxism and Feminism: can the "unhappy marriage" be saved?', *Journal of Political Ideologies*, Vol. 9, No. 1.

Bubeck, D. (1995) *Gender, Care and Justice* (Oxford: Clarendon Press).

Buckley, M. (1989) *Women and Ideology in the Soviet Union* (New York and London: Harvester Wheatsheaf).

Ebert, T. (1996) *Ludic Feminism and After: Postmodernism, Labor and Desire in Late Capitalism* (Ann Arbor: The University of Michigan Press).

Elster, J. (1986) *An Introduction to Karl Marx* (Cambridge: Cambridge University Press).

Engels, F. (1978) *The Origin of the Family, Private Property and the State* (Peking: Foreign Languages Press).

Fine, B. (1991) 'Production', in T. Bottomore (ed.) *A Dictionary of Marxist Thought*.

Firestone, S. ([1970] 1979) *The Dialectic of Sex* (London: Women's Press).

Foner, P. (ed.) (1984) *Clara Zetkin: Selected Writings* (New York: International Publishers).

Gardiner, J. (1997) *Gender, Care and Economics* (Basingstoke: Macmillan).

Grant, J. (1993) *Fundamental Feminism: Contesting the Core Concepts of Feminist Theory* (London: Routledge).

Hartmann, H. (1986) 'The Unhappy Marriage of Marxism and Feminism: Towards a More Progressive Union', in L. Sargent (ed.) *The Unhappy Marriage of Marxism and Feminism*.

Himmelweit, S. (1991) 'Reproduction', in T. Bottomore (ed.) *A Dictionary of Marxist Thought*.

Holt, A. (1977) *Alexandra Kollontai: Selected Writings* (London: Allison and Busby).

Jackson, S. (1999) 'Marxism and Feminism', in A. Gamble, D. Marsh and T. Tant (eds) *Marxism and Social Science* (Basingstoke: Macmillan).

Mandel, E. (1983) 'Economics', in D. McClellan (ed.) *Marx: The First 100 Years* (Oxford: Fontana).

Marx, K. (1986) 'Introduction' to the *Grundrisse*, in J. Elster (ed.) *Karl Marx: A Reader* (Cambridge: Cambridge University Press).

Marx, K. and Engels, F. (1968) *Selected Works* (London: Lawrence and Wishart).

—— (1982) *The German Ideology* (London: Lawrence and Wishart).

Mies, M. (1998) *Capitalism and Accumulation on a World Scale: Women in the International Division of Labour* (London and New York: Zed Press).

Millett, K. (1985) *Sexual Politics* (London: Virago).

Mitchell, J. ([1966] 1984) *Women: The Longest Revolution* (London: Virago).

—— (1971) *Woman's Estate* (Harmondsworth: Penguin).

—— (1974) *Psychoanalysis and Feminism* (London: Allen Lane).

O'Brien, M. (1981) *The Politics of Reproduction* (London: Routledge and Kegan Paul).

Pollert, A. (1996) 'Gender and Class Revisited; or, the poverty of "patriarchy"', *Sociology*, Vol. 30, No. 4.

Rockmore, T. (2002) *Marx After Marxism: The Philosophy of Karl Marx* (Oxford: Blackwell).

Rosenberg, C. (1989) *Women and Perestroika: Present, Past and Future for Women in Russia* (London: Bookmarks).

Sargent, L. (ed.) (1986) *The Unhappy Marriage of Marxism and Feminism: A Debate on Class and Patriarchy* (London: Pluto Press).

Shaffer, R. (1979) 'Women and the Communist Party U.S.A. 1930–1940', *Socialist Review*, Vol. 9, No. 3.

Stites, R. (1981) 'Alexandra Kollontai and the Russian Revolution', in J. Slaughter and R. Kern (eds) *European Women on the Left: Socialism, Feminism and the Problems Faced by Political Women 1880 to the Present* (Westport, Con. and London: Greenwood Press).

Vogel, L. (1983) *Marxism and the Oppression of Women* (London: Pluto Press).

Weigland, K. (2001) *Red Feminism, American Communism and the Making of Women's Liberation* (Baltimore and London: Johns Hopkins University Press).

Wilson, E. (1980) *Only Halfway to Paradise: Women in Postwar Britain 1945–1968* (London and New York: Tavistock).

Wood, E.M. (1995) *Democracy Against Capitalism: Renewing Historical Materialism* (Cambridge: Cambridge University Press).

Young, I. (1986) 'Beyond the Unhappy Marriage: A Critique of the Dual Systems Theory', in L. Sargent (ed.) *The Unhappy Marriage of Marxism and Feminism*.

9
Revolution[1]

Paul Blackledge

Every great radical political movement tends to face a common dilemma: can progressives utilise the existing state to help realise their goals, or must they overthrow this structure? The contemporary anti-capitalist movement is, in this respect at least, unexceptional: the perennial debate between reformists and revolutionaries has been rekindled (Callinicos 2003:86 ff; Kingsnorth 2003:229 ff; Neale 2003:127; Monbiot 2003:67). However, the anti-capitalist movement has differentiated itself from many previous movements in at least two ways: first, it has reestablished the concept of anti-capitalism at the centre of contemporary political discourse; second, it has provided a framework within which many diverse individuals and groups have been able to unite around the slogan 'another world is possible'. Nevertheless, if the movement is to progress beyond this promising start, it must develop a strategy that is adequate to the task of realising this demand.

Unfortunately, some within the movement have confused a healthy scepticism towards received dogma with a celebration of confusion. Thus, Susan George, while embracing the slogan 'another world is possible', has insisted that she has not 'the slightest idea what "overthrowing capitalism" means in the early twenty first century' (George 2001:3, 9). In contrast to this suggestion of strategic paralysis, others have recommended strategies of one form or another. So, Hilary Wainwright of *Red Pepper* magazine has outlined a militantly reformist strategy for the left: she believes that anti-capitalists should aim to 'reclaim the state', and use it to 'tie down the private economic forces that have undermined the power of the vote' (Wainwright 2003:xix). Alternatively, Alex Callinicos draws on the revolutionary Marxist tradition to argue that human liberation demands that modern capitalist states must be overthrown; they are neither 'ours' to reclaim, nor could we hope to use them to foster the general good (Callinicos 2003:90–2).

Indeed, revolutionaries insist that the problems associated with the modern world-system cannot be overcome without instituting qualitative changes in the way that society is organised: another world requires a revolution to free it from the existing order. Moreover, Marxists argue that a revolution is a necessary process through which people must pass if they are to become fit to rule themselves; for it is only through the mass activity associated with revolutions that ordinary people begin to break with the culture of subservience within which they have been socialised, and upon which the reproduction of capitalist relations of production depends. Unfortunately, many anti-capitalists hold back from accepting this thesis as they associate the revolutionary project with the experience of Stalinism. Indeed, for many radicals, Stalinism has so tainted the Marxist vision of a qualitative break with capitalism that their political imagination seems limited to the belief that the best that can be hoped for in the present circumstances are reforms of the existing system (Anderson 2000). This is regrettable, for not only did Stalinism mark the negation of both Marxism and the socialist aspirations of 1917 (Cliff 2003), but Marx's democratic vision of socialism from below probably expresses the sentiments of many within the contemporary anti-capitalist movement, including large numbers of those influenced by reformist arguments. In this chapter I stress this democratic core of revolutionary socialist thought, before moving on to reevaluate the utility and power of classical revolutionary theory in the light of contemporary debates.

REVOLUTION: EVOLUTION OF A CONCEPT

The word revolution first entered the English language in the fourteenth century, when it was used to denote the technical process of revolving; while the denotation of revolution in the sense of social and political transformation evolved in a complex process from the fifteenth century onwards (Williams 1976:226; Hill 1991:88). Hill points out that 'revolution' took on its modern denotation from the mid seventeenth century, as the language of the 'revolutionaries' and their foes evolved to make sense of the great social upheavals of the age. However, there were two revolutions in seventeenth-century England: 1649 and 1688; and while the modern denotation of revolution arose to explain the first of these, in eighteenth-century England the term revolution was almost exclusively applied to the second. This elision lent itself to later ambiguity, as 1649 was the culmination of a mass movement, while the 'Glorious Revolution' of 1688 did not involve '"the people" at all' (Hill 1991:101). This conceptual vagueness was compounded as Cromwell's earlier revolution was labelled the 'Great Rebellion' by the eighteenth-century English. It was only with the American and French revolutions that the concept 'revolution' attained its modern denotation (Williams 1976:228; Hobsbawm 1977). From then on battle lines were firmly drawn: Burke and the conservatives located themselves resolutely against revolution; while progressives such as Paine saw events in America and France as heralding the birth of a new 'age of reason'. However, if Paine and others welcomed the political and social revolutions of their epoch, the processes through which the new bourgeois era would generate its own class divisions remained obscure. And while, in the 1780s, the American Federalists had a much more acute sense of these divisions, even they could not have imagined how industrialisation would produce such misery alongside hitherto unknown levels of wealth. It was Marx's contribution to political theory to argue that industrialisation created both the material conditions for the overthrow of the rule of scarcity, and the agency through which such an advance for humanity might be achieved: a new workers' revolution against capitalist social relations was necessary if the aspirations of the *Declaration of the Rights of Man* were to be realised.

MARXISM: FREEDOM AND REVOLUTION

'Freedom', Marx wrote, 'is so much the essence of man that even its opponents realise it' (quoted in Dunayevskaya 1988:53). Marx inherited his understanding of freedom from Hegel, and he utilised it to critique both the alienation of humanity under capitalism, and apologetic reductions of freedom to either the free market, or to its equation with negative freedom: the argument that freedom can be defined as the absence of restrictions upon the individual. In contrast, Marx insisted that freedom was a potential inherent in humanity that came to be realised through history; it was thus something that evolved over time through a process of collective struggles, and these struggles could best be understood against the background of the development of humanity's productive forces. Freedom thus should not be reified as either one moment of this process, or as an attribute of individuals against the social. Rather, the meaning of freedom evolves through history, as both the material parameters for its realisation expand, and as groups form through struggle to fight for the realisation of these expanding demands (Fromm 1966).

Marx distinguished himself from other socialists of his day through the link he drew between socialism and the democratic struggle from below: before Marx, the utopian socialists had supposed that elites could act as the agency of the transition from capitalism to socialism (Draper 1977:59). Where Marx differed from these thinkers was in the trajectory through which he arrived at the case for socialism: he was originally an extreme democrat who came to socialism in the course of his involvement in the increasingly radical campaign for democracy in Germany. In throwing himself into this struggle, Marx realised that the working class acted as the most resolute arm of the democratic movement, and in so doing added a social depth to the demands of the movement. It should be stressed, however, that Marx did not develop his theory of proletarian revolution through abstract reasoning alone. It was his experience of workers' struggles in Germany and France that acted as the catalyst, pushing him to the conclusion that Hegel's critique of proletarianisation was one-sided: where Hegel argued that this process merely created a fragmented rabble, Marx suggested that workers could move, through their engagement in combined struggles for a better life, from being an atomised and dehumanised group towards becoming a potential collective agency of universal social and political emancipation.

Importantly, Marx insisted that working-class struggles are neither unexpected eruptions of primeval anger, nor are they caused by the seemingly ubiquitous 'outside agitators' so beloved of the bourgeois press. Rather the class struggle is grounded in workers' experiences of capitalism: the process of class formation was predicated upon prior changes in society's social basis, such that Marx's theory of revolution itself was related dialectically to his theory of social evolution (Blackledge 2002): 'At a certain stage of development, the material productive forces of society come into conflict with the existing relations of production ... From forms of development of the productive forces these relations turn into their fetters. Then begins an era of social revolution' (Marx 1970:20).

For Marx, then, the forces of production tended to develop over time, and, as they did so, where once relations of production aided this process they eventually begin to hinder it. Thus a contradiction develops at society's material base which could only be resolved through a revolution. Moreover, the level of development of the forces of production sets the parameters for the viable outcome of the revolution. But why was a revolution, rather than reform, necessary to overcome this contradiction?

At a most elemental level, Marx's answer to this question is based upon the proposition that the contradiction between the forces and relations of production is a systemic problem that cannot be overcome without fundamentally transforming the relations of production: mere reforms of the system would be an inadequate response to the crisis. Under capitalism, the contradiction between forces and relations of production is expressed through the tendency of the rate of profit to decline. This tendency is itself rooted in the capital accumulation process, and thus cannot be resolved short of a revolutionary transformation of society (Callinicos 2003:35–40). Additionally, a reform strategy could not hope to inaugurate a fundamental transformation of social relations, as the ruling class would fight to maintain its privileged position. However, despite the power of these arguments against the practicality of reformism, Marx and Engels developed a much more profound case for the socialist revolution; for while it is true that 'the ruling class cannot be overthrown in any other way', they suggested that 'the class overthrowing it can only in a revolution succeed in ridding itself of all the muck of ages and become fitted to found society anew' (Marx and Engels 1974:95).

This latter element to Marx's case for revolution is absolutely central to his thought, for he believed that a revolution was necessary because it was, above all else, only through the act of making a revolution that working people, socialised by their class location to assume subservient roles, could become fit to rule. Indeed, he suggests that workers, in tending to rebel against the process of their dehumanisation, begin to act as potential agents not only for their own liberation, but also for the universal liberation of humanity (Marx and Engels 1975b:36–7). In fact, the class analysis of the coming revolution so informed Marx and Engels' social theory that, rather than use the abstract word socialism to describe their goal, they usually wrote more concretely of the class rule of the proletariat (Draper 1978:24). However, they insisted that this form of class rule would undermine its own conditions of existence: workers' power would necessarily be but a moment in the dissolution of class society, as it would gradually wither away into communism. But how could a particular class emancipate the whole of humanity? Marx answered this question through a sketch of the history of the struggles for democracy.

Where Hegel had located the bureaucracy as a class that would act in the universal interest, Marx suggested a historical model of the relationship between a particular and a universal class. He argued that at different points in history, different classes would, in fighting for their particular interests, act for the universal interest. Thus, during the Great French Revolution, the revolutionary bourgeoisie, by acting in its own selfish interests, actually acted as a universal class in as far as they broke the fetters which feudalism had placed on general social development. However, as capitalist society evolved, the bourgeoisie became increasingly conservative, to the point where the revolutionary baton was taken up by the new class of proletarians. The proletariat would then take up the mantle of universality, until its own dissolution in the wake of the workers' revolution:

> The role of *emancipator* therefore passes in a dramatic movement from one class ... to the next, until it finally reaches that class which no longer realises social freedom by assuming certain conditions external to man and yet created by human society, but rather by organising all the conditions of human existence on the basis of social freedom. (Marx 1975:255)

The proletariat was therefore a universal class at a historically specific moment. Moreover, it would not achieve this universality immediately, but would acquire it through the process of revolution: in struggling for its own narrow particular interests, it would develop from an atomised 'class in itself' to become an organised and universal 'class for itself'.

Marx located the key material barrier to the victory of the proletariat in the class war as the capitalist state. The Paris Commune of 1871, he wrote, had proved that 'the working class cannot simply lay hold of the ready-made state machinery, and wield it for its own purposes' (Marx 1974:206). However, in contradiction to anarchism, Marx believed that after 'smashing' the bourgeois state, workers would need to create a state of their own, the dictatorship of the proletariat, through which they could ensure their victory over the forces of counter-revolution. Such a state would differ fundamentally from its bourgeois predecessor for, where the capitalist state rested upon the suppression, indoctrination and passivity of the masses, the dictatorship of the proletariat was built upon the active creativity of workers. The importance of this distinction was such that Marx placed the concept of the dictatorship of the proletariat at the centre of his mature political theory (Marx and Engels 1975a:64).

Three points are worth stressing with regard to the concept of the dictatorship of the proletariat. First, Marx understood it to be the dictatorship of a class that was, like the bourgeoisie in the Great French Revolution, historically universal: its victory would be in the interests of the whole of humanity. Second, unlike its bourgeois predecessor, since the proletariat neither exploited nor oppressed any other class below it, it could not be expected to develop a long-term antagonistic relationship to other classes. Therefore, once the opposition of the bourgeoisie had been finally subdued, the new form of state would 'wither away'. So, by contrast with modern connotations of the word dictatorship, the proletarian dictatorship could be expected to be both a temporary phenomenon and one that was largely benign. Third, in contrast to the way that dictatorship and democracy are placed at opposite poles of the political spectrum in liberal political theory, Marx understood any form of class rule to be a dictatorship. So, while modern liberal democracies mask the real dictatorship of the bourgeoisie, the dictatorship of the proletariat was, in a sense, the modern form taken by classical democracy – the rule of the poor (Ste. Croix 1983:75). So the dictatorship of the proletariat represented a moment in the process of the working class's 'self emancipation'.

However, while capitalism's crisis-prone nature would continuously generate class struggles, and while these struggles would tend in the direction of workers' power, Marx did not believe that the victory of the working class could be anticipated as a mechanical consequence of the evolution of bourgeois society. Four key factors mediated against this eventuality. First, the bourgeoisie can be expected to use the full coercive powers of the state to maintain its control over society. Second, the bourgeoisie will also attempt to secure the ideological incorporation of workers into its worldview. Third, this ideological strategy is itself underpinned by the very structure of capitalist social relations: production carried out by wage labourers for the market tends to mystify the process of exploitation and reify social relations to create the illusion of the universality of capitalism. Fourth, while workers do indeed struggle against capital, this struggle is never uniform, and this lack of uniformity is reflected in the fragmentary and uneven nature of class consciousness within the working class.

Marxists have traditionally sought to overcome the problems of the uneven class consciousness within the working class and bourgeois hegemony, and to work towards organising the smashing of state power, through building revolutionary workers' parties. Indeed, Marx argued that 'the working class cannot act, as a class, except by constituting itself into a political party' (Marx 1974:270). While Marx and Engels laid down some general guidelines for building a workers' party, they did not develop these into a fully worked out theory: this task was taken up by later Marxists, notably Lenin, Luxemburg, Trotsky and Gramsci (Molyneux 1986). Regrettably, despite the power of these contributions to Marxist political theory, the defeats inflicted by fascism and Stalinism on the working class in the 1920s and 1930s meant that, from the 1930s to the upsurge of militancy in the 1960s, their messages largely fell on barren ground (Anderson 1976).

CONTEMPORARY ANTI-CAPITALISM

Unfortunately, a number of forces acted to stymie the blossoming of revolutionary politics after 1968. First, the revival in working-class militancy in the decade from the mid 1960s to the mid 1970s was quickly broken. Second, despite the power of many revolutionary Marxist critiques of Stalinism, revolutionaries were often found guilty by association with the Soviet experiment: the refrain 'get back to Russia' was not uncommon. Third, the collapse of the Soviet Union in the late 1980s and early 1990s threw a cloud over the viability of all projects that aimed at a qualitative break with capitalism. When these factors were combined with a move to the right in Soviet historiography that represented Stalinism as the culmination of the Marxist betrayal of the hopes embodied in the revolts of 1917, then it seemed only natural that revolutionary Marxism should be on the defensive in the 1980s and 1990s.

However, the marginalisation of revolutionary thought within the academy had less to do with the power of competing paradigms than it did with the inhospitable political context within which these criticisms were made. Thus, Kristeva's argument that revolutionary Marxism necessarily gave rise to totalitarian consequences because it imposed a non-existent homogeneity upon heterogeneous revolts was far less radical than it would at first appear (Kristeva 1998:125). Indeed, as Žižek has forcibly argued, this supposedly radical critique of revolutionary politics involves its own paradoxical betrayal of radicalism: for any attempt to reject revolution in the name of revolt

precludes any actual radical change: the existing political regime is never effectively undermined or overturned, just endlessly 'questioned' from different marginal 'sites of resistance', since every actual radical change is in advance dismissed as inevitably ending up in some form of 'totalitarian' regression. (Žižek 2000:182)

Despite the power of this defence of the case for revolution, Žižek's argument does not address the tactical question of the relationship between the struggle for revolution and more mundane struggles for reforms. Some reformists have seized upon this necessary conceptual gap between the notions of reform and revolution to misrepresent revolutionaries as dogmatic opponents of reform (Kingsnorth 2003:230). However, while this caricature might fit a few ultra-leftist sectarians, it is unsustainable as a characterisation of the practice of Europe's main revolutionary organisations, the International Socialist Tendency and the Fourth International, both of which trace their ancestry back to the classical Marxists.[2] Amongst these, Lenin denounced simplistic refusals to work in bourgeois institutions as 'infantile'; while Rosa Luxemburg went to great lengths to explore the ways in which struggles for reforms evolved into revolutionary movements (Lenin 1993; Luxemburg 1986:29–30 and 1989:21). In fact, revolutionaries have not criticised reformists for working in parliament and other bourgeois institutions, but have objected to their reification of this work, and for thus subordinating the struggles of the oppressed to it. The point is not that revolutionaries refuse to work in institutions such as parliament, and certainly not that they reject the struggle for reforms, rather, they seek to marry these struggles to the long-term goal of overthrowing the state through mass working-class struggles; in Lukács' phrase the 'actuality of the revolution' informs their every act (Lukács 1977:9).

Whereas Lukács wrote as a participant in the great revolutionary wave that shook Europe after the First World War, today's anti-capitalist movement has generated a number of attempts to rehabilitate some of the key concepts associated with Marx's theory of revolution. Indeed, Žižek claims that one of these texts, Hardt and Negri's *Empire*, can be read as a 'rewriting of *The Communist Manifesto* for the twenty-first century' (Žižek 2002a:331). *Empire* is undeniably an inspiring and optimistic read, in which Hardt and Negri develop a powerful defence of the politics of class struggle. To this end, they broaden the Marxist conception of the proletariat to include 'all those exploited by and subject to capitalist domination', and insist that we are witnessing the 'emergence of a new quality of social movements' associated with the struggles of this 'multitude' against 'empire', capital's latest organisational form (Hardt and Negri 2000:53, 56).

Without doubt, one of the key strengths of *Empire* lies in Hardt and Negri's rejection of the arguments that the working class is in decline, and that it has ceased to be a potential agent of revolutionary change (Hardt and Negri 2000:402). However, there are problems with the alternative position they formulate, which relate to their utilisation of Deleuze and Guattari's treatment of 'the nomad as the model of all resistance to power' (Callinicos 2001a:47). Similarly, Hardt and Negri take the nomad to be the epitome of revolutionary agency; and they argue that the nomadic desire for freedom on the part of the multitude underpins the class struggle as the motor of history (Hardt and Negri 2000:124). Indeed, they suggest that such disparate processes as the globalisation of the world economy, the collapse of the Soviet Union, and the economic crisis of the 1970s can best be understood as the unintended consequences of the multitude's struggles to meet its desire to flee for freedom against authority (Hardt and Negri 2000:43, 262, 277). Unfortunately, this approach to recent history not only risks confusing offensive and defensive struggles on the part of the working class; it also leads Hardt and Negri to misunderstand the difference between proletarian victories and defeats. Thus, they not only suggest that the process of globalisation marks an opaque victory of proletarian internationalisation over capital – 'what they fought for came about despite their defeat'; but they seem to hide their heads in the sand when discussing the condition of the American working class: 'Against the common wisdom that the US proletariat is weak because of its low party and union representation with respect to Europe and elsewhere, perhaps we should see it as strong for precisely those reasons' (Hardt and Negri 2000:50, 269). Whatever the power of the implied critique of traditional workers' organisations expressed in these lines, this argument elides over the American working class's experience of defeat over the last few decades. This elision is dangerous, as other socialists have argued, because it fails adequately to ground contemporary strategic thought in an understanding of past working-class defeats (Callinicos 2001a:44; Gindin and Panitch 2002:37).

Holloway has gone further than this critique to argue that beneath Hardt and Negri's optimism lurks the danger of a resurrected functionalism: while workers' struggles may be ubiquitous, they seem to posit a model of capitalism that ascribes to it the permanent ability to restructure and adapt in response to these struggles (Holloway 2002a:83–5). Holloway suggests that the basic weakness with Hardt and Negri's whole approach lies in their rejection of any form of humanism. This, he argues, undermines their claim to outline an emancipatory project: 'The problem with this approach, surely, is that neither ants nor machines revolt. A theory that is grounded in revolt has little option but to recognise the distinctive character of humanity' (Holloway 2002b:172).

From a position that is deeply sympathetic to many of the themes in *Empire*, Holloway insists that anti-capitalists should reaffirm the anti-statist core of Marx's humanist politics, and he powerfully criticises those for whom the collapse of Stalinism represented the death of the socialist alternative to capitalism (Holloway 2002b:11–18). Nevertheless, just as Hardt and Negri's general model of class struggle appears to leave them unable to fully comprehend the ways in which its multi-levelled ebb and flow relates to changes in class consciousness, so Holloway's approach leads to his own strategic impasse.

Against Hardt and Negri's argument that it is the power of the working class that determines capitalist development, Holloway insists that what workers exercise is 'anti-power': an ever-present characteristic, or so he claims, of class-divided societies. Holloway sheds some light on the concept of anti-power through the repetition of an Ethiopian proverb: 'When the great lord passes, the wise peasant bows deeply and silently farts' (Holloway 2002b:157). Regrettably, and paralleling weaknesses associated with Kristeva's critique of revolution, and Hardt and Negri's idea of freedom noted above, Holloway does not seem to possess the resources that might facilitate a deeper understanding of a shift from this subservient act of rebellion to a socially transformative revolutionary movement. Indeed, given his goal of changing the world without taking power, it is only logical that he dismisses past Marxist movements for aiming to take power: they became, he suggests, as bad as the powers they challenged (Holloway 2002b:11).

In formulating his argument thus, Holloway dismisses the great schism experienced throughout the international socialist movement in 1914. This break led to a reappraisal of the Kautskyite orthodoxy that dominated the Marxist movement up to the war, which culminated in the publication of Lenin's *The State and Revolution* in 1917 – a vociferous critique of any attempt to utilise the bourgeois state as an agency of the socialist transformation of society. In this book Lenin returned to the works of Marx and Engels, who, he argued, insisted that it was incumbent upon the framers of the socialist party's programme to spell out clearly to workers that the transition to socialism could come only 'by force': 'our party and the working class can only come to power under the form of a democratic republic. This is even the specific form of the dictatorship of the proletariat' (Marx and Engels 1990:226–7). Holloway evades the issue of the structure of proletarian political power in the transitional period between capitalism and communism, and therefore, like the Marxists of whom Lenin was so critical, he fails to deal adequately with the issue of revolution.

This conclusion to Holloway's work is informed by his rejection of the 'elitist' notion of building socialist parties, on the grounds that Leninism led to Stalinism (Holloway 2002b:215). While this anti-party perspective remains strong within the anti-capitalist movement, it rests upon a combination of bad history and a shared Stalinist and liberal myth of Leninism.[3] By contrast, Žižek has argued:

> the key 'Leninist' lesson today is: politics without the organisational form of the Party is politics without politics, so the answer to those who want just the (quite adequately named) 'New Social Movements' is the same as the Jacobins' answer to the Girondin compromisers: 'You want revolution without a revolution!' (Žižek 2002a:297)

Žižek places the word 'Leninist' in this sentence within inverted commas to signify its Stalinist providence, which, he insists, should be distinguished from the actual democratic practice of the Bolshevik party (Žižek 2002a:193). In contrast to the Stalinist bastardisation of Leninism, Žižek rightly argues that, for Lenin, a revolutionary party is not an authoritarian top-down command structure, but rather reflects a 'new type of knowledge linked to a collective political subject' (Žižek 2002a:188). A successful revolutionary socialist party, according to this model, is not a grouping of the elite whose role it is to tell ordinary people what they should think; rather, it is the collective expression of the growing class consciousness of the most advanced sections of the anti-capitalist movement. Moreover, such a party can only be built given the realisation of the socialist assumption that, in contrast to those secularised versions of the original sin myth which naturalise the tendency to bureaucratic degeneration in all political parties, ordinary people actually lead both within the party, and within the anti-capitalist struggle more generally (Barker 2001). Indeed, as Žižek has argued elsewhere, the need to build such a party is of the utmost political importance today: 'the ten-year honeymoon of triumphant global capitalism is over … The problem now is the strictly Leninist one – how to *actualise* the media's accusations, how to invent the organisational structure which will confer on this unrest the *form* of universal political demand. Otherwise the momentum will be lost' (Žižek 2002b:96).

Unfortunately, Žižek's is an idiosyncratic Leninism from which some of the analytical power of Lenin's original is lost. For where Lenin attempted to ground revolutionary practice in a scientific analysis of the contemporary world, Žižek's equation of capitalism with Lacan's concept of the Real, risks, as Callinicos argues, displacing that scientific element from the revolutionary project. So where, for Žižek, the Real is that which exists beyond language, and which we can prove thus exists, but which we cannot know 'in its positive determination' (Žižek 2002c:91), Marxists insist that, despite the opacity of language, a scientific comprehension of the world is possible (Murray 1988). This difference is important, because the Marxist perspective allows the revolutionary to know capitalism to a degree that is impossible for the Lacanian; and this knowledge in turn informs and deepens her struggle against it. Thus, in contrast to the image of Lenin who comes alive on the pages of the biographies of Cliff, Harding, Le Blanc and Liebman, Žižek's Lenin is somewhat weakened as he fails fully to comprehend the profound link between politics and a developing analysis of capitalism (Callinicos 2001b:392).

A more powerful approach to revolutionary politics can be found in the works of the classical Marxists. For, despite the common caricature of Marx's political theory as mechanical, Marxists insist that their scientific analysis of capitalism does not imply that the success of anti-capitalist struggles can be guaranteed by some mythical 'iron law of history'. Thus, according to Bensaïd, while Lenin understood that 'his was the "era of war and revolutions"', he was also quite clear that 'the rest was a matter for politics, not prediction' (Bensaïd 2002:50). So, while the socialist political project is informed by a scientific analysis of capitalism, it cannot be reduced to this. Moreover, the key intellectual shift in Marxism from theory to practice is not a mechanical process of deduction, but is rather a movement 'from science to art' (Cliff 1986:254). Similarly, Callinicos, in a project that builds upon Marx's claim that truth can only be demonstrated 'in practice', underpins an impressive commitment to practice with sophisticated scientific analyses of both the dynamic of capitalist development, and the contemporary balance of class forces (Callinicos 2003; Marx and Engels 1974: 121). Indeed, in sharp contrast to the dominant vision of Marxism as a one-sidedly materialist doctrine, Ernest Mandel, in a powerful rejection of the mechanical conceptualisation of the relationship between politics and economics, has insisted that if the Marxist hope for a better world is to be actualised, socialist practice must be informed by an imaginative, and indeed utopian, component (Mandel 2002).

CONCLUSION

Only a few years ago, voices critical of global capitalism were few in number, and politically marginal. Today, by contrast, even a former chief economist at the World Bank can write that globalisation 'is not working for many of the world's poor ... for much of the environment ... for the stability of the global economy' (Stiglitz 2002:214). The author of these lines believes that the global elite can institute reforms through which these problems might be conquered, if only it be given the correct advice. On the other hand, Brenner, writing from within the Marxist tradition, suggests that the problems associated with capitalism are structural, and cannot be so easily overcome (Brenner 2002). Whether these socio-economic and environmental issues are deep-seated or epiphenomenal to capitalism, they have helped foster the growth of anti-capitalism (Klein 2000:266); and it is from within this movement that a debate is growing about how they might be overcome. If the movement is to have any hope of realising its goals, then it needs to bring these arguments into the open, so that it might attain a degree of strategic clarity. Žižek, Holloway, and Hardt and Negri have made powerful contributions to the revolutionary side of this debate. However, while their arguments are to be welcomed, it is important to read them alongside the Marxist classics. For, while Hardt and Negri's rehabilitation of class analysis, Holloway's humanism, and Žižek's Leninism mark a series of steps forward beyond the various forms of postmodernism that have dominated radical politics in recent years, radicals can, as Callinicos and Bensaïd have shown, still learn much from Marxism's powerful method for grounding political practice within a scientific analysis of capitalism, for developing nuanced analyses of the balance of class forces, and for outlining the strategically central distinction between capitalist and workers' states (Callinicos 2003; Bensaïd 2002).

GUIDE TO FURTHER READING

The best short introduction to Marx's thought is by Alex Callinicos (1996); while Hal Drapers' four-volume work (1977–90) is superbly comprehensive. Amongst the best commentaries on Marx's politics are Alan Gilbert (1981), Michael Löwy (2003), August Nimtz (2000), and Henry Collins and Chimon Abramsky (1965). Perhaps the best places to start amongst the classic texts are Marx and Engels' *The Communist Manifesto*, Marx's *The Critique of the Gotha Programme*, Lenin's *The State and Revolution*, Luxemburg's *The Mass Strike*, Gramsci's *Lyons Theses*, and Trotsky's *What Next?* These can all be found online at www. marxists.org. Of the more recent literature, Alex Callinicos (2003) develops a Leninist perspective for the movement, while an anti-Leninist Marxist standpoint is articulated by John Holloway (2002a and b). For a defence of Leninism that is typically idiosyncratic see Slavoj Žižek (2002c), which includes an excellent selection of Lenin's writings from 1917. A more orthodox Lenin can be found in the three volumes of Tony Cliff's political biography (1985–87), the first volume of which should be required reading for all anti-capitalists. Finally, Chris Harman provides a critical overview of the anti-capitalist literature from a revolutionary Marxist perspective. This can be downloaded from http://www.swp.org.uk/ISJ/HARM88.HTM.

NOTES

1. Thanks to Johnny, Matty and Zoë Anne Marsden for their help with this chapter.
2. For contemporary examples of their interpretations of Marxism see Callinicos (2003), and Bensaïd (2002).
3. For a powerful critique of similar accounts of Lenin's thought and practice see Molyneux (1998).

REFERENCES

Anderson, P. (1976) *Considerations on Western Marxism* (London: New Left Books).
—— (2000) 'Renewals', *New Left Review,* No. 1.
Barker, C. (2001) 'Robert Michels and the "Cruel Game"', in C. Barker et al. (eds) *Leadership and Social Movements* (Manchester: Manchester University Press).
Bensaïd, D. (2002) *Marx for Our Times* (London: Verso).
Blackledge, P. (2002) 'From Social Evolution to Social Revolution', in P. Blackledge and G. Kirkpatrick (eds) *Historical Materialism and Social Evolution* (London: Palgrave).
Brenner, R. (2002) *The Boom and the Bubble* (London: Verso).
Callinicos, A. (1996) *The Revolutionary Ideas of Karl Marx* (London: Bookmarks).

—— (2001a) 'Toni Negri in Perspective', *International Socialism*, Vol. 2, No. 92.

—— (2001b) 'On Slavoj Žižek', *Historical Materialism*, Vol. 8.

—— (2003) *An Anti-Capitalist Manifesto* (Cambridge: Polity Press).

Cliff, T. (1985) *Lenin: All Power to the Soviets* (London: Bookmarks).

—— (1986) *Lenin: Building the Party* (London: Bookmarks).

—— (1987) *Lenin: The Revolution Besieged* (London: Bookmarks).

—— (2003) *Marxist Theory After Trotsky* (London: Bookmarks).

Collins, H. and Abramsky, C. (1965) *Karl Marx and the British Labour Movement* (London: Macmillan).

Draper, H. (1977) *Karl Marx's Theory of Revolution I: State and Bureaucracy* (New York: Monthly Review Press).

—— (1978) *Karl Marx's Theory of Revolution II: The Politics of Social Class* (New York: Monthly Review Press).

—— (1986) *Karl Marx's Theory of Revolution III: The Dictatorship of the Proletariat* (New York: Monthly Review Press).

—— (1990) *Karl Marx's Theory of Revolution IV: Critique of Other Socialisms* (New York: Monthly Review Press).

Dunayevskaya, R. (1988) *Marxism and Freedom* (Columbia: Columbia University Press).

Fromm, E. (1966) *Marx's Concept of Man* (New York: Ungar).

George, S. (2001) 'What Now?', *International Socialism*, Vol. 2, No. 91.

Gilbert, A. (1981) *Marx's Politics* (Oxford: Martin Robertson).

Gindin, S. and Panitch, L. (2002) 'Gems and Baubles in Empire', *Historical Materialism*, Vol. 10, No. 2.

Hardt, M. and Negri, A. (2000) *Empire* (London: Harvard University Press).

Hill, C. (1991) *A Nation of Change and Novelty* (London: Routledge).

Hobsbawm, E. (1977) *The Age of Revolution* (London: Abacus).

Holloway, J. (2002a) 'Going in the Wrong Direction: Or, Mephistopheles – Not Saint Francis of Assisi', *Historical Materialism*, Vol. 10, No. 1.

—— (2002b) *Change the World Without Taking Power* (London: Pluto Press).

Kingsnorth, P. (2003) *One No, Many Yeses* (London: The Free Press).

Klein, N. (2000) *No Logo* (London: Flamingo).

Kristeva, J. (1998) 'The Necessity of Revolt', *Trans*, No. 5.

Lenin, V.I. (1993) *Left-wing Communism: An Infantile Disorder* (London: Bookmarks).

Löwy, M. (2003) *The Theory of Revolution in the Young Marx* (Boston: Brill).

Lukács, G. (1977) *Lenin* (London: New Left Books).

Luxemburg, R. (1986) *The Mass Strike* (London: Bookmarks).

—— (1989) *Reform or Revolution* (London: Bookmarks).

Mandel, E. (2002) 'Anticipation and Hope as Categories of Historical Materialism', *Historical Materialism*, Vol. 10, No. 4.

Marx, K. (1970) *A Contribution to the Critique of Political Economy* (Moscow: Progress Publishers).

—— (1974) *The First International and After* (Harmondsworth: Penguin).

—— (1975) *Early Writings* (Harmondsworth: Penguin).

Marx, K. and Engels, F. (1968) *Selected Works in One Volume* (Moscow: Progress Publishers).

—— (1974) *The German Ideology* (London: Lawrence and Wishart).

—— (1975a) *Selected Correspondence* (Moscow: Progress Publishers).

—— (1975b) *Collected Works*, Vol. 4 (London: Lawrence and Wishart).

—— (1990) *Collected Works*, Vol. 27 (London: Lawrence and Wishart).

Molyneux, J. (1986) *Marxism and the Party* (London: Bookmarks).

—— (1998) 'How Not to Write about Lenin', *Historical Materialism* Vol. 3.

Monbiot, G. (2003) *The Age of Consent* (London: Flamingo).

Murray, P. (1988) *Marx's Theory of Scientific Knowledge* (London: Humanities Press).

Neale. J. (2003) *You are G8, We are 6 Billion* (London: Vision).

Nimtz, A. (2000) *Marx and Engels: Their Contribution to the Democratic Breakthrough* (New York: Monthly Review Press).

Ste. Croix, G.E.M. de (1983) *The Class Struggle in the Ancient Greek World* (London: Duckworth).

Stiglitz, J. (2002) *Globalisation and its Discontents* (Harmondsworth: Penguin).

Wainwright, H. (2003) *Reclaim the State* (London: Verso).

Williams, R. (1976) *Keywords* (London: Fontana).

Žižek, S. (2000) 'Postface: George Lukács as the Philosopher of Leninism', in G. Lukács *A Defence of History and Class Consciousness: Tailism and the Dialectic* (London: Verso).

—— (2002a) 'Afterword: Lenin's Choice', in S. Žižek (ed.) *Revolution at the Gates* (London: Verso).

—— (2002b) 'A Cyberspace Lenin – Why Not?', *International Socialism*, Vol. 2, No. 95.

—— (2002c) *For They Know Not What They Do* (London: Verso).

10
Working-Class Internationalism

Mark O'Brien

The 1848 *Communist Manifesto* is probably best known for its clarion call, addressed to the workers of the world, to rally around the banner of international solidarity. When Marx and Engels wrote the manifesto they were part of a distinctly international scene of radical politics, based in London. From that time internationalism has become one of the touchstones of left radicalism in the working-class and socialist movements. This chapter will look briefly at the historical development of internationalist politics in the working class. It will also explore current perspectives on labour internationalism and, finally, will consider its contemporary state and some of the controversies within it.

MARXIST INTERNATIONALISM

In *The Communist Manifesto* Marx and Engels describe the relentless expansion of capitalism around the globe. For every part of the world the introduction of modern industry becomes a 'life and death question'. The sheer productivity of capitalist manufacture compared to previous forms of production, and the cheapness of its goods, breaks down barriers and local prejudices against the new system. Finally: 'It compels all nations, on pain of extinction, to adopt the mode of production; it compels them to introduce what it calls civilization into their midst; i.e. to become bourgeois themselves. In one word, it creates a world after its own image' (Marx and Engels 1998:39–40).

Consequent upon the spread of capitalism was the growth of an international working class whose labour it exploited. As capitalism developed, so in more and more countries the capital–labour nexus was the dominant factor in determining social relations. In this situation the social experience of a worker in a factory in Belgium would be very similar to that of a worker in a factory located in the

North of England. It was this commonality in the experience of workers from one country to the next that gave Marx and Engels hope in the emergence of the working class as a revolutionary class on a world scale.

The launch in 1866 of the international campaign for the eight-hour working day – almost simultaneously, though independently, in the USA and in Europe – vindicated the expectations that socialists had had of the international character of the struggle against capitalism. Marx was delighted at this development. For him it was evidence that a common class consciousness and programme could emerge 'instinctively out of the conditions of production themselves' (Foner 1986:12).

For Marx and Engels, however, working-class internationalism was not something that could be left to develop spontaneously. It was something that would have to be actively organised. They were intensely involved in the International Working Men's Association which had been founded in 1864. The First International, as it became known, was first and foremost an instrument of solidarity. Although the working class were more numerous than their exploiters, this would not in and of itself guarantee victory in the class war. As Marx was to point out, 'numbers weigh only in the balance, if united by combination and led by knowledge' (Marx 1987a:536). Without international coordination and solidarity workers would be 'chastized by the common discomfiture of their incoherent efforts' (Marx 1987a:536–7).

Through the First International Marx also propagated the principle of working-class support for the oppressed peoples of the capitalist colonies. This was no philanthropic principle, however. What Marx stressed was the interdependence of the struggles against colonial oppression abroad and the class struggle waged at home against those same capitalist exploiters. To the extent that workers in the imperialist countries did not side with those struggles abroad they remained in mental bondage to their capitalist exploiters at home. As Marx put it in relation to the question of Ireland: 'for them [the workers of England] the national emancipation of Ireland is no question of abstract justice or humanitarian sentiment but the first condition of their own social emancipation' (Marx 1987b:592).

A new chapter in working-class internationalism opened with the emergence of forms of mass socialist politics in Europe in the late 1880s. The Second International was established following the founding Paris Congress held on Bastille Day, 1889. Internationalism was a key theme. The internationalism of millions of workers in this period was genuine and enthusiastic, as is evidenced by the enormous May Day rallies of the early 1890s (Wrigley 1996). International May Day demonstrations became an established part of the socialist and working-class movement calendar in almost every part of the world. In 1909 American socialists organised the first International Woman's Day with the Europeans following in 1911 (Kaplan 1988).

The essentially national-state focus of each of the various socialist parties in this era, however, warped the development of this internationalism. The result was a political culture in which nationalist as well as internationalist sentiments competed for expression. This compromised and ambivalent form of internationalism was put to its ultimate test by the onset of war in 1914. Against a background of massive anti-war demonstrations in Germany, Austria, Italy, France and Belgium, the parties of the Second International, with the notable exceptions of the Italian Socialist Party and the Russian Bolshevik Party, collapsed behind the war chauvinism of their respective nation-states.

The Third International was founded by the Russian Bolshevik leadership in 1919. Its original purpose was the export of revolution across the world. It became a training school for fledgling communist parties which had been established in Europe and throughout the colonial world. The policy of the Third International was summed up by Lenin, advocating support for the ill-fated Irish rising of 1916: 'We would be very poor revolutionaries if, in the proletariat's great war of liberation for socialism, we did not know how to utilise *every* popular movement against *every single* disaster imperialism brings in order to intensify and extend the crisis' (Lenin 1977:161).

The Third International's trade union adjunct, the Red International of Labour Unions (RILU), was launched in 1921. In its programme of action RILU declared that unions must make general 'every local uprising, every local strike, and every small conflict' (Nicholson 1986:66). In the colonies the task of the 'red' unions was also to fight for the leadership of predominantly peasant anti-colonial movements.

The failure of workers' states to establish themselves in other countries, and the consequent isolation of the revolution, were to have profound implications for the direction of politics within Russia itself. Under the increasingly tight grip of Stalin, the international ambitions of the revolution gave way to the doctrine of 'Socialism in One Country'. It was against this policy that Trotsky was to wage war, from his exile in 1929 up until his assassination by Stalin's agents in 1940.

Trotsky argued that socialism could not be built in Russia alone because the capitalist system was integrated on a world scale. Russia could not survive as a socialist island in a hostile sea of capitalism. The productive forces of capitalism had 'long ago outgrown ... national boundaries' (Trotsky 1971:22). A socialist Russia, already economically underdeveloped and cut off from world markets and advances in productive technique, would perish. This did not mean that the revolution was doomed. Trotsky had long held that the world revolution could begin in the least economically developed countries that were dominated by the imperialist powers. This reversed the logic of the theorists of the Second International who had argued that socialism could arise only after a long historical period of capitalist economic development that raised production to adequate levels. Such revolutions, however, against colonial rule and for democratisation, would not be able to sustain themselves as fledgling independent democratic capitalist states. Rather, their revolutions, given the small size of their indigenous bourgeoisies, would be compelled to grow into workers' revolutions. These new workers' states, in their turn, could only survive as the preludes to revolutions in the advanced capitalist world. This was Trotsky's theory of Permanent Revolution.

Trostsky's perspective, then, remained thoroughly internationalist. This meant that the struggles of the colonised peoples of the world for liberation were intimately tied up with the struggles of workers in the imperialist countries against their exploitation. Speaking of British imperialism Trotsky argued: 'the internationalism of the British and Indian proletariats does not at all rest on an *identity* of conditions, tasks and methods, but on their indivisible *interdependence*. Successes for the liberation movement in India presuppose a revolutionary movement in Britain and vice versa' (Trotsky 1971:26).

What was at stake in this conflict was nothing less than the fate of the world revolution. Since that time the theme of what internationalism means has been contested in every historical phase of working-class struggle and organisation. The Spanish Civil War, the period of worldwide working-class rebellion and revolution from 1968–75, the struggle against South African apartheid in 1976–94, etc., have all had their international dimension. Controversy continues today. In the rest of this chapter we will consider current perspectives and developments on working-class internationalism.

PERSPECTIVES ON LABOUR INTERNATIONALISM

The question of whether political ideology or economic interest should be given the greater weight in understanding and interpreting internationalism in the working class has been a point of dispute. Logue, in his *Towards a Theory of Trade Union Internationalism* (1980), sees it as rooted in economic interests. With special focus on the chemical, metal and transport industries, Logue traces the evasion of national-state control by companies and the consequent increase in the need for cooperation between the international bodies of these sectors. The emphasis on economic factors behind labour internationalism is very strong also in Levinson's *International Trade Unionism* (1972), which established something of a paradigm for the field in the 1970s. In Levinson's view, changes in the structure of capitalism force trade unions to prioritise international activity. Levinson had hopes particularly in the growth in significance of multinational collective bargaining and the striking of world company contracts. This notion of the rise of a more internationalised world labour movement driven by changes in capitalism was similar to that put forward by Edo Fimmen, the leader of the International Transport Federation during the interwar years, in his book *Labour's Alternative* (1924).

An exclusive focus on economic factors in understanding labour internationalism often stems from an over-emphasis on the adaptation to capitalist structures that does, partially, characterise trade unionism. The assumption is often that it is only by following the internationalising tendencies of capitalism that labour will itself become more internationalist. What this misses, however, is the other side of trade unionism that has more to do with expressing the moods, views and perceptions of worker members of trade unions. A more complete view leads us to also consider these, less institutional, factors.

Some have been more questioning of economic motivations in their accounts of working-class internationalism. Olle and Schoeller (1977), criticising Levinson, argued that trade union internationalism would not simply emerge by adaptations to structural changes within capitalism. In their analysis, the international activities of national trade union centres actually replicated and even reinforced inequalities created by uneven levels of capitalist development. Haworth and Ramsey (1988) have argued that a common political vision is indispensable in the creation of labour internationalism. This perspective grows out of a certain analysis of the dynamic of working-class consciousness. For Haworth and Ramsey, worker consciousness has its origins in the particular and immediate experience of the workplace. A similar view is put forward by Hyman (1999a). In this view, the further away from the experience and solidarity of the workplace, the weaker exclusively working-class identity becomes. A unifying ideology therefore becomes necessary for the emergence of an effective trade union internationalism.

The historical significance of ideology in international trade unionism is explored by McShane (1992). McShane argues that the 1949 split in the briefly unified World Federation of Trade Unions had its roots in the ideological battles that occurred within the world trade union movement before the Second World War. This perspective contradicts a common view that it was a direct result of tensions introduced by the early phase of the Cold War. For McShane, keen to trace the problems of international labour back to the days of Lenin, it was suspicions and irritations introduced by the tactics of the RILU which led to the split.

Gumbrell-McCormick (2001), in her summary of the purposes of labour internationalism, makes a distinction between political self-interest and the much more complex area of ideology. Much of the literature regarding political interest (for example, Wedin 1970; Carew 1987; McShane 1992) has been drawn from studies of organised labour during the Cold War. Against these approaches Gumbrell-McCormick points to a cluster of related concepts which suggest different interpretations of working-class internationalism. Solidarity and identity as well as ideology, she argues, provide a 'framework for the mediation of individual interests and motivations' (2001:19) and have informed other studies (Hyman 1999b; Munck 2000; Waterman 1998). The real strength of an emphasis on 'solidarity' and 'identity', however, is that it shifts the focus away from the, at times, corrupting bureaucratic practice of the official leaderships and towards a discussion of what internationalism means for worker members of trade unions when they support the struggles of workers in other countries or when they themselves receive such support. The notion of working-class internationalism as something that is ethically uplifting, or even transformative, is touched upon by some authors on the subject. McShane, for example, identifies a 'universal-inspirational' labour internationalism as opposed to 'regulatory-functional' and 'diplomatic-national' forms (McShane 1992:10). Johns (1998) distinguishes between 'accommodationist' forms of trade unionism which adapt to changing capitalist arrangements and 'transformatory' forms of cross-border solidarity. This latter view of labour internationalism suggests an understanding that has more to do with activism, social movements, rank-and-file democracy and emancipatory idealism than it has to do with institutional responses to capitalist restructuring or bureaucratic pragmatism. But even within this approach there are a number of key questions that are arousing controversy today. We will consider three.

ISSUES IN LABOUR INTERNATIONALISM

Is there a 'new' labour internationalism?

A name long associated with the study of labour internationalism in general and the question of a 'new' labour internationalism in particular is that of Peter Waterman (1984; 1986; 1998). In his more recent publications (for example 1998:72–3) Waterman has described what he means by a new labour internationalism. These are some of its attributes: face-to-face encounters between workers; decentralised communications networks; a shift away from the 'aid' model of trade union beneficence towards workers in the poor countries to a more genuine solidarity based on common identities; a shift from rhetorical gestures to more political and practical activity; an energetic grass-roots activism. Munck (2002) has also argued that trade unions are making transitions both domestically and in terms of their international orientations. These transitions are throwing up 'new repertoires' in terms of strategy and sites of struggle. This new terrain, for Munck, is one on which the practices of the old bureaucratic and diplomatic forms of labour internationalism mix with the new, networked and 'informationalised' practices of more global union orientations.

One of the most extraordinary examples of new internationalist formations is that of the Southern Initiative on Globalisation and Trade Union Rights (SIGTUR). This has been described by Lambert and Webster (2001). SIGTUR grew out of a relationship of practical solidarity between the Congress of South African Trade Unions (COSATU) and the Western Australian Trade and Labour Council. At its sixth conference in South Korea, in November 2001, representatives from trade unions of 14 southern hemisphere countries were in attendance. The national union centres that have affiliated are of the leftward leaning, social movement variety. At the Seoul congress the delegates devoted a full day's discussion to exploring the relationship between their own struggles and mobilisations such as that at Genoa in 2001. As Lambert and Webster (2003) have shown, SIGTUR is more than a purely bureaucratic phenomenon and has demonstrated an ability to mobilise and to provide political coordination on an impressive scale. On the occasion of its fourth congress, held in Calcutta in 1997, 20,000 workers, organised by the Congress of Indian Trade Unions, participated in the opening events, and 'banners and posters lined Calcutta's crowded streets' (Lambert and Webster 2003:337–62). On May Day of 2001, SIGTUR affiliates organised around the common issues of job security and the effects of global neo-liberalism. Four million workers in South Africa, 2 million workers in India and 100,000 workers in South Korea took part in these strikes. It has also mobilised actions in relation to industrial campaigns such as that of the International Chemical, Energy and Mining Federation against the mining giant Rio Tinto. Contradicting the notion that workers of the 'political North', in countries such as Australia, cannot unite with workers of the South, it seems clear that what SIGTUR represents is the beginning of nothing less than a new southern hemisphere based, action orientated, trade union international.

New orientations are also evident in parts of the world where traditions of trade union practice are deeply entrenched. In Europe, a number of transnational actions have been staged by organised workers in recent years. Actions by car workers against factory closures in Belgium in 1997 and in the UK in 2001, transport workers in 1998, dockworkers in 2001 and retail workers in 2001 have all had a strong European dimension.

In interpreting such actions, the distinction between changes in trade union structures and official orientations and shifts in worker consciousness should be understood as primarily analytical. In reality a mix of the two themes usually occurs and the balance between them must be determined concretely. Trade unions do adapt to capitalism to one degree or another depending on their form of organisation and traditions. This does not, however, capture the totality of the experience for worker members of those organisations. For example a distinctively European trade unionism is emerging through the process of European capitalist regionalisation, the development of the European Trade Union Confederation and associated structures such as the European Works Councils (Visser 1998; Wills 2001). Europe-wide action by workers, however, creates an experience that can go beyond an exclusivist European solidarity. Whether this potential for a thoroughgoing, global worker internationalism is realised depends on the politics of the organisations, the speakers and the activists involved in the process, and crucially on the conclusions that workers themselves reach on the basis of what they already know and what they have heard. The same could be said for those occasions where trade unions have participated officially in the giant international mobilisations against the institutions of global capitalism and against war that have occurred in recent years.

Does internationalism constitute a strategy for the working class?

The question of the effectiveness of international solidarity in the actual outcome of industrial battles is one that cautions against generalisation. On the one hand, the occurrence of international support for workers in struggle, whether in the form of finance, blacking or solidarity strike action obviously demonstrates an internationalism on the part of those workers giving such support which can be inspiring for those receiving it. In this sense internationalism is an end in itself. Within the socialist tradition internationalism is a historical principle, and when it happens it is celebrated as such. However, there are times when appeals to internationalism are not so benign. Indeed it is often the emotional power of such appeals that can create the possibility of a misplaced belief in the industrial power of internationalist strategies to determine the result of a particular dispute. We have to look carefully and critically at each particular case in order to ascertain what the internationalism involved really represents.

There are circumstances in which international solidarity really is a life and death matter. A recent and highly significant example of such a struggle is that of the Sintraemcali workers in Columbia. These workers launched a successful, 36-day occupation of their company head office buildings beginning on Christmas Day 2001. This act of resistance against plans for sweeping privatisation of government services was heroic in a country which has one of the worst records of human rights abuses against trade unionists. A key role of international support in this case was literally to make the murder of leading trade unionists more difficult for the state sponsored paramilitaries.

International solidarity is often also of vital importance to the ability of workers to withstand long, bitter confrontations with their employers. In the great London dock strike of 1889, the arrival of £30,000 from the Australian 'wharfies' and dockers of Brisbane saved the strike from collapsing through starvation. During the British miners' strike of 1984–85, solidarity from abroad played an important role in the extraordinary ability of mining communities to withstand that one-year-long dispute. Mazur (2000) has explained the role that internationalism as a tactic played in the turning-point victory for North American UPS workers in 1997. The setting up of the World Council of UPS unions the year before the strike and the organising of the UPS World Action Day, which saw 150 'job actions or demonstrations worldwide' and which included actual strike action by workers in Italy and Spain and planned action by French workers at Orly airport, played a significant role in the company's climbdown.

And yet the note of caution remains. In 1889, the Australian donation was also the occasion of the lifting of the 'No Work' call for a general strike across London which might have seen substantial solidarity action more locally. Similarly, nearly a century later, donations to the British miners from abroad kept spirits high and stomachs full. However the miners remained isolated in their action politically and industrially by the official trade union movement.

This matter has been the subject of debate in relation to the Liverpool dockworkers dispute of 1995–98 (Lavalette and Kennedy 1996; Radice et al. 1997). Debate was sharpened by the awareness of everyone who took part of the courage and sacrifice of the dockers and their families in that gruelling three-year campaign. Internationalism was a very practical issue within the dispute and significant resources were put into sending pickets to ports all over the world. These efforts did generate solidarity. Indeed some of these actions, as in the case of the strikes staged by west coast harbour workers in the United States, were, fleetingly, magnificent (Moody 1997).

Despite the enormous efforts that went into this solidarity action, however, the hard truth is that it did not secure the dockers and their families the victory they so obviously deserved. The fact that the leadership of the dockers' union refused to make the dispute official meant that within the UK it remained isolated. One result of this was that when a change of government occurred in 1997, with the New Labour landslide, the pressure on the new government to settle with the dockers was not sufficient and their struggle was eventually defeated. At best then, the 'international strategy' was no substitute for more locally based strategies to confront what was, after all, a locally based employer. At worst it was actually a diversion from the difficult questions of how to achieve wider action that might have been of more immediate effect in the face of secondary action laws and a reluctant trade union leadership.

If there is any general lesson to be learned from this experience it is that whilst internationalism is an ethical principle of the working-class movement its practical application should not follow any dogmatic formula. Tactical orientations cannot be determined according to simple, once-and-for-all choices such as 'global or local?' The form that internationalism takes in the course of working-class struggle, and even the priority that it is given, must be determined locally and this may involve internal conflict. Such conflict will often reflect different understandings of how to win in any given dispute. It may also reflect deeper tensions related to the political directions of the struggle and in this sense be secondary to questions of leadership.

What is the political vision of labour internationalism today?

Today the politics of labour internationalism is in a fluid state. This should not surprise us, given the ways in which the organisations of international labour were structured by the divisions of the Cold War (McShane 1992; Kjeld 2001). At the official level, the World Federation of Trade Unions of the ex-Stalinist countries has declined whilst the International Confederation of Free Trade Unions has grown through attracting new affiliate organisations. Some have seen in this post-Cold War world the possibility of a unity within world labour based on a new non-political pragmatism (for example Hyman 1999b). Indeed this is a widely expressed opinion within international labour organisations. This view, however, underestimates the highly political issues that confront the working-class movement today. Just because the old Cold War division in world labour is now a thing of history does not mean that capitalism will not seek to create new divisions. The 'war against terror', the bombing of Afghanistan, the war against Iraq and the general political offensive launched since the September 11 attacks have all tested the internationalism of the labour movement. So far, organised workers in most countries have demonstrated an internationalism over these issues and have been present in significant numbers on anti-war mobilisations.

These practical displays of anti-war sentiment, however, have been just one element of a more complex process which is creating the potential for new political directions within the working-class movement. A great deal of interest has been generated in recent years by the phenomenon of new alliances formed between trade unions and social movements. The spectacular growth of the anti-capitalist movement since the protests in Seattle at the end of 1999 has seen organised labour marching alongside of human rights and social justice groups of varying sorts (Thomas 2000; Danaher 2000). The fact that this is a phenomenon that involves unions, movements and NGOs at the transnational and global levels has also been widely discussed (Waterman 1998; Nedverdeen Pieterse 2000; Pollack 1999; Taylor 1999; O'Brien et al. 2000). Certainly a number of the most notable mobilisations including those at Seattle in 1999, Nice in 2000, Genoa in 2001, Florence in 2002, Evian in 2003 and Mumbai in 2004 have seen strong showings from trade unions.

A significant development within which labour is playing a role is what we might call the 'social forum' movement. Gagnon (2000) has traced the roots of the Hemispheric Social Alliance which was founded at the Santiago Summit of the Peoples of America in 1998. Growing out of opposition to the North Atlantic Free Trade Area and its 'fast track' version, it was made up of the now familiar coalitions and networks of human rights groups and trade unions. Since then, through initiatives by Partido dos Trabalhadores – the Brazilian Workers' Party – and the French ATTAC movement, Porto Alegre in Brazil has become the home of the ever-larger World Social Forum. In Europe, the first European Social Forum held in Florence in November 2002 attracted over 60,000 delegates. The second European Social Forum held in Paris in 2003 was similarly successful. The Asian Social Forum held in Hyderabad in January 2003 and the 2004 World Social Forum held in Mumbai in January 2004 signalled the further expansion of this movement as a truly global phenomenon. Local social forum events have also proliferated around the world.

As a separate though potentially complementary development, some have speculated on the significance of new forms of 'social movement' trade unionism which take struggles and campaigns beyond the workplace and network with other movements in society. Social movement unionism is seen by some (for example, Moody 1997; Lambert 1999) as an effective trade union form in the era of neo-liberalism and as something which, from its origins in South Africa, South Korea and Brazil, could be replicated globally.

None of the developments described above amount to a new alternative social vision for international labour – yet. However, it is the very ideological flux and practical experimentation within the movement itself which is so refreshing and so full of potential. The first socialists in the 1820s revolted against the corrosive anti-social tendencies of capitalism and insisted that human beings, rather than being reduced to brute economic survival, needed social bonds to sustain them – in other words they needed 'society'. Today, the language of the social forum movement expresses revulsion at the devastating effects of neo-liberalism the world over. Just as the new socialist workers in the Europe of the 1880s and 1890s gathered and marched with feelings of excitement and euphoria at the possibility of a better world, so today the enormous mobilisations occurring the world over are generating similar feelings of hope. How this new 'social-*ism*' will develop politically is uncertain. But the fact that such questions are on the historical agenda once more suggests that the new horizons so urgently needed by the international labour movement are in the process of being formed.

CONCLUSION

Internationalism has been a part of the development of the working-class movement for most of its history. At its strongest, the effect of this internationalism is to lift mental horizons above the struggle for daily survival and to break down the divisions created by capitalists to aid their rule. Where a strong internationalist political culture exists, the effect is also to undercut racism and nationalism within workplaces and communities. On a more practical level, such solidarity often enables workers to survive long battles with their employers and to transmit the lessons of struggle to workers around the world. In this sense, it is the political and organisational unevenness of workers' movements in different parts of the world that makes international solidarity necessary.

Internationalism forms a tradition within the working class. Rather than being a purely historical phenomenon, however – a sort of interesting exhibit in the museum of organised labour – it is a tradition that is very much alive. Indeed, working-class internationalism has, over the course of the 1990s and 2000s, come back into its own with new forms of expression, new motivations and new problems. But it is this very newness which is its most interesting and exciting aspect. As it grows and develops it shows signs of contributing significantly to the process of labour – and possibly even socialist – renewal.

GUIDE TO FURTHER READING

Moody (1997) still provides one of the best introductions to the emergence of new forms of international trade unionism, especially that of social movement unionism at the global scale. For overviews of some of the most interesting developments and issues in labour internationalism Peter Waterman and Jane Wills (2001) and Ronaldo Munck (2002) are good places to start. Chris Harman (2002) takes on many of the arguments about the supposed decline of organised labour head-on. Many of the classic issues in labour internationalism are explored by Roger Southall (1995). Eric Lee (1996) provides a very readable introduction to the impact of innovations in communications technology for world trade unionism.

REFERENCES

Carew, A. (1987) *Labour Under the Marshall Plan* (Manchester: Manchester University Press).

Danaher, K. (2000) *Globalize This!* (Monroe, Maine: Common Courage Press).

Fimmen, E. (1924) *Labour's Alternative: The United States of Europe or Europe Limited* (London: Labour Publishing Company).

Foner, P. (1986) *May Day: A Short History of the International Workers' Holiday 1886–1986* (New York: International Publishers).

Gagnon, M. (2000) 'Trade Union Cooperation in the NAFTA Area', *Transfer*, Vol. 6, No. 1.

Gumbrell-McCormick, R. (2001) *The International Confederation of Free Trade Unions: Structure, Ideology and Capacity to Act* (University of Warwick: unpublished PhD thesis).

Harman, C. (2002) 'The Workers of the World', *International Socialist Journal*, Vol. 2, No. 96.

Haworth, N. and Ramsey, H. (1988) 'Workers of the World Undermined: International Capital and Some Dilemmas in Industrial Democracy', in R. Southall (ed.) *Trade Unions and the New Industrialisation of the Third World* (London: Zed Press).

Hyman, R. (1999a) 'Imagined Solidarities: Can Trade Unions Resist Globalisation?', in P. Leisink (ed.) *Globalisation and Labour Relations* (Cheltenham: Elgar).

—— (1999b), 'National Industrial Relations Systems and Transnational Challenges', *European Journal of Industrial Relations*, Vol. 5, No. 1.

Johns, R. (1998) 'Bridging the Gap between Class and Space: US Worker Solidarity with Guatemala', *Economic Geography*, No. 74.

Kaplan, T. (1988) 'On the Socialist Origins of International Women's Day', in F. Holthoon and M. van der Linden (eds) *Internationalism in the Labour Movement* (Leiden: Brill).

Kjeld, J. (2001) 'Rethinking the International Confederation of Free Trade Unions and its Inter-American Regional Organisation', *Antipode*, Vol. 33, No. 3.

Lambert, R. (1999) 'The Movement's New Unity', *South Africa Labour Bulletin*, Vol. 23, No. 4.

Lambert, R. and Webster, E. (2001) 'Southern Unionism and the New Labour Internationalism', *Antipode*, Vol. 33, No. 3.

—— (2003) 'What is New in the New Labour Internationalism: A Southern Perspective', paper presented at the *International Trade Unionism in a Network Society* Conference, Leeds Metropolitan University, May 2–3.

Lavalette, M. and Kennedy, J. (1996) *Solidarity on the Waterfront* (Liverpool: Liver Press).

Lee, E. (1996) *The Labour Movement and the Internet: The New Internationalism* (London: Pluto Press).

Lenin, V. (1977) *Questions of National Policy and Proletarian Internationalism* (Moscow: Progress Publishers).

Levinson, C. (1972) *International Trade Unionism* (London: Allen and Unwin).

Logue, J. (1980) *Towards a Theory of Trade Union Internationalism* (Gothenburg: University of Gothenburg).

Marx, K. (1987a) 'Inaugural Address to the First International', in D. McLellan (ed.) *Karl Marx, Selected Writings* (Oxford: Oxford University Press).

—— (1987b) 'Letter to Meyer and Vogt, 9th April 1870', in D. McLellan (ed.) *Karl Marx: Selected Writings* (Oxford: Oxford University Press).

Marx, K. and Engels, F. (1998) *The Communist Manifesto* (London: Verso).

Mazur, J. (2000) 'Labor's New Internationalism', *Global Policy Forum – Journal of Foreign Affairs*, <www. globalpolicy.org/socecon/global/labor.htm>.

McShane, D. (1992) *International Labour and the Origins of the Cold War* (London: Clarendon).

Moody, K. (1997) *Workers in a Lean World* (London: Verso).

Munck, R. (2000) 'Labour in the Global', in R. Cohen and S. Rai (eds) *Global Social Movements* (London: The Athlone Press).

—— (2002) *Globalisation and Labour* (London: Zed Press).

Nedverdeen Pieterse, J. (2000) 'Globalisation and Emancipation: From Local Empowerment to Global Reform', in B. Gills (ed.) *Globalisation and the Politics of Resistance* (London: Macmillan).

Nicholson, M. (1986) *The TUC Overseas: The Roots of Policy* (London: Allen and Unwin).

O'Brien, R. et al. (2000) *Contesting Global Governance* (Cambridge: Cambridge University Press).

Olle, W. and Schoeller, W. (1977) 'World Market Competition and Restrictions of Trade Union Policies', *Capital and Class*, Vol. 2.

Pollack, A. (1999) 'Transnational New Internationalism in the Making: Encounters, Networks, Alliances', *Associations*, No. 4.

Radice, H. et al, (1997) <www.labournet.org/docks/9704/GLOBAL.HTM>.

Southall, R. (1995) *Imperialism or Solidarity? International Labour and South African Trade Unions* (Cape Town: UCT Press).

Taylor, R. (1999) *Trade Unions and Transnational Industrial Relations* (Geneva: International Institute for Labour Studies).

Thomas, J. (2000) *The Battle in Seattle* (Colorado: Fulcrum).

Trotsky, L. (1971) *'The Permanent Revolution' and 'Results and Prospects'* (London: New Park Publications).

Visser, J. (1998) 'Learning to Play: The Europeanisation of Trade Unions', in P. Pasture (ed.) *Working Class Internationalism and the Appeal of National Identity* (Oxford: Oxford University Press).

Waterman, P. (ed.) (1984) *For a New Labour Internationalism* (Brussels: International Labour Education, Research and Information Foundation).

—— (1986) 'A Note on Labour Internationalism and the New Social Movements', *Newsletter of International Labour Studies*.

—— (1998) *Globalisation, Social Movements and the New Internationalisms* (London: Mansell).

Waterman, P. and Wills, J. (eds) (2001) 'Place, Space and the New Labour Internationalism', *Antipode*, Vol. 33, No. 3 (special issue).

Wedin, Å. (1970) *International Trade Union Solidarity, ICFTU 1957–65* (Stockholm: LO).

Wills, J. (July 2001) 'Uneven Geographies of Capital and Labour: The Lessons of the European Works Councils', *Antipode*, Vol. 33, No. 3.

Wrigley, C. (1996) 'The Early May Days: 1890, 1891 and 1892', in A. Charlesworth et al. (eds) *An Atlas of Industrial Protest in Britain 1750–1990* (London: Macmillan).

11
Equality

Brendan Evans

Equality is a complex and diverse concept, but one that has been ubiquitously employed in progressive political discourse. Classical liberals use the term to advocate formal political and legal equality for citizens. This is a reductionist version of the concept which is endorsed by all democratic political parties.

The focus here is on more advanced versions of the concept, drawn from the socialist tradition. It is perhaps too Procrustean to classify these more radical theories into three categories, but there is heuristic merit in distinguishing between Marxist (or needs based), social democratic (equality as an ultimate evolutionary goal) and social liberal (creating equal opportunities) conceptions. This chapter argues that the currently hegemonic equal opportunities movement derives its philosophy from social liberalism. The dominance of equal opportunities over the wider concept of equality results in a dilution of the concept. While equal opportunities has brought to the political mainstream a recognition of inequalities affecting minorities and women which were neglected by traditional socialism, it serves to drain the concept of its radical potency. The progressive left should, however, retain the term equality as a core ideological value or ideal (Eagleton 2000:176).

As an ideal, equality is highly adaptable. Particular meanings can prevail according to time, place and purpose. What all exponents of equality share is their commitment to a *value*. Equality might be regarded by Marxists as historically inevitable; by social democrats as the correlate of rational modernity; and by exponents of equal opportunities as just. Yet even for the revolutionaries of the late eighteenth century, the cry 'all men are created equal' was an unverifiable proposition. For the left, however, equality must be a core ideological value.

THE HISTORY AND DEVELOPMENT OF THE CONCEPT

To explain the trajectory of the concept of equality it is necessary to differentiate American and British versions, and to consider the contribution of Marxism to the equality debate.

Marxism and equality

Marx was undoubtedly a proponent of equality. While rejecting bourgeois theories of 'equal rights' he asserted that 'differences of brain and intellectual ability do not imply any differences in the nature of the stomach and of physical needs' (Marx and Engels 1977:566). Yet he scorned capitalist and social democratic theories of equality. Under capitalism, according to Marx, there is an ostensible equality because in all exchange relationships each of the exchangers is in an equal position (Marx 1971b:245). Yet beneath the surface the reality is different, since under capitalist relations of production the capitalist appropriates the surplus value generated by the worker and the workers have no choice but to sell their labour (Marx 1971b:163).

Marx also condemned social democratic theories of justice as historical products lacking enduring significance. He referred to the 'defects' of the social democratic theory of 'equal rights' (Marx 1971a:23). Marx advanced a more comprehensive concept of equality, and regarded the social democratic version as 'one-sided'. As Marx proclaimed the class struggle to be the motor of history, he argued that social democrats were deluded in urging the goal of eliminating all inequalities without first overthrowing existing class relations. In his comments on the Gotha Programme of the German Unity Party, he argued that only with the abolition of all class distinctions 'would all social and political inequality arising from them disappear of itself' (Marx 1971a:27). Once the proletarian revolutionaries had fulfilled their mission of overthrowing the bourgeoisie and installing the dictatorship of the proletariat, there would occur a transitional period of fading bourgeois ideological horizons before society could proclaim on its banners a needs-based version of a truly egalitarian communism. Future communist society should 'inscribe on its banners, from each according to his ability to each according to his needs' (Marx 1971a:18). Equality was not, therefore, about equal outcomes, or the current equal opportunities mantra of 'equal pay for equal work'; it was about contributions and extractions to and from society on the basis of capacity and need.

Marx rejected the social democratic commitment to an 'equal right' of workers to the products of labour. First, the notion of 'equal right' was a bourgeois concept. This was symbolised by the social democratic demand for 'universal and equal elementary education by the state'. Marx argued that in existing society education could never be equal, and under capitalism is necessarily distorted, since 'who educates the educators?' (Larrain 1979:26). Second, there are many members of society who are necessarily inactive, whether young, old or sick, whose needs should also be provided for. Wealth should not simply be divided on the basis of economic contributions. Even to reward on the basis of merit is to reward luck, and individual achievement is a product of the contributions of others to the training received by an individual (Verma 2000:82). Third, it is only possible to distribute that which is left when the requirements of society have been addressed. These requirements include the provision of public services and the replacement of the means of production (Marx 1971a:15). Marx described ideas about 'fair distribution' as 'trash', as they treated distribution independently of the means of production. Distribution is 'itself a product of production ... the specific kind of participation in production determines the specific forms of distribution' (Marx 1971a:18). Marx complained that social democrats, by splitting distribution from production, were failing to understand the real relations in society. Finally, the social democrats retained the capitalist assumption that labour is a burden to be endured. Under the alienating conditions of capitalist production this was understandable. In future communist society, however, labour would not be simply a criterion for reward, but 'life's prime want' (Marx 1971a:18). The dehumanisation of capitalist production would be superseded. This remains a challenging version of equality that contemporary socialists can never cavalierly discard.

Some comments by Engels can be interpreted as rejecting the concept of equality. For example, he asserted that there would always be inequality in the conditions of life, as exemplified by the different experiences of Alpine dwellers from those who live on the plain. He argued that the socialist preoccupation with equality resulted from French Revolutionary slogans (quoted in Marx 1971a:36). But Marx's rejection of inequality is clear from his theory of surplus value. He simply opposed limited conceptions of equality. Marx's ultimate vision of self-realisation in a cooperative community rejected a narrow construction, within which social democrats were trapped.

It was the non-occurrence of proletarian revolution which led many social democrats to reject Marx. Since they eschewed the revolution, they pursued what Marx would regard as a distorted version of equality by failing to recognise that the dynamic of capitalism lies in unequal rewards.

Equality in the American context

Throughout the history of the United States, Americans have proclaimed equality as a rhetorical ideal and some have reached beyond liberal 'bourgeois' views to advocate social liberal or social democratic versions of the concept. Tom Paine was an early influence on American thought, and argued that the coexistence of rich and poor was like 'dead and living bodies chained together' (Keane 1995:426). The Founding Fathers of the Constitution regarded all white males as equal in dignity (Skidmore 1978:158). Abraham Lincoln stated that equality is the principle on which the United States was built (Pole 1976:149).

The political appeal to the interests of 'the common man' from Thomas Jefferson, through Andrew Jackson, to Franklin Roosevelt's New Deal, has been about maintaining opportunity for all when it was under challenge. De Tocqueville in the 1840s asserted that 'the passion for equality ... is ... the chief and constant object of Americans' (quoted in Pole 1976:33). But the Jacksonians contributed to equality by asking only 'that all people be given an equal chance', and that the established rich should not dominate (Bennett 1990:32). It is striking that even American socialists were so conditioned by their environment that to them egalitarianism was about opportunity. This is evidenced by Spargo's definition, as an early twentieth-century American socialist leader, of American socialism as not about 'human equality, but equality of opportunity, to prevent the creation of artificial inequalities by privilege'. Spargo was adamant that socialism was not about uniformity, but about removing constraints on talent (Pole 1976:220). The American communist leader Earl Browder's statement that communism equated to 'twentieth-century Americanism' demonstrates the same phenomenon (Browder 1938:249). Yet even de Tocqueville, who asserted that 'the general equality of conditions in America was the fundamental fact from which all others seemed to be derived', feared the threat that equal opportunity would permit 'a permanent inequality of conditions', and that if aristocrats emerged again, 'it may be predicted that this is the gate by which they will enter' (quoted in Pole 1976:33). These versions of equality, therefore, were far removed from producing egalitarian outcomes. It is notable that, when in 1972 the liberal Democrat George McGovern advanced a substantial egalitarian policy, including placing income redistribution on the Democratic Party agenda, he was annihilated in the presidential election. Evidently, Americans subscribe to the idea of a society based on egalitarian principles, but reject a society of equals. Yet other Americans have echoed de Tocqueville in perceiving the difficulty with equality of opportunity, as it conceals 'the elementary contradiction between rights to an equal start and rights to equal degrees of fulfilment'; and equality also lost meaning when the economic opportunities which the American frontier had offered were all appropriated (Croly 1909:183).

More recently, the American debate has taken place between supporters and opponents of Equal Opportunities and Affirmative Action programmes. This is essentially a debate between liberals and social liberals, and is discussed later.

Social democratic conceptions of equality in the UK

The programme of the German Unity Party foreshadowed European continental social democratic theories of equality. British social democratic thinkers share many of the values of their counterparts in other European countries, although they were also affected by nineteenth-century domestic radicalism.

Matthew Arnold (1822–1888) protested against inequality. He considered devotion to inequality a particularly British trait, like social snobbery. He argued that equality was the foundation of a good society, that inequality was incompatible with human dignity and that it hampered the privileged and underprivileged alike by respectively 'pampering' and 'depressing' them (Tawney 1964:42). Progressively, nineteenth-century social democratic theorists retreated from common ownership and installed equality as their central goal, since their roots were in the British radicalism of Arnold and not in Marxism. Dickens (1812–1870) and Ruskin (1819–1900) joined Arnold in deploring the indolence of the leisured and wealthy. J.S. Mill (1806–1873) also deplored the contrast between the rewards for the industrious and the idle (Wolfe 1975:9). British socialism is, therefore, an extension of radicalism. It was later ethical socialists such as Tawney (1880–1962) who exercised the profoundest influence on social democratic thought, but Tawney too drew upon earlier radicalism in Britain.

Tawney's ethical socialism was patently non-Marxist, but, as a member of the Labour Party, his ideas deserve re-examination because they demonstrate a contrast with New Labour's virtual abandonment of social democracy. Wright also correctly argues that Tawney's resolution of the dilemma of reconciling equality with liberty remains the 'reference point' for the entire debate (Wright 1987:165). Tawney's was a democratic route to greater equality, achieved by persuasion, but sustained by its moral superiority. He regarded the British political system as formally democratic but hierarchical in practice. He rejected attempts to secure equality for the working class by 'hose piping them to their salvation by coercive leadership, however enlightened' (Barker 1978:145). He shared with Marx a critique of the effects of concentrated economic power, recognised the equation of economic with political power and understood that the victimised in society contribute to the prevalence of capitalistic values. Tawney asserted that 'capitalism is maintained, not only by capitalists, but by those who ... would be capitalists if they could, and that injustices survive, not merely because the rich exploit the poor, but because, in their hearts, too many of the poor admire the rich' (Tawney 1964:42). He also makes a similar claim to that of Marx regarding the reification of capitalism, when he asserts that every generation regards as natural the institutions to which it is accustomed.

Tawney advocated equality of worth; but this moral stance carried radical connotations. He asserted that the humanity of all people warranted that the 'good things of life', culturally and educationally, should be available to all; and argued that '... social institutions, property rights, and the organisation of industry, and the system of public health and education – should be planned, as far as possible, to emphasise and strengthen, not the class differences which divide, but the common humanity which unites them' (Wright 1987:49). In an unequal society people are 'too far from each other, and society becomes not the affirmation of a common humanity, but the scene of social injustice' (Barker 1978:145). Tawney urged redistribution, objected to the acquisition of property for its own sake, and argued that if it did not serve a social function it degenerated into 'improperty'. He condemned public schools for perpetuating inequality. But even equality of opportunity merely represented 'the impertinent courtesy of an invitation offered to unwelcome guests, in the certainty that circumstances will prevent them from accepting it' (Tawney 1964:42). Tawney rejected equality of opportunity as 'the tadpole philosophy', in which a small minority of tadpoles become frogs.

Tawney argued that liberty and equality are inextricably linked. An economic system which grades people into groups ensures that liberty becomes the privilege of a class. Liberty cannot occur where economic power is maldistributed. He acknowledges that 'the enlargement of the general liberty involves the curtailment of such particular liberties as may conflict with it' (Tawney 1964:233). He exemplified this by such policies as increasing taxes, collective welfare provision, the control of investment, and the abolition of fees in education (Tawney 1964:234). Rights must not merely be formal, like 'the right of all who can afford it to dine at the Ritz, but must be capable of being exercised …. Social arrangements which enable only some groups to do much what they please, may possess their virtues; but freedom is not among them' (Tawney 1964:235).

The Labour minister and writer Anthony Crosland has been the guru of social democratic thought in Britain since the publication of *The Future of Socialism* in 1956. He maintained Tawney's commitment to freedom, but his main continuity with Tawney was his advocacy of equality. Many socialists reject Crosland's central propositions that capitalism has been changed by the division of ownership from control, that society can be equalised by redistributive taxation and public expenditure and that comprehensive schooling breaks down class barriers. Crosland's arguments for equality had an extrinsic character; for example, that inequality leads to social bitterness. He also argued that inequality is socially and economically wasteful and fails to extract the maximum value from the population (Crosland 1956:146). Crosland proposed 'large egalitarian changes in our education system, the distribution of property, … social manners and style of life, and the location of power within industry; and perhaps some, but certainly a smaller change in respect of incomes from work' (Crosland 1956:148). Crosland sought more than equality of opportunity but his arguments lacked a commitment to the intrinsic merit of equality.

To demonstrate that Crosland was characteristic of social democrats, in the 1960s another Labour minister and writer, Douglas Jay, developed Crosland's argument that 'equality mattered more than common ownership' (Jay 1962:5). His objection to public ownership was that 'a massive transfer from private to public ownership could be carried out in certain ways, and very little fundamental redistribution of incomes, or approach to social justice, achieved at all – as many employed in British publicly-owned enterprises would now be the first to admit' (Jay 1962:45).

Another Labour politician and academic, Evan Luard, in 1979 challenged entrenched myths surrounding the case for inequality, for example, the need for incentives. He rejected the argument for differentials based upon the amount of training required in a job – as, for example, with doctors – since apprentices have a stronger case, owing to the long and arduous nature of their training. Luard also criticised the claim that some professionals such as doctors possess greater skill, and since skill is a privilege, it is unlikely that doctors would wish to relinquish it in order to become factory workers. In any event, skill is hard to measure, as signalmen and electricians are also skilled, and work in occupations with consequences for life and death (Luard 1979:73). Luard is unconvinced by pleas about the varying responsibilities of occupations, as there is great pressure on those working on assembly lines, and company directors or senior managers may actually enjoy the responsibilities that they carry. In any event, psychological burdens vary between individuals in the same occupation (Luard 1979:74). So Luard is correct to argue that traditional differentials are flimsily justified and only survive because of existing social expectations. One consequence of these expectations is that the responsibilities involved in caring work are not reflected in adequate remuneration.

Social liberal conceptions of equality in the UK and the USA

The social liberal conception of equality derives from such writers as John Rawls and Ronald Dworkin. It also includes the 'thinkers' behind New Labour in Britain and the 'new' Democrats in the United States. The personal adherence of the British Prime Minister, Tony Blair, to this position is evident from his claim that he has been as much influenced by Lloyd George and Beveridge as by Keir Hardie. This fusion of social democracy with social rather than classical liberalism exemplifies Blair's position in the centre of the spectrum.

Rawls, the political theorist, in 1973 advanced practical policies to assist the poorest members of society, but allowed incentives for wealth creators. He enunciated the three principles of liberty, equality of opportunity, and socio-economic differences and argued that inequalities are defensible if they enable the worst off members of society to become better off. The radical feature of Rawls' theory was that he put the onus on the defence of inequality. As he explained, 'primary goods – liberty and opportunity, income and wealth, and the bases of self respect – are to be distributed equally unless an unequal distribution of any or all of these goods is to the advantage of the least favoured' (Rawls 1973:75). Differentials are to be kept to the minimum necessary to improve the lot of the poorest. Rawls added the rider that assisting the poor should not be at the expense of the just savings principle, in which individuals by their savings ensure that society invests in its future (Rawls 1973:285). Sometimes he appears to straddle the principles of equality of opportunity and those of 'fair shares'. His objective is 'to ensure fair equality of opportunity and to regulate the social and economic system so that social resources are properly used and the means to the citizens' ends are produced efficiently and fairly shared' (Rawls 1973:368).

Rawls leaves open the type of society that follows from his theory of justice, accepts private property and leaves open the degree to which incentives in income are necessary. In response, Barry claims that 'not since Locke's theory of property have such potentially radical premises been used as the foundations for something so little disturbing to the status quo' (quoted in McCormick 1982:84). This refers to Locke's shift from the view that the land is given in common to his defence of the sanctity of private property. McCormick also doubts if privileging of savings is egalitarian (McCormick 1982:100).

Yet latterday egalitarians have attempted a more radical interpretation of Rawls' theory. Cohen argues that the socio-economic difference principle need not require incentives, but that the worst off in society can be assisted by the internalisation of a social duty ethos by society's productive members (Cohen 1997:127). He recognises that an egalitarian society can operate with low living standards and poor public services, but hopes that a market economy can maximise economic growth without generating major inequalities. His argument differs from that of Rawls as he asserts that people can only claim to be motivated by justice if they do not demand material incentives to assist the worst off. People have a duty to work hard and a right to see the fruits of their production distributed equally. Meckled-Garcia takes issue with Cohen, asserting that 'to expect the most able or productive members of society to spend their lives raising production levels without incentives, when they might choose to spend their time differently, is to create a form of social bondage' (Meckled-Garcia 2002:779). For example, two miners should be differentially rewarded if one is more talented at producing coal. The merit of the theory of incentives over that of social duty is its optional nature. This gives the game away. Rawls' solution depends upon the readiness of individuals to contribute, and it endorses inequality as a means of advancing social justice. As a theory of justice it lacks relevance to the goal of equality.

Dworkin's egalitarianism is within the social liberal tradition and is based upon the cut between choice and chance, or personality and circumstance. He argues that where individual disadvantage is the result of chance, then corrective action is warranted. He urges equality for those who are disadvantaged for reasons beyond their control, but not for those whose situation results from personal responsibility (Dworkin 2000:286). The individual who is poor because of expensive tastes cannot expect compensation through distributional equality, as could someone who is the victim of 'brute luck'. Dworkin's position is liberal, but conservatives could also adopt his 'cut' with its connotations of the 'deserving' and the 'undeserving' poor (Matravers 2002:564). This academic controversy reflects the essential debate within social liberalism about the role of personal responsibility.

There is an evident link between Rawls and Dworkin and New Labour in Britain. Like Rawls, Blair claims that his objective of attacking social exclusion is compatible with some individuals in society earning very high incomes. He even fails to add the proviso about the high earners contributing to the alleviation of the poorest (Blair 2001). Blair's vision is a grandiosely expressed version of equality of opportunity. 'Not equal incomes ... But true equality: equal worth, an equal chance of fulfilment, equal access to knowledge and opportunity. Equal rights, equal responsibilities. The class war is over' (Blair 1999). The connection between equal opportunities and New Labour is clear. Jack Straw asserts that the policy of equal opportunities is 'part of our programme to ensure that the public sector sets the pace in this drive towards equality' (Equal Opportunities Commission 2000:1).

EQUAL OPPORTUNITIES

The current ubiquity of the term 'equality', in the context of equal opportunities legislation, represents a degradation of the concept. One sign is the recent tendency for the term 'equal opportunities' to be replaced in Human Resources jargon with the term 'diversity'. Diversity means that in a workplace employers welcome and exploit the benefits that flow from the recruitment of a diverse workforce, in terms of ethnicity, gender, sexuality and creed. Yet employers are persuaded to adopt diversity by appeals to their need to overcome skills shortages. Diversity enables employers to 'improve performance' (Department of Trade and Industry 2003). Concealed within progressive verbiage, this might mark a reaction against affirmative action in the United States, and lead to the removal of the legal requirements to practise equal opportunities and anti-discrimination policies in the labour market (Singh 2000:460).

The use of the concept of equality within the equal opportunities industry is confined to providing opportunity, and does not address worsening inequality in society. It merely aims to spread the disadvantages of inequality on a basis free of gender, racial and other particular forms of discrimination, which happen to be high on the agenda at any given time. This is consonant with Dworkin's view, as it is based upon cosmic chance, rather than individual responsibility. Equal opportunities can be criticised philosophically, and in practical terms, and can be condemned from both within and without its own norms.

From Tawney's perspective, altering which tadpoles have the opportunity to become frogs leaves behind a majority of tadpoles. On a Marxist interpretation, 'equal opportunities is a cross class alliance within capitalism. Globalisation produces such alliances' (Butler 2000:1). It is true that the equal opportunities movement has raised consciousness about issues such as sexual harassment and racial abuse, and drawn attention to the plurality of social struggles. It may demonstrate the multiplicity of sites of resistance, but to many Marxists it lacks ontological depth, and displaces attention from the centrality of the contradiction between capital and labour. There are many social conflicts involving race, gender and sexuality, but to Marxists they cannot be separated from the central contradiction. The oppression of women is widespread, but 'assumes forms which are specific to and determined by the fundamental contradiction developed by each mode of production' (Larrain 1983:167). Indeed, if the conflicts addressed by the equal opportunities movement result in fragmenting or alienating the political practice of the proletariat, then that helps to conceal the main contradiction lacerating capitalist society.

It is conceivable that the steps now being taken will convert equal opportunities to a more radical programme (see the earlier chapter by Mary Davis). In 2002, for example, the British Commission for Racial Equality called for a more unified approach, best underpinned by a single Equality Act, and for the formation of a single Equality Commission (Commission for Racial Equality 2002). The government supports this (Cabinet Office 2002). Yet this radical tone is undermined by the fact that government conferences promoting the Equality Act are sponsored by companies like the Reed Partnership; and Barclays Bank is cited as an exemplar organisation. Greater enlightenment by employers about diverse recruitment is welcome, but it is in business self-interest to find new talent, to develop customers among minorities and to gain approval from government. It is true that equal opportunity policies can mean a more self-confident, productive society with fresh human capital available, but how much more might society benefit if a fuller equality were achieved?

Equal opportunities practice in the UK can also be criticised against its own performance. In May 2002, 40 per cent of local councils had not produced a Racial Equality Strategy. A local government commentator asserts that the 'real concern is that equal opportunities is being sidelined' (Bailey and Jones 2001:1). An Audit Commission report demonstrates that after 'thirty years of work on equal opportunities, some parts of local government have barely changed'. It also revealed that nationally only 22 per cent of senior managers are women (Audit Commission 2002). Even this figure is higher than in other sectors of employment.

Equal opportunities legislation has assisted individuals, and it should be recognised that New Right elements in the United States regard it as a threat. The Republican Party has pronounced that 'equal opportunities rely on quotas, to exclude some individuals in favour of others' (Ansell 1997:195). It is an insight into political language that supporters of affirmative action refer to 'targets' and opponents to 'quotas'. Senator Dole argued that existing discrimination cannot be cured by introducing other forms through equal opportunities (Ansell 1997:209). Some American opponents argue that equal opportunities collapses into equality of results, because it denies 'the principle that all men should be judged and treated according to their individual merits' (Ryan 1981:44). These anxieties are misplaced. It is debatable whether equal opportunities is an incremental step towards equality, or is detrimental to it – by imposing a modest liberal hegemonic meaning of equality on contemporary society.

To protect its position, the equal opportunities movement should widen its focus. It is necessary in Europe and the United States to recognise that the extent of popular support for policies depends upon the benefit derived from them. If equal opportunities policy were to benefit the poor it would garner more supporters, so 'class must be brought back into the analysis' (Bagilhole 2002:560). Crosland asserted that equality of opportunity merely rewards intelligence, but since there are other virtues, why concentrate on only one human trait?

New Labour draws from the social liberal rather than Tawneyan version of equality. It is also motivated by extrinsic arguments about efficiency and reflects the contrast between New Labour modernisers who regard equality as outmoded, and the previous right-wing Labour position, which condemned equality of opportunity for compelling people to 'proceed through life racing against each other to amass as much wealth as possible' (Gaitskell 1956:3). Yet New Labour would not go as far as some opponents of equality, in arguing that the poor can only be assisted by making everybody richer, or that to seek equality of opportunity is like imposing a policy of facial justice in which the better looking members of society are disfigured to remove the benefit of luck (Joseph and Sumption 1979:7).

THE CASE FOR EQUALITY

Equality as a *value* ranges from cautious equality before the law, through vacuous equality of worth, to aspirations for equality of outcomes. The last version is utopian, but it is possible to think beyond the confines of the status quo. What is regarded as utopian varies according to historical circumstance. Nor is it correct that people are currently contented. People are 'less likely to turn to socialism for solutions than to theosophy,' but they are willing to protest, 'if only about asylum seekers' (Eagleton 2000:174). Eagleton argues that socialists should become coherent, offer solutions to popular concerns and agitate against inequality. For the left, despite practical and theoretical difficulties with the idea of equal outcomes, this means a more robust version of equality than that offered by adherents of liberalism, social liberalism, New Labour and even equal opportunities.

Equality must address redistribution. The relativities in British society are vast. Even a social democrat like Will Hutton complains that 'more than half the people who are eligible to work are living either on poverty incomes or in conditions of permanent stress and insecurity' (Hutton 1995:107–8). With such a disparity, even 'equal opportunities' is currently a misnomer.

Turner asserts that modern social citizenship is incompatible with inequality (Turner 1986:18). But arguments for equality must demonstrate the process by which progress can be achieved. The Rawlsian perspective that good reason has to be shown for treating people differently has merit, and even advocates of a utopian approach should not be deflected by the 'straw man' of a total and dreary equality of outcomes, in which everyone consumes the same degree of protein daily and reads four books a year. The need is for a *quest for greater equality*, and for the principle of an equal right (not opportunity) of access to the material and non-material aspects of human existence. Socialists need to act as if inequality can be abolished.

Extending the public sector advances equality. There are common resources. People share the same parks, but equality does not mean that the local park should be divided up into equal lots for all. There should be equal access to libraries, but everybody need not borrow the same books (Ryan 1981:30). Weale argues that welfare provision can be determined by egalitarian principles. In health care, treatment must be free of charge, financed from progressive taxation, with no marked regional variation in the quality of the service provided. People should not be exempt from paying for the benefits that they do not utilise; as such a system would necessarily reduce the standards of public provision (Weale 1978:103). Advantage in the sphere of wealth need not translate into inequality in other areas, such as health or education (Walzer 1983).

To generate greater equality, however, income and wealth redistribution must be considered. A New Labour supporter is correct to argue that today people want strong reasons or evidence to believe in anything, including egalitarianism. If there are any sympathies with the goal of equality then they tend to be linked to notions of 'desserts', or of allowing all people access to such basics as food and shelter, but not foreign holidays (Mulgan 1994:45). This still permits retaining the ultimate goal of equality of results together with the achievement of a transitional aspiration, for example, a three-to-one ratio of wealth ownership. The case must, however, be strongly made. In Britain the objective of equality of worth cannot be attained without dealing with elite fee-paying schools, as Tawney and Crosland insisted. Formal equality and equality of worth remain important, but steps in the direction of equality of outcomes are more practicable than the inherently contradictory chimera of equality of opportunity.

Finally, it can be argued that there is a continuum from social liberal to Marxist conceptions. The link between liberal and social democratic perspectives is apparent from the advocacy of equality of opportunity. More surprising are the connections between social democrats and Marxism. Marx stressed the importance of drawing from the common pool of resources to provide public services, his goal of self-realisation demonstrated his support for personal liberty and his theory of surplus value is rooted in the context of nineteenth-century radicalism which led ethical socialists to deplore the contrast between the industrious and the idle. Marx too, despite his protestations, ultimately perceived of equality as a *value*.

GUIDE TO FURTHER READING

The best volume on equality is by Callinicos (2000) whose approach is substantially different from this chapter, but where there is overlap he is able to go into greater detail. Rees (1972) provides an excellent theoretical discussion which is very little dated. Both Turner (1986) and Ryan (1981) offer arguments for equality, but from different perspectives and using distinct methodologies.

REFERENCES

Ansell, A. (1997) *New Right, New Racism* (London: Macmillan).

Audit Commission (July 2002) *Equality and Diversity: learning from audit, inspection and research*, <www.auditcommission.gov.uk>.

Bagilhole, B. (2002) 'The American Welfare State at Twilight', *Journal of Social Policy*, Vol. 31.

Bailey, D. and Jones, A. (2001) 'Evaluating Equalities', *Local Government Studies*, Vol. 27, No. 2.

Barker, R. (1978) *Political Ideas in Modern Britain* (London: Methuen).

Bennett, D. (1990) *The Party of Fear* (New York: Vintage).

Blair, T. (September 1999) Labour Party Conference Speech, Bournemouth.

—— (May 2001) Newsnight Interview, BBC TV.

Browder, E. (1938) 'Revolutionary Background of the United States Constitution', in *The People's Front in the United States* (London: Lawrence and Wishart).

Butler, A. (2000) *Globalisation and the Enlargement of the European Union* (London: Routledge).

Cabinet Office (May 2002) *Equality in the Twenty First Century*, <www.womenandequalityunit.gov.uk>.

Callinicos, A. (2000) *Equality* (Cambridge: Polity Press).

Cohen, G.A. (1997) 'Where the Action Is: On the Site of Distributive Justice', *Philosophy and Public Affairs*, Vol. 26.

Commission for Racial Equality (2002) News Release, <www.cre.gov.uk/media>.

Croly, H. (1909) *The Promise of American Life* (New York: Macmillan).

Crosland, C.A.R. (1956) *The Future of Socialism* (London: Cape).

Department of Trade and Industry (October 2003) *Conference Publicity for Diversity in Britain*.

Dworkin, R. (2000) *Sovereign Virtue: The Theory and Practice of Equality* (Cambridge, Mass.: Harvard University Press).

Eagleton, T. (2000) 'Equality', *New Left Review*, No. 4.

Equal Opportunities Commission (2000) *Equal Opportunities Review*.

Gaitskell, H. (1956) *Socialism and Internationalism* (London: Fabian Society).

Hutton, W. (1995) *The State We're In* (London: Cape).

Jay, D. (1962) *Socialism in the New Society* (London: Longman).

Joseph, K. and Sumpton, J. (1979) *Equality* (London: Murray).

Keane, J. (1995) *Tom Paine and Political Life* (London: Bloomsbury).

Larrain, J. (1979) *The Concept of Ideology* (London: Hutchinson).

—— (1983) *Marxism and Ideology* (Basingstoke: Macmillan).

Luard, E. (1979) *Socialism Without the State* (Basingstoke: Macmillan).

Marx, K. (1971a) *The Critique of the Gotha Programme* (Moscow: Progress Publishers).

—— (1971b) *Grundrisse* (Harmondsworth: Penguin).

Marx, K. and Engels, F. (1977) 'The German Ideology', in D. McClellan *Karl Marx: Selected Writings* (Oxford: Oxford University Press).

Matravers, M. (2002) 'Responsibility, Luck and the "Equality of What" Debate', *Political Studies*, Vol. 50, No. 3.

McCormick, N. (1982) *Legal Right and Social Democracy* (Oxford: Clarendon).

Meckled-Garcia, S. (2002) 'Why Work Harder? Equality, Social Duty and the Market', *Political Studies*, Vol. 50, No. 4.

Mulgan, G. (1994) *Politics in an Anti-Political Age* (Cambridge: Polity Press).

Pole, J. (1976) *The Pursuit of Equality in American History* (Berkeley: University of California Press).

Rawls, J. (1973) *A Theory of Justice* (Oxford: Oxford University Press).

Rees, J. (1972) *Equality* (London: Macmillan).

Ryan, W. (1981) *Equality* (New York: Pantheon).

Singh, R. (2000) *Governing America: The Politics of a Divided Democracy* (Oxford: Oxford University Press).

Skidmore, M. (1978) *American Political Thought* (New York: St. Martin's Press).

Tawney, R. (1964) *Equality* (London: Unwin).

Turner, B. (1986) *Equality* (London: Tavistock).

Verma, V. (2000) *Justice, Equality and Community: An Essay in Marxist Political Theory* (London: Sage).

Walzer, M. (1983) *Spheres of Justice* (Oxford: Blackwell).

Weale, A. (1978) *Equality and Social Policy* (London: Routledge).

Wolfe, W. (1975) *From Radicalism to Socialism* (Yale: Yale University Press).

Wright, A. (1987) *R. H. Tawney* (Manchester: Manchester University Press).

12
Democracy

Georgina Blakeley

By the time Marx began writing his critique of bourgeois democracy in the early 1840s, the concept of democracy had already travelled a long way in its life and had changed its meaning significantly. This chapter begins by briefly tracing the journey of democracy from its Athenian roots to its present-day form as liberal democracy. It continues by examining Marx's powerful critique of bourgeois democracy and his vision of a future communist, democratic society. The main conclusion is that much can still be learned from Marx's theory of democracy. First, his critique of bourgeois democracy is a powerful reminder that liberal democracy is not democracy per se but is a historically specific form of democracy which capitalism has both facilitated and constrained. Without this historical specificity, it is difficult to envisage an alternative to liberal democracy. Second, the ways in which any alternative can be put into practice will result, not from abstract theorising, but from the practical application of Marxist theory to the reality around us.

DEMOCRACY'S LONG JOURNEY

The concept of democracy has its roots in the ancient city-states of fifth-century BC Greece, of which Athens is one of the most well documented examples. Athenian democracy meant direct rule by the *demos*. What is key, in this definition, is the fact that *demos* meant simultaneously the people and the plebs; in other words, Athenian democracy was not just rule by the people, it was also rule by the poor. Democracy in its original sense, as Wood argues, 'always had class connotations', as its critics were only too well aware (1986:67). Wood highlights the fact that Plato and Aristotle's firm rejection of Athenian democracy was based on the recognition that democracy did not just mean rule by the majority, it also meant rule by the poor who were the majority (Wood 1986:68). No wonder then, that the powerful, property-owning classes viewed democracy with horror.

For a long time, this view of democracy as 'mob rule' dominated, and the property-owning classes continued to regard democracy

192

with hostility. It is worth emphasising, for example, that James Madison (1751–1836), one of the Founding Fathers of the American Constitution, was under no illusion that the political system he advocated for the United States was a democracy: such an idea would have filled him with horror given that at that point democracy's association with the poor was still axiomatic. In The Federalist Paper No.10, Madison recommended for the United States a model of representative republicanism, which he regarded as a superior form of government, suitable for an extended territory with considerable diversity, in contrast to pure democracy, which was considered not only unsuitable for America but also undesirable. For Madison:

a pure democracy, by which I mean a society consisting of a small number of citizens, who assemble and administer the government in person ... have ever been spectacles of turbulence and contention; have ever been found incompatible with personal security or the rights of property; and have in general been as short in their lives as they have been violent in their deaths. (1987:126)

Later generations, however, have muddied the definitional waters with the result that democracy now refers to the representative republicanism established by Madison, thereby allowing even the most conservative of property-owning elites to embrace a definition of democracy that is now disassociated from its class connotations. Democracy today is generally taken to mean liberal democracy. What made this unique formula possible was the development of capitalist relations of production and the resulting formal separation between economic power (the private sphere) and political power (the public sphere). With this separation, formal political equality could be enjoyed within the public sphere without disturbing the exploitative relations between capital and labour, and the inequalities arising from this, within the private sphere.

Our democracies today are therefore made up of two elements: liberalism and democracy. Liberalism is associated above all with the framework of political institutions that serve to limit government and thereby preserve the rights of the individual. Thus, the separation of powers, and freedoms of speech and association, are all seen as liberal devices designed to limit government and to protect the individual from state encroachment. The key question, however, was who exactly was to count as an individual. When early liberal thinkers such as John Locke (1632–1704), and later liberal thinkers such as Jeremy Bentham (1748–1832) and James Mill (1773–1836), talked about the popular control of government they were far from including all the people in that designation. Women and those without property were generally excluded from the suffrage. Thus, the 'abstract' individual underpinning liberal theories was not abstract at all: in fact, this abstract individual was invariably a white, bourgeois male. What is important to note, therefore, is that the liberal element in many western states developed long before they could be described as democracies, that is to say, before the vote was extended to the majority of the population. Universal suffrage followed much later in liberalism's footsteps, centuries later in some cases, and only after significant and often violently crushed struggles by working-class and feminist activists.

THE CRITIQUE OF BOURGEOIS DEMOCRACY

Marx's critique of bourgeois democracy centres precisely on the split between the illusory political world of the state and the real economic world of civil society which capitalist relations of production made possible and upon which bourgeois democracy is based. Freedom and equality exist in the illusory, political world of the state but not in the real, economic world of civil society. Marx wrote in the 'Critique of Hegel':

> It is an historical advance which has transformed the *political* estates into *social* estates, so that, just as the Christians are equal in heaven, but unequal on earth, so the individual members of the nation are *equal* in the heaven of their political world, but unequal in the earthly existence of *society*. (Marx and Engels 1975:79; italics in the original)

Although political distinctions were abolished in the illusory world of political society, the equality of political society remained compromised by the inequalities of the real world of civil society where differences in property and wealth become differences in real freedom and real equality.

Through this separation between political life and civil society, man leads a contradictory existence in which he is both a communal being in the state and a private, egoistical individual in civil society. Marx describes this contradiction in his article 'On the Jewish Question':

Where the political state has reached its true form, man leads a double life, a heavenly life and an earthly one, not only in thought, in consciousness, but in *reality*, in life itself. He leads a life within the *political community* ... in which he is himself a *communal being* ... and he leads a life in *civil society* in which he acts as a *private individual*, regarding other people as means, so that he becomes the football of alien powers. (1983:102; italics in the original)

Moreover, it is the man as a member of civil society, as an egoistic individual, which is the true man: 'The sphere in which man conducts himself as a communal being is degraded, put below the sphere in which he conducts himself as a sectional being. Finally man as a *bourgeois* and not man as a *citoyen* is taken to be the *essential* and *true* man' (Marx 1983:110; italics in the original).

Thus, 'political emancipation' is only partial because 'political emancipation is the reduction of man to a member of civil society, to an *egoistic independent* individual' (Marx 1983:114 italics in the original). Marx therefore notes: 'the so-called *rights of man*, the *droits de l'homme* as distinguished from the *droits du citoyen*, are nothing but the rights of the *member of civil society*, i.e., of egoistic man, of man separated from other men and from the community' (1983:107; italics in the original).

The separation within each man, and the separation of each man from another, conditions the freedom and equality in the real world of civil society. Freedom in this context is 'the liberty of man as an isolated monad withdrawn into itself' and equality is merely the right of every man to be 'equally regarded as a self-sufficient monad' (Marx 1983:108–9). Liberty in civil society is 'not based on the linking of man with man but rather on the separation of man from man. ... It allows every man to find in other men not the *realization* of his freedom, but rather the *limitation* of it' (Marx 1983:108; italics in the original).

DEMOCRACY IN A COMMUNIST SOCIETY

In Marx's future communist democracy, this separation between state and civil society, the separation of man from others, and man's own contradictory existence as both citizen and bourgeois, would disappear. For Marx, real liberty and equality can only be achieved by healing the split between state and civil society, by healing the division between man as abstract citizen and as egoistical individual, because only then, 'when actual, individual man has taken back into himself the abstract citizen and has become a *species-being* in his every day life ... only then is human emancipation complete' (Marx 1983:114; italics in the original).

Moreover, it is only as a social being, in association with others, that freedom and equality can have any real significance:

> Only in community with others has each individual the means of cultivating his gifts in all directions; only in the community, therefore, is personal freedom possible. In the previous substitutes for the community, in the state, etc., personal freedom has existed only for the individuals who developed within the relationships of the ruling class, and only in so far as they were individuals of this class ... In the real community the individuals obtain their freedom in and through their association. (Marx 1983:193)

The nearest we get to a description of this 'real community' in which 'the free development of each is the condition for the free development of all', is in Marx's writings on the Paris Commune of 1871 (Marx and Engels 1970:53):

> The Commune was formed of the municipal councillors, chosen by universal suffrage in the various wards of the town, responsible and revocable at short terms. The majority of its members were naturally working men, or acknowledged representatives of the working class ... From the members of the Commune downwards, the public service had to be done at *workmen's wages* ... The Paris Commune was, of course, to serve as a model to all the great industrial centres of France. The communal *régime* once established in Paris and the secondary centres, the old centralised Government would in the provinces, too, have to give way to the self-government of the producers ... The rural communes of every district were to administer their common affairs by an assembly of delegates in the central town, and these district assemblies were again to send deputies to the National Delegation in Paris, each delegate to be at any time revocable and bound by the *mandat impératif* (formal instructions) of his constituents. (Marx and Engels 1970:287–8; italics in the original)

From this description we can see that Marx's future communist democracy is based on a free and egalitarian association of people in which there will be common ownership of the means of production. However, although the two-month Paris Commune was of key significance for Marx, it did not become a dogmatic blueprint for the road to communism. Rather, for Marx, the Commune had been 'a thoroughly expansive political form' whose true secret was that 'It was essentially a working class government, the produce of the struggle of the producing against the appropriating class, the political form at last discovered under which to work out the economic emancipation of labour' (Marx and Engels 1970: 290). Two further conclusions can be drawn. First, in Marx's description of the Paris Commune the link between democracy and the working class, as in the original Athenian meaning, is clear. A Marxist concept of democracy refers to the people in its original Athenian meaning, not only as the many, the numerical majority, but also as the poor. Second, the model of the Paris Commune was not the final stage in the transformation of society and state. The Paris Commune represented 'the political form' which would facilitate the achievement of the ultimate goal of communism under which classes and class antagonisms would be swept away.

THE CONTRADICTORY NATURE OF BOURGEOIS DEMOCRACY

It is clear from the above that Marx provides a powerful critique of bourgeois democracy and an indication, albeit a deliberately vague one, of how his future democratic society would differ from this. Nevertheless, Marx was not consistently negative about bourgeois democracy in general and universal suffrage in particular. Although later Marxists like Lenin would see parliamentary democracy as inimical to the interests of the working class and would therefore reject the possibility of a 'democratic road' to socialism, Marx held an altogether more ambivalent view. Moreover, such an ambivalent view towards bourgeois democracy should not surprise us because, as Fernbach highlights, Marx did not have to confront, until very late in life, the phenomenon of a representative state with universal suffrage, let alone one in which the working classes had gained electoral supremacy (Marx 1973b:14).

Thus, in 'The Class Struggles in France' Marx writes, with reference to the Constitution of the French bourgeois democratic republic in 1848:

the most comprehensive contradiction in the Constitution consists in the fact that it gives political power to the classes whose social slavery it is intended to perpetuate: proletariat, peasants and petty bourgeoisie. And it deprives the bourgeoisie, the class whose old social power it sanctions, of the political guarantees of this power. It imposes on the political rule of the bourgeoisie democratic conditions which constantly help its enemies towards victory and endanger the very basis of bourgeois society. (1973a:71)

Moreover, in an article on 'The Chartists', Marx acknowledged the value of universal suffrage particularly in the context of England where:

universal suffrage is the equivalent for political power for the working class of England, where the proletariat forms the large majority of the population ... The carrying of universal suffrage in England would, therefore, be a far more socialistic measure than anything which has been honoured with that name on the Continent. (1973b:264)

Marx did, however, see clearly the limitations of bourgeois democracy, which resulted primarily from the split between state and civil society mentioned above. Marx recognised the partial 'political emancipation' of bourgeois democracy, in contrast to the much fuller 'human emancipation'; the freedom and equality won in the political sphere were limited by the fact that they left untouched the lack of freedom and equality in the economic and social spheres. Thus, for Marx, 'the social antagonisms that survive political emancipation cannot be resolved by pure reason or the vote of representatives within this particular emancipated sphere' (1973b:13). Marx did not suffer from the 'parliamentary cretinism' that afflicted many around him whereby 'magical power' was attributed to universal suffrage. Rather, Marx recognised that the enfranchisement was of real value to the working class, but that its value was ultimately limited.

Marx's ambiguous stance with regard to bourgeois democracy had a number of consequences. On the one hand, ambiguity lent support to conflicting positions amongst later theorists. Marx's ambiguity furnished a split between advocates of the 'parliamentary road to socialism' like Kautsky, and critics such as Lenin who disagreed profoundly that socialism could ever be achieved by the ballot box. On the other hand, Marx's ambiguity was itself seen as proof of his own ambivalence towards democracy and was used by those, like Lenin, who wished to drive home the view that bourgeois democracy was nothing but a 'sham'. Lenin's interpretation of Marx's ideas certainly gained the upper hand not the least because Marxism-Leninism sustained the communist regimes of the twentieth century, leading theorists such as Graham to argue: 'the terrible fate which befell Marx was that he was Leninised' (1986:203).

Whilst it is not necessary to be as damning in our interpretation of Lenin, a more important point concerns the way in which theorists, both past and present, tend to approach the ambiguities in Marx's work. The problem with these various ambiguities is not that they exist, but that many theorists following in Marx's footsteps try to resolve them. This is to miss the point. Marx was alive to ambiguity and contradiction because this better reflected the messy world around him. Although theory in the abstract could be presented in simple terms, concrete analysis of the 'real' world had, by definition, to be complex. The point therefore is not to resolve the ambiguities in Marx's work by providing definitive interpretations of their significance; the point is to take Marx's theory and concepts as a starting point and apply them to the messy world around us. No doubt this is why, according to Engels, 'Marx used to say, commenting on the French "Marxists" of the late [eighteen-] seventies: "All I know is that I am not a Marxist"' (Marx and Engels 1970:679).

POST-MARXISM

The dominance of Lenin's thought and, more importantly, the dominance of the regimes it underpinned, did much to discredit Marx's contribution to democratic theory. By the late 1970s, a general collapse of faith in Marxism, which Wood (1986) summed up as a general 'retreat from class', became apparent. Democratic theorists, critical of classical Marxism, proliferated under a variety of labels such as the 'new revisionists', the 'new true socialists' and 'the new left'. Whatever the differences amongst them, all questioned the centrality of the working class within Marxism and, more generally, abandoned all interest in questions of political economy. Two authors emblematic of this trend are Laclau and Mouffe, who state, in their book *Hegemony and Socialist Strategy*, that 'we are now situated in a post-Marxist terrain' (1990:4). They acknowledge, however, that their project of radical democracy is inspired by their Marxist roots, and affirm that: 'It has been through the development of certain intuitions and discursive forms constituted within Marxism, and the inhibition or elimination of certain others, that we have constructed a concept of hegemony which, in our view may be a useful instrument in the struggle for a radical, libertarian and plural democracy' (1990:4).

Much of their inspiration comes from the work of the Italian Communist, Antonio Gramsci (1891–1937). Laclau and Mouffe argue that Gramsci is the only Marxist theorist to accord any autonomy to the political and ideological realms. This is because Gramsci talked in terms of the formation of a historical bloc, not specifically related to the material realm. His theory of hegemony, in which a class struggles for ascendancy not only in the economic realm but also in the social, political and ideological spheres, posits that a class cannot become hegemonic by restricting itself only to class interests. On the contrary, in the struggle for hegemony, all the popular and democratic struggles of the people, which may embrace a wide variety of different struggles not specifically related to class – such as peace movements, green movements, student movements, etc. – must be 'knotted together' (Simon 1991:43–6). Gramsci, however, was still a Marxist. Although he paved the way for the autonomy of politics and ideology, by recognising the diversity of struggles within civil society, in the last instance he returned to the determinacy of class. We should not forget that Gramsci's concept of hegemony was a 'strategy for revolution' in which civil society, with its diverse political and cultural struggles, became the battleground in the contest for hegemony between the working class and the capitalist class (Adamson 1987/8:324). Thus, although the 'basic concepts of Gramscian analysis' provide the basis for Laclau and Mouffe's project of radical democracy, they argue that 'it will be necessary to radicalise them in a direction that leads us beyond Gramsci' (1990:136).

In contrast to the reductionist picture they paint of classical Marxism, Laclau and Mouffe offer a theory of radical democracy that renounces 'final closure' and instead starts 'from a plurality of political and social spaces which do not refer to any ultimate unitarian basis' (1990:140). They reject the explanatory primacy accorded to the relations of production and refute any link between the material on the one hand and politics and ideology on the other. Having divorced the interests of the working class from their class character, it follows logically that, for Laclau and Mouffe, the working class has no particular status within capitalist society and thus no special role to play in its demise. Instead, they exhort the working class to 'abandon its class ghetto and transform itself into the articulator of a multiplicity of [antagonisms and] demands stretching beyond itself' (1990:58). In turn, having rejected the privileged position of the working class, the struggle for socialism becomes absorbed into a much wider struggle for radical democracy within which a multiplicity of antagonisms occurs with no single one having any ontological centrality over another (1990:167–8). For Laclau and Mouffe, plurality is all. There is no privileged subject; there is a plurality of subjects whose identities are discursively, and not materially, constructed. Moreover, it is the 'democratic discourse' itself, whose origin they locate within the French revolution of 1789, which makes it possible 'to articulate the different forms of resistance to subordination' and to therefore 'struggle against different types of inequality' (1990:154). From this, they arrive at the conclusion that socialism is 'a moment internal to the democratic revolution' (1990:156).

There is much to criticise here. To begin with, there is the obvious objection that if plurality is all, we may be left with no ability to explain anything. As Geras argues, 'it is integral to the very act of explanation that some things are picked out, given prominence' (Geras 1990:11). Second, there is the questionable location of the democratic principle in the French revolution, which omits the original Greek meaning of democracy with all its class connotations. More important, however, is Laclau and Mouffe's thesis that until the arrival of democratic discourse, workers could not have recognised their own material conditions as oppressive because the discursive conditions did not exist to construct them as such. It follows from this that working-class oppression does not result from capitalist relations of production but rather is created as a result of liberal democratic discourse, in short, the very discourse that 'mystifies and obscures' capitalist exploitation (Wood 1986:47–75 and Geras 1988). By this stage, it appears as if we have entered the world of Alice in Wonderland where words can mean just what we want them to mean – neither more, nor less.

Untied from its Marxist moorings, an impoverished theory of democracy remains. First, in Laclau and Mouffe's model of 'radical democracy' the association between democracy and class has been completely severed. Not only does the socialist conception of democracy lose its class base by virtue of the fact that socialism becomes a 'moment internal to the democratic revolution'; at the same time, the class base of liberal democracy is also obscured by denying the location of its roots in the class struggles of capitalism (Wood 1986:68–9). Without recourse to Marxist tools of analysis we are apt to forget, as Laclau and Mouffe do, the historical specificity of liberal democracy as a particular form of democracy and capitalism as a particular mode of production, both constituted by class conflict, rather than by discursive means. We thus remain unable to see an alternative to either. Both assume a class-transcending universality that does not allow us to understand the workings of actually existing, capitalist, liberal democratic regimes. Thus, we live in a world where Fukuyama's 'end of history' exhorts us to believe that this is as good as it gets.

Second, without understanding the historical specificity of liberal democracy, which a Marxist analysis demands, we remain stuck at the level of abstract, and often simply baffling, theory, and thereby reproduce 'continually the elitist division between theory and practice' (Thompson 1978:195). And yet Marx himself, as Graham argues, 'should be taken as warning against the treatment of ideas and theory in a vacuum' (1986:175). As Shaw argues, historical materialism 'is best interpreted as an empirical theory'. It is an approach that 'rests not on philosophically derived abstractions or dogmas, but rather on observation and an accurate depiction of real conditions; in short, on premises that "can thus be verified in a purely empirical way"' (Shaw 1983:206). What is therefore astonishing is that Marxist theorising tends to become bogged down in sterile theoretical debate in which for every post-Marxist rejecting Marxist premises we have a classical Marxist restating them, thereby locking both into a zero-sum situation. Neither side, however, appears keen to apply Marxist concepts and tools of analysis to the empirical reality around them. That kind of 'continual dialogue', of the kind recommended by E.P. Thompson, between theoretical pronouncements and the 'phenomena of material and social existence' is of course the difficult part (Thompson 1978:201, 205). To turn from abstract theory to concrete analysis is to turn from the simple to the complex. As Thompson argued in 1978 about Louis Althusser, the French 'neo-Marxist' philosopher, it appears that Marxist theorists have:

> retired to the rituals of their own secluded observatory. As if an astronomical observatory should be made without any windows, and the astronomer within should arrange the starry universe solely by pen, ink and paper, so M. Althusser, in his Observatory (and there are many like it) had no need to cast an eye upon the teeming myriads of human beings around him, but could settle

all their destinies on a slate, and wipe out all their tears with one dirty little bit of sponge. (1978:384)

INTERPRETING THE WORLD

Marx's theory helps us to interpret the world by providing the tools to analyse the particular form of democracy that capitalism made possible and the particular constraints that capitalism imposes on a more substantive democracy. At this point, it is worth recalling that liberal democracy is not democracy *per se*. At best, Harrison ventures, it is 'a subspecies of the genus' (1995:129). So accustomed are we to the formula 'liberal democracy', however, that we forget just how novel this combination is, and how distant it is from democracy in its original Athenian sense.

What can explain this collective amnesia regarding the accurate meaning of democracy? First, from a hegemonic viewpoint, it is expedient for elites to embrace a concept which bestows upon them a mantle of legitimacy which, having been shorn of all substantive content, presents little threat to the prevailing order. Second, we commit the same error as those 'bourgeois economists' whom Marx criticised for regarding economic categories 'as eternal and not as historical laws' through our tendency to see the formula of liberal democracy as 'fixed and eternal', thereby forgetting the specificity and historicity of both liberalism and democracy (Marx and Engels 1970:664).

The specificity of capitalism lies in its conceptual separation of the political and economic. Moreover, it is this very distinction, specific to capitalism, not 'eternal or fixed', that facilitated the extension of democracy to the majority of the population. Wood argues: 'Capitalism, to put it simply, can afford a universal distribution of political goods without endangering its constitutive relations, its coercions and inequities' (1995:14). This separation of the political and economic under capitalism devalues political goods in contrast to earlier systems such as Athenian democracy or feudalism in which the lack of a separation between the political and economic endowed political goods with much greater significance and, accordingly, restricted their distribution. *Pace* Laclau and Mouffe, there is no determinism or teleology here. What we have here is the specificity of capitalism and the particular form of democracy it has rendered feasible. Wood continues: '"Formal" democracy and the identification of democracy with liberalism would have been impossible in practice and literally unthinkable in theory in any other context but the very specific social relations of capital. These social relations have both advanced and strictly limited democracy' (1995:14–15).

CHANGING THE WORLD

Marx is frequently criticised for failing to leave a blueprint for the future or for leaving one that was utopian. Both criticisms miss the point. Any Marxist vision of the future is by definition utopian. Marx's concept of democracy rests deliberately on a profound and revolutionary transformation of society, which would require key changes in the organisation of production and social relations and in the pattern of people's working lives. As Graham argues: 'It is no objection to Marx's conception of a system where citizens rule themselves that it fails to fit in with prevailing circumstances. On the contrary, that is his point' (1986:192).

Moreover, far from lamenting the lack of a clear blueprint for future action, we should be grateful that no such straitjacket has been imposed. Marx constantly warned of the need to study the complex world around us anew. Marx provides the starting point for analysis, not the end point. Concepts are not just abstract theoretical categories that can be taken off the shelves and applied easily without further ado; concepts must be dragged painfully from the analysis of political phenomena. In a letter to Schmidt, Engels explained:

> In general, the word 'materialistic' serves many of the younger writers in Germany as a mere phrase with which anything and everything is labelled without further study, that is, they stick on this label and then consider the question disposed of. But our conception of history is above all a guide to study, not a lever for construction ... All history must be studied afresh ... (Marx and Engels 1970:679)

Nevertheless, although there is no blueprint, Marx does provide the tools to interpret the world around us and to change it. Recognising the ways in which democracy is both advanced and limited by capitalism has consequences for political activity. It means recognising that the structural and false separation of the political from the economic in capitalism allows a variety of struggles to occur in the political arena, which have a minimal impact on inequalities in the economic and social realms. Thus: 'In capitalism, a great deal can happen in politics and community organisation at every level without fundamentally affecting the exploitative powers of capital or fundamentally changing the decisive balance of social power' (Wood 1995:275).

The state's role in this is crucial and requires acknowledgement, for without an understanding of the state's role political action remains uninformed. Without wishing to enter the rather sterile debate (see the earlier chapter by Andrew Taylor) over whether Marx believed the state was simply a tool of the bourgeoisie, a position clearly stated in *The Communist Manifesto*, or whether Marx granted the state a degree of autonomy from the bourgeoisie, as exemplified in *The Eighteenth Brumaire*, we can conclude that there are important limits to state action within capitalist societies, which affect the possibilities of democracy. To be effective, political action must unfold with that firmly in mind. Held writes:

> If state intervention undermines the process of capital accumulation, it simultaneously undermines the material basis of the state; hence, state policies must be consistent with the capitalist relations of production. Or, to put the point another way: constraints exist in liberal democracies – constraints imposed by the requirements of private capital accumulation – which systematically limit policy options. (1996:136)

Nor, it is worth emphasising, do you have to be a Marxist to subscribe to this view. The neo-pluralist Lindblom argued:

> Any government official who understands the requirement of his position and the responsibilities that market-oriented systems throw on businessmen will therefore grant them a privileged position. He does not have to be bribed, duped or pressured to do so. He simply understands, as is plain to see, that public affairs in market-oriented systems are in the hands of two groups of leaders, government and business, who must collaborate and that to make the system work government leadership must often defer to business leadership. (1977:175)

In short, we return to Marx's powerful critique of bourgeois democracy and the question of whether we can really have political equality when that is constrained by the very different economic and social resources at our disposal. Marxism gives us the tools to analyse this 'bourgeois democratic' reality by its emphasis on the historical specificity of capitalism as a form of production and liberal democracy as a form of political organisation. Simply by stressing this historical specificity, we can envisage an alternative. At the same time, acknowledging historical specificity influences how we try to put that alternative into practice. This is not to be cavalier about the difficulties entailed, but it is to argue for a clear analysis of what precisely these difficulties are. Thus, in order to 'illuminate the points at which political action could most effectively intervene' such action has, to quote Wood again, to be 'organised and conducted in the full recognition that capitalism has a remarkable capacity to distance democratic politics from the decisive centres of social power and to insulate the power of appropriation and exploitation from democratic accountability' (1995:19, 275).

The task of Marxist analysts, therefore, should not be to immerse ourselves in what E.P. Thompson graphically described as 'Capital navel-scrutinising' (1978:384), but rather to apply Marxist theory to the messy reality around us. The solution should lie in 'public action' rather than 'the dialectical rotations' of our own minds (Marx and Engels 1970:667). In a letter to Bloch, Engels remarks that theory at the abstract level or the need to 'emphasise our main principle vis-à-vis our adversaries' is one thing, 'but when it came to presenting a section of history, that is, to making a practical application, it was a different matter and there no error was permissible' (Marx and Engels 1970: 683).

Abstract theorising must not substitute for concrete analysis which is correspondingly complex. Moreover, the challenge lies in applying Marxism to non-western nations. Fernbach laments:

It was unfortunate for the development of Marx's politics that he found himself exiled in a country that was, in the third quarter of the nineteenth century, the most stable and crisis-free in the bourgeois world ... The sluggish English environment undoubtedly acted as a brake on the development of Marx's politics ... Revolutionary political theory *can* only develop in response to the new problems and tasks raised by mass struggle, and this was completely lacking in Marx's England. (Marx 1973b:19)

Thus, the 'new problems and tasks raised by mass struggle' that will furnish radical political theory are not to be found in 'the sluggish

English environment' but in those parts of the world where capitalism appears in its most blatant form. Bobbio writes:

The poor and forsaken are still condemned to live in a world of terrible injustices, crushed by unreachable and apparently unchangeable economic magnates on which the political authorities, even when formally democratic, nearly always depend. In such a world the idea that the hope of revolution is spent, that it is finished just because the communist utopia has failed, is to close one's eyes so as not to see ... Democracy, let us admit it, has overcome the challenge of historical communism. But what means and what ideals does it have to confront those very problems out of which the communist challenge was born? (1991:5)

A Marxist theory of democracy provides the 'means and ideals' to confront those very problems. It provides no definitive answer, but it does provide a good starting point.

GUIDE TO FURTHER READING

Laclau and Mouffe (1990) detail the case for post-Marxist democracy; Geras (1988 and 1990) and Wood (1986) provide the clearest rebuttal. Wood (1995) is an excellent restatement of Marx's position on democracy. Graham (1986), Harrison (1995) and Held (1996) all have good chapters on Marxist theory and democracy.

REFERENCES

Adamson, W.L. (1987/8) 'Gramsci and the Politics of Civil Society', *Praxis International*, Vol. 7, No. 3/4.
Bobbio, N. (1991) 'The Upturned Utopia', in R. Blackburn (ed.) *After the Fall: The Failure of Communism and the Future of Socialism* (London: Verso).
Geras, N. (1988) 'Post-Marxism?', *New Left Review*, No. 163.
—— (1990) 'Seven Types of Obliquy: Travesties of Marxism', *Socialist Register*.
Graham, K. (1986) *The Battle of Democracy* (Brighton: Wheatsheaf Books).
Harrison, R. (1995) *Democracy* (London: Routledge).
Held, D. (1996) *Models of Democracy* (Cambridge: Polity Press).
Laclau, E. and Mouffe, C. (1990) *Hegemony and Socialist Strategy* (London: Verso).
Lindblom, C.E. (1977) *Politics and Markets* (New York: Basic Books).
Madison, J., Hamilton, A. and Jay, J. (1987) *The Federalist Papers*, edited by K. Kramnick (Harmondsworth: Penguin).

Marx, K. (1973a) *The Revolutions of 1848*, edited by D. Fernbach (Harmondsworth: Penguin).

—— (1973b) *Surveys From Exile*, edited by D. Fernbach (Harmondsworth: Penguin).

—— (1983) *The Portable Karl Marx*, edited by E. Kamenka (Harmondsworth: Penguin).

Marx, K. and Engels, F. (1970) *Selected Works* (London: Lawrence and Wishart).

—— (1975) *Collected Works*, Vol. 3 (London: Lawrence and Wishart).

Shaw, W.S. (1983) 'Historical Materialism', in T. Bottomore (ed.) *A Dictionary of Marxist Thought* (Oxford: Blackwell).

Simon, R. (1991) *Gramsci's Political Thought: An Introduction* (London: Lawrence and Wishart).

Thompson, E.P. (1978) *The Poverty of Theory* (London: Merlin Press).

Wood, E.M. (1986) *The Retreat from Class* (London: Verso).

—— (1995) *Democracy Against Capitalism* (Cambridge: Cambridge University Press).

Notes on Contributors

Paul Blackledge is a Senior Lecturer in Politics at Leeds Metropolitan University and an editor of the journal *Historical Materialism*. He is the author of *Perry Anderson, Marxism and the New Left* (Merlin 2004), and co-editor of *Historical Materialism and Social Evolution* (Palgrave 2002).

Georgina Blakeley is Head of Politics at the University of Huddersfield. She is the author of *Democratization and Participation in Spain: Building Democracy in Barcelona* (Edwin Mellen Press 2004). She has published and presented papers on democracy and civil society in Spain as well as on aspects of Spanish politics more generally. With Valerie Bryson, she is the editor of *Contemporary Political Concepts: A Critical Introduction* (Pluto 2002).

Valerie Bryson is Professor of Politics at the University of Huddersfield. She teaches and researches on feminist theory and women and politics. Her publications include *Feminist Political Theory: An Introduction* (Palgrave Macmillan, revised edition 2003) and *Feminist Debates: Issues of Theory and Political Practice* (Macmillan 1999). With Georgina Blakeley, she is the editor of *Contemporary Political Concepts: A Critical Introduction* (Pluto 2002).

Mary Davis is Professor of Labour History, Head of the Centre for Trade Union Studies and Deputy Director of the Working Lives Research Institute at London Metropolitan University. She has broadcast and published on a wide range of issues around the labour movement, British imperialism and racism, women's history and equal pay. Her books include *Comrade or Brother?: The History of the British Labour Movement 1789–1951* (Pluto 1993), *Sylvia Pankhurst: A Life in Radical Politics* (Pluto 1999), *Fashioning a New World: A History of the Woodcraft Folk* (Holyoake Press 2000), and *Marxism and Struggle: Towards the Millenium* (ed. with Marj Mayo, Praxis Press 1998).

Brendan Evans is Professor of Politics and until recently was Pro Vice Chancellor for Academic Affairs at the University of Huddersfield. He has published widely on British politics, with a particular focus on ideology and policy-making. His books include *Radical Education: A Political Critique* (Croom Helm 1987), *The Politics of the Training Market* (Routledge 1992), *From Salisbury to Major* (Manchester University Press 1996, with Andrew Taylor) and *Thatcherism and British Politics* (Sutton Publishing 1999).

Keith Faulks is Reader in Citizenship and Director of Research in the Department of Education and Social Science at the University of Central Lancashire. He is the author of four books, including *Citizenship* (Routledge 2000), and a variety of papers exploring aspects of political sociology and social theory. He is currently working on a book for Edinburgh University Press entitled *Theories of Citizenship: Classical and Contemporary Perspectives*.

Graham Harrison is Senior Lecturer in Politics at the University of Sheffield. He is currently researching donor involvement in good governance in Uganda and Tanzania and also the international political economy of development, Mozambican politics, and corruption. His publications include *The Politics of Democratization in Rural Mozambique* (Edwin Mellen Press 2000), *Issues in the Contemporary Politics of Sub-Saharan Africa: The Dynamics of Struggle and Resistance* (Palgrave 2002), and *The World Bank and Africa: The Construction of Governance States* (Routledge 2004).

Renzo Llorente is Chair of the Department of Humanities and Social Sciences, Saint Louis University, Madrid Campus. His current research interests are in three areas: the philosophy of work (specifically the status of work in egalitarian social theory); the relationship between the normative foundations of animal liberation and the ethical foundations of Marxism; and the 'ethical turn' in recent analytical Marxism. He has published a number of refereed articles and book chapters, mainly in these areas. His PhD was on the division of labour.

Peter McLaverty is Reader in Public Policy at The Robert Gordon University, Aberdeen. His research interests are in the areas of the theory and practice of democracy and public participation. He has published widely on issues around local government, housing policy and participation, and is the author of *The Politics of Empowerment?* (Dartmouth 1996) and editor of *Public Participation and Innovations in Community Governance* (Ashgate 2002).

Mark O'Brien is a Research Director in Social Policy at the University of Liverpool. His PhD research is in the area of contemporary labour internationalism. He has published a number of book chapters on aspects of social history and class struggle and is the author of *Perish the Privileged Orders*, a narrative history of the Chartist movement (Redwords 1995) and *When Adam Delved and Eve Span*, a history of the Peasants' Revolt of 1381 (New Clarion Press 2004).

Andrew Taylor is Reader in Politics at the University of Sheffield. His main publications include *The Politics of the Yorkshire Miners* (Croom Helm 1984), *Trade Unions and Politics* (Palgrave Macmillan 1989) and *From Salisbury to Major: Continuity and Change in Conservative Politics* (Manchester University Press 1996, with Brendan Evans) and *The NUM and British Politics: Volume 1, 1944–1968* (Ashgate 2003) and *The NUM and British Politics: Volume 2, 1969–1995* (Ashgate 2004). His current research interest is on theories of governance.

Philip Wood is Associate Professor and coordinator of Graduate Admissions in the Department of Political Studies, Queen's University, Kingston, Ontario. His main research interests lie in regional and historical political economy. Recent research deals with politics, race and economic development in the American South, globalisation and industrial restructuring, and the prison-industrial complex and prison privatisation in the United States. He is the author of *Southern Capitalism: The Political Economy of North Carolina, 1880–1980* (Duke University Press 1986).

Index

Compiled by Sue Carlton